MW00979000

Other books in The Princeton Review Series

Cracking the ACT
Cracking the GMAT
Cracking the GRE
Cracking the LSAT
Cracking the MCAT
Cracking the System: College Admissions
Study Smart
The Student Access Guide to Paying for College
The Student Access Guide to the Best Colleges
Word Smart: Building a Better Vocabulary
Word Smart II: How to Build a More Educated Vocabulary

Also available on cassette from Living Language
Word Smart
Grammar Smart

THE **PRINCETON** REVIEW

CRACKING THE SAT® & PSAT

1993/94 EDITION

1993/94 EDITION

THE **PRINCETON** REVIEW

CRACKING THE SAT® & PSAT

1993/94 EDITION

BY ADAM ROBINSON
AND JOHN KATZMAN

with a foreword by David Owen

VILLARD BOOKS NEW YORK 1993

 Published in the United States by Villard Books, a division of Random House, Inc., New York, and simultaneously in Canada by Random House of Canada Limited, Toronto. This is a revised edition of a book first published in 1986 and updated in 1989.

ISSN 1049-6238
ISBN 0-679-74676-5

SAT questions: p. 29, #25; p. 30, #1; pp. 64–65, Passage; pp. 65–66, #33–37; p. 74, #33; p. 75, #37; p. 76–77, #34, #35, #36; pp. 97, #1, #2; p. 99, #6, #7; p. 100, #6; p. 101, #10; p. 102, #4; p. 103, #10, #9; p. 104, #8, #9; p. 112, #4; pp. 113–14, #1, #2, #3; p. 114–115, #1, #2, #3; p. 115, #5; p. 116, #4; p. 134, #25; p. 136, #24; p. 138, #24; p. 171, #11; p. 172, #18; p. 174, #3; p. 175, #17; p. 176, #17, #25; p. 178, #15; p. 181, #12, #20; p. 206, #10, #13; p. 207, #29; p. 214, #25; p. 219, #24; p. 230, #22; p. 233, #21.

All other questions in the book were created by the authors.

Manufactured in the United States of America on recycled paper

9 8 7 6 5 4 3 2

Third Revised Edition

FOREWORD

The publishers of the Scholastic Aptitude Test don't want you to read this book. For nearly sixty years they have claimed that the SAT cannot be coached, and this book proves that it can be.

Cracking the SAT & PSAT contains information that could help you raise your SAT scores substantially and improve your chances of being admitted to the college of your choice. It also contains information that should make you think twice before boasting about a high SAT score or becoming depressed about a low one. The SAT, you will discover, is not the test that your teachers, guidance counselors, parents, and friends may have led you to believe. Despite its reputation as an "objective" examination, the SAT doesn't measure much more than your ability to take the SAT.

Unfortunately, though, your ability to take the SAT could have a significant impact on the course of your life. Virtually all the nation's most selective colleges—and a great many less selective ones—require their applicants to submit SAT scores. (Many other schools require scores from the SAT's chief competitor, the ACT, published by the American College Testing Program.) Most admissions officers won't understand how to interpret the scores you send them, but this won't keep them from speculating freely about your intelligence and even your personality on the basis of how you do. Where you spend the next four years of your life may be determined in part by what they decide. The test's effect can even carry over into the years beyond college. More than a few employers require recent college graduates to submit their high-school SAT scores when applying for jobs. This practice is illegal, but some companies do it anyway. For the time being, anyway, you're probably stuck with the SAT.

Since you are, you owe it to yourself to learn as much as you can about the test. If you're like most of the 1.3 million high-school students who will take it this year, you probably don't have a very clear idea of what you're in for. You may have glanced at an SAT preparation book or even taken a coaching course. But most coaching materials don't have much to do with the real SAT. Partly because most available materials are so bad, many teachers and guidance counselors believe that it is impossible for students to improve their SAT scores through coaching. Another reason they believe this is that the test's publishers have always told them coaching doesn't work. The College Board, which sponsors the test, has claimed that score gains resulting from coaching "are always small regardless of the coaching method used or the differences in the students coached." The Educational Testing Service (ETS)—which has written and administered the SAT for the College Board since 1947—says the same thing: "The abilities measured by the SAT develop over a student's entire academic life, so coaching—vocabulary drill, memorizing facts, or the like—can do little or nothing to raise the student's scores."

Despite all the official denial, though, the SAT can very definitely be coached. The only "aptitude" you need to make your scores go up is your aptitude for understanding how ETS's question-writers think.

Cracking the SAT & PSAT is different from other coaching guides because it contains strategies that really work on the SAT. These strategies are taught at a new coaching school called The Princeton Review. The school is based in New York City and has branches in a growing number of other cities. The strategies were developed by Adam Robinson, formerly a private SAT tutor, and John Katzman, the founder of the school. Although The Princeton Review is just a few years old, it has already become legendary among many high-school and college students. A guidance counselor at an exclusive private academy in New York once told me that most of her juniors were enrolled at The Princeton Review and that their SAT scores had risen so much that she was no longer certain how to advise them about where they ought to apply to college. At Harvard not long ago, a freshman was overheard saying, "Yeah, he got a 750 on the verbal, but it was only a Princeton Review 750."

If you read this book *carefully,* you will have a huge advantage when you actually take the SAT. In fact, students who take the test without knowing these strategies are, in effect, taking it blindfolded.

ETS often refers to the SAT as an "objective" test, meaning that the score you receive on it isn't just one person's judgement (the way a grade in a course is) but is arrived at "scientifically." Few people stop to think that the word *objective* in this case applies only to the mechanical grading process. Every question still has to be written—and its answer determined—by highly subjective human beings. The SAT isn't really an "objective" test. Banesh Hoffmann, a critic of standardized testing, once suggested that a better term for it would be "child-gradable," because marking it doesn't require any knowledge or intelligence. The principal difference between the SAT and a test that can't be graded by a child is that the SAT leaves no room for more than one correct answer. It leaves no room, in other words, for people who don't see eye to eye with ETS.

In 1962, Banesh Hoffman wrote a wonderful book called *The Tyranny of Testing*. It begins with a letter reprinted from the *Times* of London:

> *Sir,——Among the "odd one out" type of questions which my son had to answer for a school entrance examination was: "Which is the odd one out among cricket, football, billiards, and hockey?"*
>
> *I said billiards because it is the only one played indoors. A colleague says football because it is the only one in which the ball is not struck by an implement. A neighbour says cricket because in all the other games the object is to put the ball into a net; and my son, with the confidence of nine summers, plumps for hockey, "because it is the only one that is a girl's game." Could any of your readers put me out of my misery by stating what is the correct answer?*
>
> *Yours Faithfully,*
>
> *T. C. Batty*

Other answers were suggested in Hoffman's book: billiards, because it's the only one that's not a team sport; football, because it's the only one played with a hollow ball; billiards, because it's the only one in which the color of the ball matters; hockey, because it's the only one whose name ends in a vowel.

The "odd one out" problem is an "objective" question: A grading machine will mark it the same way every time, whatever the answer really is. But you won't be able to answer it correctly unless you know what the testers had in mind when they wrote it. If you aren't on the same wavelength they were on, you won't come up with the answer they wanted.

The same is true with the SAT. In order to do well, you need to understand how the test-makers at ETS were thinking when they sat down to write the questions. *Cracking the SAT & PSAT* will teach you how to do precisely that.

— David Owen,
author of *None of the Above: Behind the Myth of Scholastic Aptitude*

ACKNOWLEDGMENTS

An SAT course is much more than clever techniques and powerful computer score reports; the reason our results are great is that our teachers care so much about their kids. Many of them have gone out of their way to improve the course, often going so far as to write their own materials, some of which we have incorporated into our course manual as well as into this book. The list of these teachers could fill this page, but special thanks must be given to Lisa Edelstein, Thomas Glass, Len Galla, Rob Cohen, Fred Bernstein, and Jayme Koszyn.

Princeton Review would never have happened without the advice and support of Bob Scheller. Many of the questions on our diagnostic tests are the result of our joint effort. Bob's program, Pretest Review, provides the best sort of competition; his fine results make us work all the harder.

Finally, we would like to thank the people who truly have taught us everything we know about the SAT: our students.

CONTENTS

INTRODUCTION

Welcome to the 1993/94 edition of *Cracking the SAT & PSAT*. This book is for anyone planning to take the SAT in the fall of 1993 or January 1994. If you are planning to take the SAT in the spring of 1994, stop. As of March 1994 , the SAT will be given in a slightly different format, and you should be reading the 1994 version of *Cracking the System*. Go exchange this book wherever you bought it before you bend the cover or crinkle a page. *If you've recently bought this book, and you've already crinkled a page, send the book (with receipt) to us at TPR Publishing, 2315 Broadway, New York, NY 10024, and we'll swap it for you.*

If you're a high school junior, you may be thinking that you should take the SAT this November or December, before the test changes. Relax and wait until spring. The changes are small, and should actually make the test easier to prepare for. Besides, the math and reading you do in school this year will help you more than the changes will hurt.

So why did ETS change the test anyway? And what does that mean about the test you'll be taking?

The changes themselves are pretty trivial. First, ETS (the Educational Testing Service, which writes and administers the SAT) and the College Board (which sponsors the test) have finally admitted that the SAT doesn't measure intelligence, so they've changed its name from the Scholastic Aptitude Test to the Scholastic Assessment Test I. Some schools ask you to take a few one-hour Achievement tests in addition to the SAT; these Achievements will be renamed the Scholastic Assessment Test II.

Inside the SAT, antonym items will be dropped from the verbal section. Both the sentence completions and reading comprehension sections will include more questions that test vocabulary.

In the math section, students will be permitted to use calculators. Also, ETS and the College Board will include ten questions in which students will fill in their answers in a little grid. ETS suspected that this format would be confusing, and they were right. According to their own statistics, 20,000 students a year will answer these questions incorrectly because they don't understand the format.

You may have heard that the new, improved SAT would have an essay section, but it won't. Finally, the odious Test of Standard Written English will be dropped. We've never felt that this so-called "placement test" belonged on the SAT, anyway. Now it appears that ETS and College Board have come around to our point of view.

In other words, the SAT, though different, will be as flawed as ever. We've been lobbying for real change for a long time, and we're a little disappointed. What we'd like to see the SAT encompass are the three foundations of any valid test:

> *A valid test should include a statement of intent and content.* What is the SAT supposed to measure? It seems like an easy question (it's obvious that a vision test measures sight and a driver's test measures driving ability), but we've never heard an answer. Is this a test of intelligence? Of math skills? Of the ability to do college-level work? Which questions measure which skills? How do they do that?

> *A valid test should be disclosed after it's given.* Only students at a third of SAT administrations are able to get back their test booklets to examine the questions and answers. It's tough to see if ETS has fulfilled its goals if you can't look at the evaluated test. By the way, if ETS's question-and-answer service is available at your administration, you should definitely sign up for it!

> *A responsible test company should prove that the test has measured what it claims to measure.* To our knowledge, there is no evidence that the SAT measures intelligence, reasoning, college readiness, sex drive, or anything else. And yet students in the United States spend $100 million a year taking and preparing for it.

Even though the announced changes in the SAT won't take effect until 1994, the test does change subtly every year. The Princeton Review spends almost a million dollars every year improving our materials. We send fifty teachers into each test administration to make sure nothing slips by us. The 1993/94 edition of *Cracking the SAT & PSAT* incorporates our observations, giving you the most up-to-date information possible.

The Princeton Review has grown from fifteen kids in 1981 to 50,000 in 1991 because we do what almost no one else does: raise scores. Students in our SAT course improve their test scores a lot (independent studies show an average improvement of 110–160 points).

Our approach involves more than great techniques. Classes are small (eight to twelve in a group), and they're grouped by shared ability, so each student receives personal attention. When students don't understand something in class, we work with them in even smaller groups, and then in one-on-one tutoring.

We realize, however, that many kids can't get to our courses. That's why we wrote *Cracking the SAT & PSAT*. Although the book is no substitute for small classes and great teaching, it can help you improve your score. Make sure you take your time and do the drills carefully. The techniques are too complex to try them out the week before the SAT, so give yourself four or five weeks to practice our suggestions. We recommend that you devote six to ten hours a week to studying our techniques. You should practice these techniques on real tests (ETS publishes books of previously administered SATs; they're available in bookstores).

Furthermore, this is *not* a textbook; anyone charging you for a course that uses this book is probably ripping you off. You're better off just buying the book in a bookstore.

So relax. Work hard and get the SAT scores that the colleges you care about will love. And if you need more intense work than a book can offer, give us a call at 1-800-995-5585. Whatever you do, we wish you good luck.

John Katzman
President and Co-founder

Adam Robinson
Co-founder

We [illegible] [illegible] [illegible] that many kids can't get to our courses. [illegible] [illegible] we wrote [illegible] the SAT [illegible] [illegible] [illegible] [illegible] [illegible] weeks [illegible]

[illegible] [illegible] [illegible] [illegible] [illegible] [illegible] [illegible] [illegible] [illegible] [illegible] [illegible] this [illegible] [illegible] [illegible] [illegible] [illegible]. You're [illegible] [illegible] [illegible] [illegible] [illegible]

[illegible] we will [illegible] [illegible]

PART ONE

ORIENTATION

What Is the Scholastic Aptitude Test?

The Scholastic Aptitude Test (SAT) is a three-hour multiple-choice test divided into six sections:

1. a 45-question verbal section
2. a 40-question verbal section
3. a 50-question Test of Standard Written English
4. a 25-question math section
5. a 35-question math section
6. an experimental section

Each of these sections lasts 30 minutes. Only the two verbal sections and the two math sections count toward your SAT scores. Scores on the Test of Standard Written English (TSWE) aren't supposed to be used in college admissions, although they usually are (we'll tell you more about this in Part Four). The experimental section on your SAT may look like a verbal section, a math section, or a TSWE, but it won't be scored; ETS just uses it to try out new SAT questions and to determine whether the test you are taking is harder or easier than ones that have been given in the past.

The verbal SAT contains four different types of questions:

1. analogies
2. reading comprehensions
3. antonyms
4. sentence completions

The math SAT also contains four types of questions:

1. arithmetic
2. algebra
3. geometry
4. quantitative comparisons

The Test of Standard Written English contains two kinds of questions:

1. usage
2. sentence completion

Each of these question types will be dealt with in detail later in the book.

All the techniques discussed in this book also apply to the PSAT, or Preliminary Scholastic Aptitude Test, which is usually administered in eleventh grade. The PSAT is arranged a little differently from the SAT. It contains just one 50-minute verbal section and one 50-minute math section. The questions in these sections, though, are exactly like the ones on the SAT; in fact, PSAT questions are taken from old SATs.

Where Does the SAT Come From?

The SAT is published by the Education Testing Service (ETS) under the sponsorship of the College Entrance Examination Board (College Board). ETS and the College Board are both private companies. We'll tell you more about them in Chapter One.

How Is the SAT Scored?

Four or five weeks after you take the SAT, you will receive a report from ETS containing three scores:

1. your verbal SAT score
2. your math SAT score
3. your TSWE score

Verbal and math scores are reported on a scale that runs from 200 to 800, with 800 the best possible score. The third digit is always a zero, which means that scores can go up or down only ten points at a time. In other words, you might receive a 490, a 500, or a 510 on the verbal; you could never receive a 492, a 495, or a 507. Every question on the SAT is worth about ten points. (The actual value ranges from 0 to 20 points. The number of points is determined not by the difficulty of the question but by the number of other questions you have answered correctly.)

TSWE scores are reported on a scale that runs from 20 to 60+, with 60+ the best possible. You can miss four or five questions on the TSWE and still earn a score of 60+.

PSAT scores are reported on a scale that runs from 20 to 80. This is exactly like the SAT scale, except that the final zero has been removed.

(If you think this sounds needlessly complicated, you're right. There is no reason in the world why SAT, TSWE, and PSAT scores could not be reported on the same kind of scale.)

Raw Scores and Percentiles

You may hear about two other kinds of scores in connection with the SAT: raw scores and percentile scores. Here's what they mean:

1. Your raw score is simply the number of questions you answered correctly, minus a fraction of the number of questions you answered incorrectly. It is used in calculating your final "scaled" score. We'll tell you more about raw scores in Chapter Two.

2. A percentile score tells you how you did in relation to everyone else who took the test. If your score is in the 60th percentile, it means you did better on the test than 60 percent of the people who took it. People who are disappointed by their SAT scores can sometimes cheer themselves up by looking at their percentile scores.

What Is the Princeton Review?

The Princeton Review is the nation's fastest growing test preparation school. We have branches in dozens of cities, and our list of locations is constantly expanding. We prepare more students for the SAT and PSAT than any other coaching school. We also prepare students for the ACT, GRE, GMAT, and LSAT.

The Princeton Review's techniques are unique and powerful. We developed them after scrutinizing dozens of real SATs, analyzing them with computers, and proving our theories with our students. Our methods have been widely imitated, but no one else achieves our score improvements.

The Princeton Review's techniques for beating the SAT will help you improve your SAT scores by teaching you to:

1. think like the test writers at ETS
2. take full advantage of the limited time allowed
3. find the answers to questions you don't understand by guessing intelligently
4. avoid the traps that ETS has laid for you (and use those traps to your advantage)

Why ETS Executives Buy Cracking the SAT & PSAT for Their Children

ETS has spent a great deal of time and money trying to persuade people that the SAT can't be cracked. At the same time, ETS has struggled to find ways of changing the SAT so that it will stop being cracked by The Princeton Review—in effect acknowledging what our students have known all along, which is that our techniques really do work. In recent years ETS has made several changes in the test intended to thwart our students. They haven't succeeded.

In 1990, ETS and the College Board revealed plans for further changes in the SAT. These changes include the addition of a brief essay test and the replacement of some multiple-choice math questions with "open-ended" questions in which students will have to fill in a blank rather than select from among five choices. According to ETS and the College Board, the changes will be made beginning in the spring of 1994. (See the Introduction to this book for more information about the changes.)

These and other changes are partly intended to make the SAT harder for Princeton Review students to crack. But don't worry. The planned essay test is the same twenty-minute no-brainer that ETS currently uses on some versions of its English Composition Achievement Test. We have an airtight method for acing this essay. We already teach it to students preparing for Achievements. And the open-ended math questions aren't as frightening as they may seem. In the first place, at least 80 percent of the math questions on the SAT will continue to be multiple choice. In the second place, we have methods for cracking open-ended questions, which have been turning up in the SAT's so-called experimental section.

When ETS and the College Board really do make these changes in the SAT, we'll make sure that you are fully prepared. No matter what the questions look like, it will still be the same old SAT, and we'll still be able to show you how to crack the system.

A Note About Score Improvements

We have found in our courses that students' scores usually don't improve gradually. Instead, they tend to go up in spurts, from one plateau to another. Our students typically achieve score gains of 100 points or more after mastering the initial concepts of the course. Their scores then often level off, only to take another jump a few weeks later when more course material has been assimilated.

If you work steadily through this book, you too will feel yourself moving from plateau to plateau. But you will have to work. You won't have one of our teachers standing over you, reminding you to review what you have learned.

A Warning

Many of our techniques for beating the SAT are counterintuitive. That is, using them will sometimes require you to violate what you think of as common sense. In order to get the full benefit from our techniques, you must *trust* them. The best way to develop this trust is to practice the techniques and convince yourself that they work.

But you have to practice them *properly*. If you try our techniques on the practice questions in most popular SAT coaching books, you will probably decide that they don't work.

Why?

Because the practice questions in those books are very little like the questions on real SATs. There may be "antonyms" and "analogies" and "quantitative comparisons" in those books, but if you compare them with the questions on real SATs you will discover that they are very different. In fact, studying the practice questions and techniques in some of the other books could actually hurt your SAT score.

We strongly recommend that you purchase either *5 SATs* or *10 SATs*. Both of these books are put out by the College Board and ETS, the companies that publish the SAT, and both contain copies of real tests that were actually given. If you don't find them in your local bookstore, you can order them directly from the College Board (see page 271 for ordering information). If you haven't already been given one, you should also ask your guidance counselor for a free copy of *Taking the SAT*, a College Board booklet that contains a full-length practice test.

By practicing our techniques on real SATs, you will be able to prove to yourself that they work and increase your confidence when you actually take the test.

Another Warning

In October of 1991, the College Board announced that the SAT would soon have what they referred to as "significant changes" in its format. You may have read about it in popular magazines, or viewed stories on the 10 o'clock news.

You should know two things about these changes:

1) They are not scheduled to be implemented until the spring of 1994.
2) It *is* possible that ETS could make minor adjustments to the format of the test at any time. In fact, the December 1991 SAT contained a 40-question verbal section with only two reading comprehension passages (as compared to the usual four). Be aware that this type of change may occur in this year's tests!

CHAPTER ONE

How to Think About the SAT

Are You a Genius or an Idiot?

If you're like most high-school students, you think of the SAT as a test of how smart you are. If you score 800 on the verbal you'll probably think of yourself as a "genius"; if you score 200 you may think of yourself as an "idiot." You may even think of an SAT score as a permanent label, like your Social Security number. The Educational Testing Service (ETS), the company that publishes the test, encourages you to think this way by telling you that the test measures aptitude—"capacity for learning"—and by claiming that you cannot improve your score through special preparation.

But this is wrong.

The Scholastic Aptitude Test Is Not a Test of Scholastic Aptitude

The SAT isn't a test of how smart you are. It isn't a test of your "scholastic aptitude." It's simply a test of how good you are at taking ETS tests.

Can you learn to be better at taking the SAT? Of course you can. That's what this book is all about. You can improve your SAT score in exactly the same way you would improve your grade in chemistry: by learning the material you are going to be tested on.

You Must Learn to Think Like ETS

If your teacher gave you a D on a chemistry test, what would you do? You'd probably say to yourself, "I should have worked harder," or "I could have done better if I'd studied more." This is exactly the attitude you should have about the SAT. If you were disappointed by your score on the PSAT, you shouldn't think, "I'm stupid"; you should think, "I need to get better at taking this test."

You also need to get better at thinking like the people at ETS who write the questions. In your chemistry class, you know how your teacher thinks and that he or she tends to ask certain kinds of questions. You also know what sorts of answers will win you points, and what sorts of answers won't.

You need to learn to think of the SAT in exactly the same terms. The testwriters at ETS think in very predictable ways. You can improve your scores by learning to think the way they do and by learning to anticipate the kinds of answers that they think are correct.

What Is ETS?

ETS is the Educational Testing Service, a big company. It sells not only the SAT but also about 500 other tests, including ones for CIA agents, golf pros, travel agents, firemen, and barbers. ETS is located outside Princeton, New Jersey, on a beautiful 400-acre estate that used to be a hunting club. The buildings where the SAT is written are surrounded by woods and hills. There is a swimming pool, a goose pond, a baseball diamond, lighted tennis courts, jogging trails, an expensive house for the company's president, a chauffeured motor pool, and a private hotel where single rooms cost more than $200 a night.

You may have been told that ETS is a government agency, or that it's a part of Princeton University. It is neither. ETS is just a private company that makes a lot of money by selling tests. The company that hires ETS to write the SAT is called the College Entrance Examination Board, or the College Board.

Who Writes the SAT Today?

Many people believe the SAT questions are written by famous college professors or experts on secondary education. But this is not true. Virtually all questions are written by ordinary company employees or by college students and others hired part-time from outside ETS. Sometimes the questions are even written by teenagers. Frances Brodsky, the daughter of an ETS vice-president, spent the summer after she graduated from high school writing questions for ETS tests.

The SAT Is Not Written by Geniuses; You Don't Have to Be a Genius to Earn a High Score

Right now, the real person in charge of writing questions for the verbal half of the SAT is named Pamela Cruise. She's a young woman who's worked at ETS for several years. The walls of her small office are covered with pictures of the New York Rangers ice hockey team. She's a nice enough person, but, like most of us, she probably isn't a genius. Writing verbal questions for the SAT is just her job.

The person in charge of writing math questions is named James Braswell. He's older than Pamela Cruise. He is a soft-spoken man who wears glasses with black plastic frames.

Why are we telling you who these people are? Because you should always remember that the test you are going to take was written by real people. The Wizard of Oz turned out not to be a wizard at all; he was just a little man behind a curtain. The same sort of thing is true about the SAT.

Forget about the "Best" Answer

The instructions for the SAT tell you to select the "best" answer to every question. What does "best" answer mean? It means the answer that ETS believes to be correct. Specifically, it means the answer that Pamela Cruise and James Braswell selected when they wrote the questions in the first place.

For that reason, we're not going to talk about "best" answers in this book. Instead, we're going to talk about "Pam's answer" and "Jim's answer." These are the only answers that will win you points. Your job on the verbal SAT is to find Pam's answer to every question; your job on the math SAT is to find Jim's.

How to Crack the System

In the following chapters we're going to teach you our method for cracking the SAT. Read each chapter carefully. Some of our ideas may seem strange at first. For example, when we tell you that it is sometimes easier to answer hard SAT questions without looking at the questions, but only at the answer choices, you may think, "That's not the way I'm taught to think in school."

The SAT Isn't School

We're not going to teach you math. We're not going to teach you English. We're going to teach you SAT.

Why do you need to know the SAT? Because knowledge of the SAT is what the SAT tests.

In the next chapter we're going to lay down a few basic principles. We're going to show you that it is possible to

1. find a correct answer by eliminating incorrect ones even if you don't know *why* your answer is correct
2. take advantage of the SAT's "guessing reward"
3. earn partial credit for partial information

CHAPTER TWO

Cracking the System: Basic Principles

A Geography Lesson

What's the capital of Malawi?

Give up?

Unless you spend your spare time reading the atlas, you probably don't even know that Malawi is a tiny country in Africa, much less what its capital is. If this question came up on a test, you'd have to skip it, wouldn't you?

Well, Maybe Not

Let's turn this question into a multiple-choice question—the only kind of question you'll find on the SAT—and see if you can't figure out the answer anyway.

> The capital of Malawi is________
>
> (A) Washington, D.C. (B) Paris
> (C) Tokyo (D) London (E) Lilongwe

The Question Doesn't Seem Hard Anymore, Does It?

Of course, we made our example extremely easy. (By the way, there won't actually be any questions about geography on the SAT.) But you'd be surprised at how many people give up on SAT questions not much more difficult than this one just because they don't know the correct answer right off the top of their heads. "Capital of Malawi? Oh no! I've never *heard* of Malawi!"

These students don't stop to think that they might be able to find the correct answer simply by eliminating all the answers they know are wrong.

You Already Know All the Answers

If someone offered to give you all the answers to the SAT before you took it, you'd probably be shocked. But the fact is that every student who takes the test gets to see the answers ahead of time.

There's nothing strange or suspicious about this. The SAT is a multiple-choice test. That means that every question on it is followed by five (or, in a few cases, four) answer choices. In every single instance, one of those choices, and only one, will be the correct answer to the question. You'll never have to come up with the answer entirely from scratch. All you'll have to do is identify it.

How will you do that?

By Looking for Wrong Answers Instead of for Right Ones

Why? *Because wrong answers are usually easier to find.* Remember the question about Malawi. Even though you didn't know the answer off the top of your head, you figured it out easily by eliminating the four obviously incorrect choices. You looked for wrong answers first.

In other words, you used the *process of elimination*, which we'll call *POE* for short. This is an extremely important concept, and one that we'll come back to again and again. It's one of the keys to improving your SAT score. When you finish reading this book, you will be able to use POE to answer many questions you don't understand.

The great artist Michelangelo once said that when he looked at a block of marble, he could see a statue inside it. All he had to do to make a sculpture, he said, was to chip away everything that wasn't part of it. You should approach difficult SAT questions in the same way, by chipping away everything that's not correct. By first eliminating the *most obviously incorrect* choices on difficult questions, you will be able to focus your attention more effectively on the smaller number of truly tempting choices that remain.

This Isn't the Way You're Taught to Think in School

In school, your teachers expect you to work carefully and thoroughly, spending as long as it takes to understand whatever it is you're working on. They want you to prove not only that you know the answer to a question, but also that you know how to derive it. When your algebra teacher gives you a test in class, he or she wants you to work through every problem, step by logical step. You probably even have to show your work. If you don't know all the steps required to arrive at the solution, you may not receive full credit, even if you somehow manage to come up with the correct answer.

But the SAT is different. It isn't like school. You don't have to prove that you know why your answer is correct. The only thing ETS's scoring machine cares about is the answer you come up with. If you darken the right space on your answer sheet, you'll get credit, even if you didn't quite understand the question.

What's the Capital of Qatar?

There won't be many questions on the SAT in which incorrect choices will be as easy to eliminate as they were on the Malawi question. But if you read this book carefully, you'll learn how to eliminate at least one choice on virtually any SAT question, and two, three, or even four choices on many.

What good is it to eliminate just one or two choices on a four- or five-choice SAT item?

Plenty. In fact, for most students, it's an important key to earning higher scores. Here's another example:

> The capital of Qatar is ______
>
> (A) Paris (B) Dukhan
> (C) Tokyo (D) Doha (E) London

On this question you'll almost certainly be able to eliminate only three of the five choices by using POE. That means you still can't be sure of the answer. You know that the capital of Qatar has to be either Doha or Dukhan, but you don't know which.

Should you skip the question and go on? Or should you guess?

Close Your Eyes and Point

You've probably heard a lot of different advice about guessing on the SAT. Some teachers and guidance counselors tell their students never to guess and to mark an answer only if they're absolutely certain that it's correct. Others tell their students not to guess unless they are able to eliminate two or three of the choices.

Both of these pieces of advice are completely incorrect.

Even ETS is misleading about guessing. Although it tells you that you *can* guess, it doesn't tell you that you *should*. And you certainly should. In fact, if you can eliminate even *one* incorrect choice on an SAT question, guessing blindly among the remaining choices will most likely improve your score. And if you can eliminate two or three choices, you'll be even more likely to improve your score.

Don't Pay Attention to ETS

ETS tries to discourage students from guessing at all by telling them that there is a "guessing penalty" in the way the test is scored. But this isn't true. There is no penalty for guessing on the SAT. Even if you can't eliminate *any* of the choices, random guessing isn't going to hurt your score in the long run.

There Is No Guessing Penalty on the SAT

When ETS's grading machines score your SAT answer sheet, they'll first give you a "raw score." ETS will later use a "scoring formula" to convert this raw score into the sort of SAT score you're familiar with, which is called a "scaled score"—the number between 200 and 800 that ETS will send to the colleges you've applied to. But we're not concerned with scaled scores at the moment.

Your raw score is just the number of questions you got right, minus a fraction of the number you got wrong. Every time you answer an SAT question correctly, you get one raw point. Every time you leave an SAT question blank, you get zero raw points. Every time you answer an SAT question incorrectly, ETS subtracts either one-fourth of a raw point (if the question had five answer choices) or one-third of a raw point (if it had four).

It is this subtracted fraction—one-fourth or one-third, depending on the kind of question—that ETS refers to as the "guessing penalty." But it's nothing of the sort. An example should help you understand. Raw scores are a little confusing, so let's think in terms of money instead.

For every question you answer correctly on the SAT, ETS will give you a dollar. For every question you leave blank, ETS will give you nothing. For every question you get wrong, you will have to give twenty-five cents back to ETS. That's exactly the way raw scores work.

Now, suppose you have five SAT questions that you can't answer and you decide to guess blindly on them. What will happen? Each of the questions has five choices: A, B, C, D, and E. On each question, therefore, you will have one chance in five of selecting the right answer by guessing. This means that, when you guess on all five questions, on average you can expect to pick the correct answer on one and incorrect answers on four. (If this seems confusing, ask your math teacher to give you a quick explanation of the laws of probability.)

Guessing Won't Hurt You

What happens to your score if you select the correct answer on one question and incorrect choices on four questions? Remember what we said about money: ETS gives you a dollar for the one answer you guessed correctly; you give ETS a quarter for each of the four questions you missed. Four quarters equal a dollar, so you end up exactly where you started, with nothing—which is the same thing that would have happened if you had left all five questions blank.

Guessing blindly didn't leave you any better off on these five problems than leaving them blank would have. *But it didn't leave you any worse off, either.* You guessed five times in a row, and you were wrong four times, and there still wasn't any guessing penalty.

In Fact, There Is a Guessing Reward

What if you had been able to eliminate one incorrect choice on each of those questions? In that case, guessing blindly from among the remaining choices would have been most likely to *raise* your score. In other words, there would have been a guessing *reward.* All you have to do to earn this reward is eliminate one choice, close your eyes, and take a shot.

Still, guessing makes a lot of people very uncomfortable, so we're going to give you yet another way to think about it. Even if you're already convinced, keep reading.

One of the most common misconceptions about the SAT is that you're better off leaving a question blank than "taking a chance" on getting it wrong. Some students even believe that they could earn a perfect score on the test by answering just four or five questions correctly and leaving all the others blank. They think that they won't lose any points unless they give an answer that is actually wrong.

Nothing could be further from the truth.

In order to earn an 800 on the SAT you have to mark an answer for every question, and every answer you mark has to be correct. If you leave one question blank, the best you can hope to score is 780 or 790; leave 40 blank and your maximum possible score is about 400.

In other words, you literally lose points for every question on the SAT that you don't answer correctly—*even if you just leave it blank.* And once those points are gone, they're gone forever. You can't get them back by doing better on some other part of the test.

Why This Is True

Here's another way to think about what we just told you. When you take the SAT, you start off each half of the test with the equivalent of $800 in the bank. If you answer all the questions on each half correctly, you get to keep all $800.

For every question you answer incorrectly, though, you lose $10. Now, here's the important part: For every question you leave blank, *you still lose $8*.

Because of the way ETS calculates raw scores on the SAT, an incorrect answer is only a tiny bit worse than a blank. The one thing you can be certain of is that if you leave a question blank, you are *definitely* going to lose $8, whereas if you guess you have a possibility of keeping $10. If you guess incorrectly, you'll lose just $2 more than you would have if you hadn't guessed at all. And if you guess correctly, you'll get to keep your money. That's not much of a gamble, is it? Remember, you *might* get it right.

Partial Credit for Partial Information

We hope we've been able to persuade you that guessing isn't going to hurt you and that, if you learn to do it well, it will help you raise your score. If you're like most people, though, you probably still feel a little funny about it. Your teachers may even explicitly forbid you to guess in class. They want you to prove that you understand what they've been trying to teach you, not trick them into thinking you know something you don't. Earning points for a guess probably seems a little bit like cheating, or like stealing: You get something you want, but you didn't do anything to earn it.

This is not a useful way to think on the SAT. It also doesn't happen to be correct. Here's an example that should help you understand what we mean.

The sun is a ____

(A) main-sequence star (B) meteor
(C) asteroid (D) white dwarf star
(E) planet

If you've paid any attention at all in school for the last ten years or so, you probably know that the sun is a star. (Don't worry; there won't be any questions about astronomy on the SAT, either.) You can easily tell, therefore, that the answer to this question must be either A or D. You can tell this not only because it seems clear from the context that "white dwarf" and "main-sequence" are kinds of stars—as they are—but also because you know for a fact that the sun is not a planet, a meteor, or an asteroid. Still, you aren't sure which of the two possible choices is correct. (It's choice A, by the way.)

Heads You Win a Dollar; Tails You Lose a Quarter

By using POE you've narrowed your choice down to two possibilities. If you guess randomly you'll have a fifty-fifty chance of being correct—like flipping a coin. Those are extremely good odds on the SAT: heads you win a dollar, tails you lose a quarter. But let's say that, in spite of everything we've told you so far, you just can't bring yourself to guess. It feels wrong to you to put down an answer when you aren't sure, so you decide to leave the question blank.

Don't You Dare Leave It Blank!

Before you decide to throw away points on this question, consider the case of another student—your best friend, let's say. Now, your best friend is a good guy and an OK friend, but he's not, to put it politely, a genius. When he comes to this question he has no idea *at all* what the sun is. Planet, asteroid, meteor—he doesn't have a clue. So he leaves it blank, too.

You know more about the sun than your friend does. You know that it's a star and he doesn't. But the two of you are going to earn exactly the same score on this question: zero. According to the SAT, you don't know any more about the sun than he does.

If you were in class, that probably wouldn't happen. Your teacher might give you credit for knowing that the sun is *some* kind of star. In math class your teacher probably gives you partial credit on a difficult algebra problem if you follow all the right steps but make a silly subtraction error and come up with an answer that's slightly off. This happens all the time in school. Your teachers very often give you partial credit for partial information.

Guessing Intelligently Will Increase Your Score

Guessing makes it possible to earn partial credit for partial information on the SAT. You won't know everything about every question on the test. But there will probably be a lot of questions about which you know *something*. Doesn't it seem fair that you should be able to earn some sort of credit for what you do know? Shouldn't your score be higher than the score of someone who doesn't know anything?

The Only Way to Make This Happen Is to Guess

How does guessing give you partial credit for partial information?

Simple. Every time you use POE to eliminate an obviously incorrect answer choice, you tilt the odds a little bit more in your favor: You give yourself an edge. Over the course of the entire test, these edges add up. You won't guess correctly on *every* question—but you will guess correctly on some. If you're 50 percent sure of the answer on each of ten questions, then the odds say you'll be most likely to guess correctly 50 percent of the time. You'll only earn half as many points as you would have earned if you'd been 100 percent certain of the answers—but that's completely fair, because you only know half as much.

Guessing is unfair only if you don't do it. Unfair to *you*, that is. Your SAT score won't be a fair indication of what you know unless you guess and earn partial credit for partial information. You'd get that partial credit if you were in class. Why shouldn't you get it on the SAT?

A Final Word before We Begin

At school you probably aren't allowed to write in your textbooks, unless your school requires you to buy them. You probably even feel a little peculiar about writing in books you own. Books are supposed to be read, you've probably been told, and you're not supposed to scrawl all over them.

Because you've been told this so many times, you are probably going to be very reluctant to write in your test booklet when you take the SAT. Your proctor will tell you that you are supposed to write in it—the booklet is the only scratch paper you'll be allowed to use; it says so right in the instructions from ETS—but you'll still feel bad about marking it up. When you come to a math problem that you can't solve in your head, you'll use your very tiniest handwriting to work it out in the most inconspicuous sliver of the margin. When you've finished, you may even erase what you've written.

This Is Completely Ridiculous!

Your test booklet is just going to be thrown away when you're finished with it. No one is going to read what you wrote in it and decide that you're stupid because you couldn't remember what 2 + 2 is without writing it down. Your SAT score won't be any higher if you don't mark any marks in your booklet. In fact, if you don't take advantage of it, your score will probably be lower than it should be.

You Paid for Your Test Booklet; Act As Though You Own It

Scratch work is *extremely* important on the SAT. Don't be embarrassed about it. Writing in your test booklet will help you keep your mind on what you're doing.

• When a problem asks you about a certain geometrical figure but doesn't provide a drawing, make one yourself. *Don't simply try to imagine it in your head.* Unless you have a photographic memory, you won't be able to keep track of all the different angles, sides, and vertices, and you'll end up wasting valuable time.

• When you work on a geometry problem that does provide a drawing, *don't hesitate to draw all over it yourself.* Many times you will find it helpful to pencil in information that is supplied in the question but not in the drawing.

• When you've used POE to eliminate an obviously wrong answer choice, *cross it out.* Don't leave it there to confuse you. If you have to come back to the question later on, you don't want to redo all the work you did the first time.

• When you answer a question but don't feel entirely certain of your answer, *circle the question* or put a big question mark in the margin beside it. That way, if you have time later on, you can get back to it without having to search through the entire section.

All this applies just as much to the verbal SAT as it does to the math. You probably think of "scratch paper" as something that is only useful in arithmetic. But you'll need scratch paper on the verbal SAT, too. The verbal sections of your booklet should be just as marked up as the math ones.

Transfer Your Answers at the End of Each Group

Scratch work isn't the only thing we want you to do in your test booklet. We also want you to mark your answers there. When you take the SAT, you should mark all your answers in your test booklet, with a big letter in the margin beside each problem, and then transfer them later onto your answer sheet. You should transfer your answers when you come to the end of each group of questions. (For example, when you answer a 15-item antonym group, you should transfer all your answers together after you come to the end of the group.)

Doing this will save you a great deal of time, because you won't have to look back and forth between your test booklet and your answer sheet every few seconds while you are taking the test. You will also be less likely to make mistakes in marking your answers on the answer sheet.

Summary

1. When you don't know the right answer to a question, look for wrong answers instead. They're usually easier to find.

2. When you find a wrong choice, eliminate it. In other words, use POE, the process of elimination.

3. ETS doesn't care if you understand the questions on the SAT. All it cares about is whether you darken the correct space on your answer sheet.

4. Despite what you've probably heard, there is no guessing penalty on the SAT. In fact, there is a guessing *reward*. If you can eliminate just one incorrect choice on an SAT question, you will most likely improve your score by guessing blindly among the remaining choices.

5. Leaving a question blank costs you almost as many points as answering it incorrectly.

6. Intelligent guessing enables you to earn partial credit for partial information. You get credit for this in school. Why shouldn't you get it on the SAT?

7. Do not hesitate to use your test booklet for scratch paper.

8. Transfer your answers to your answer sheet *all at once* when you reach the end of each group of questions.

CHAPTER THREE

Cracking the System: Advanced Principles

Putting the Basic Principles to Work

In the preceding chapter, we reviewed some basic principles about the SAT. We showed you that it is possible to

1. find correct answers by using POE, the process of elimination, to get rid of incorrect ones
2. take advantage of the SAT's "guessing reward"
3. earn partial credit for partial information

But how will you know which answers to eliminate? And how will you know when to guess?

In this chapter, we'll begin to show you. We will teach you how to

1. take advantage of the order in which questions are asked
2. make better use of your time by scoring the easy points first
3. use the Joe Bloggs principle to eliminate obviously incorrect choices on difficult questions
4. find the traps that ETS has laid for you
5. turn those traps into points

To show you how this is possible, we first have to tell you something about the way the SAT is arranged.

Order of Difficulty

If you've already taken the SAT once, you probably noticed that the questions got harder as you went along. You probably didn't think much of it at the time. But it's always true on the SAT. Every group of questions starts out easy and then gets hard.

When you take the SAT, the first verbal section will probably begin with a group of 15 antonym questions. The first of these questions will be so easy that you and virtually everyone else will almost certainly be able to answer it correctly. The second will be a little harder. The tenth will be quite a bit harder. And the 15th will be so hard that most of the people taking the test will be unable to answer it.

Is This Always True? Yes

All standardized tests are arranged this way. They always have been, and they always will be. It isn't too hard to see why. If your gym teacher wanted to find out how high the people in your gym class could jump, she wouldn't start out by setting the high-jump bar at 7 feet. She'd set it at a height that almost everyone could clear, and then she'd gradually raise it from there.

Questions on the SAT work the same way. If they were arranged differently, many students would become discouraged and give up before finding questions they were able to answer.

Easy, Medium, Hard

Every group of questions on the SAT can be divided into three parts according to difficulty:

1. *The easy third:* Questions in the first third of each group are easy.
2. *The medium third:* Questions in the middle third are medium.
3. *The difficult third:* Questions in the last third are difficult.

In the antonym group just mentioned, questions 1-5 are easy, questions 6-10 are medium, and questions 11-15 are hard.

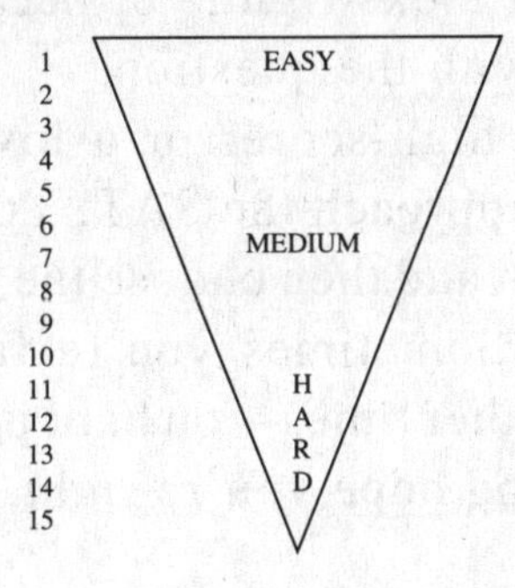

Knowing the Order of Difficulty Can Help You Improve Your Score

Knowing that SAT questions are presented in order of difficulty can help you in several ways. First, it enables you to make the best use of your limited time. You should never waste time wrestling with the fifteenth (and therefore hardest) question in the antonym group if you still haven't answered the first (and therefore easiest) in the sentence completion group, which follows it. Hard questions aren't worth more than easy ones. Why not do the easiest one first? Smart test takers save hard questions for last, after they've scored all the easy points.

We can state this as a simple rule: **Answer easy questions first; save hard questions for last.**

Knowing the Order of Difficulty Can Help You In More Important Ways as Well

Knowing how questions are arranged on the SAT can help you make the most efficient use of your time. But it can also help you find Jim's and Pam's answers on questions you don't understand.

To show you why this is true, we need to tell you something about how most people take the SAT and other standardized tests.

Choosing Answers That "Seem" Right

Most of us, when we take the SAT, don't have time to work out every problem completely, or to check and double-check our answers. We just go as far as we can on every problem and then choose the answer that *seems* correct, based on what we've been able to figure out. Sometimes we're completely sure of our answer. Other times we simply do what we can and then follow our hunch. We may pick an answer because it "just looks right," or because something about it seems to go naturally with the question.

Whether you're a high-scorer or a low-scorer, this is almost certainly the way you approach the SAT. You figure out as much of each problem as you can and then choose the answer that seems right, all things considered. Sometimes you're fairly positive that your answer is correct. But other times—on hard problems—all you can do is follow your hunch and hope you're right.

Which Answers Seem Right?

That depends on who the students are and on how hard the questions are.

Specifically, here's what happens:

1. On easy questions, Jim's or Pam's answers seem right to virtually everyone: high scorers, average scorers, and low scorers.
2. On medium questions, Jim's or Pam's answers seem wrong to low scorers, right to high scorers, and sometimes right and sometimes wrong to average scorers.
3. On hard questions, Jim's or Pam's answers seem right to high scorers and wrong to everyone else.

What we've just said is really true by definition. If the correct answer to a difficult question *seemed* correct to almost everyone, the question couldn't really be difficult, could it? If the answer seemed right to everyone, everyone would pick it. That would make it an easy question.

This is an extremely important concept. Here's a rule to help you remember it: **Easy questions have easy answers; hard questions have hard answers.** For the average student, an "easy" solution to a hard question will always be wrong.

Meet Joe Bloggs

We're going to talk a lot about "the average student" from now on. For the sake of convenience, let's give him a name: Joe Bloggs. Joe Bloggs is just the average American high-school student. He has average grades and average SAT scores. There's a little bit of him in everyone, and there's a little bit of everyone in him. He isn't brilliant. He isn't dumb. He's exactly average.

How Does Joe Bloggs Approach the SAT?

Joe Bloggs, the average student, approaches the SAT just like everybody else does. Whether the question is hard or easy, he always chooses the answer that *seems* to be correct.

Here's an example of a very hard question from a real SAT:

25. A woman drove to work at an average speed of 40 miles per hour and returned along the same route at 30 miles per hour. If her total traveling time was 1 hour, what was the total number of miles in the round trip?

(A) 30 (B) $30\frac{1}{7}$ (C) $34\frac{2}{7}$ (D) 35 (E) 40

This was the 25th problem in a 25-problem math section. Therefore, according to the order of difficulty, it was the hardest problem in that section. Why was it hard? *It was hard because most people answered it incorrectly*. In fact, only about one student in ten got it right. (Don't bother trying to work it out. The correct answer—Jim's answer—is choice C, 34 2/7).

How Did Joe Bloggs Do on This Question?

Joe Bloggs—the average student—got this question wrong.

Why?

Because if the *average* student had gotten it right, it wouldn't have been a hard problem, would it?

Which Answer Did Joe Bloggs Pick on This Question?

Joe picked choice D on this question; 35 just *seemed* like the right answer to him. Joe assumed that the problem required him to calculate the woman's average speed, and 35 is the average of 30 and 40.

But Joe *didn't* realize that he needed to account for the fact that the woman's trip didn't take the same amount of time in each direction. Her trip *to* work didn't last as long as her trip *home*. The answer could be 35 only if the woman had driven for a half-hour at 40 miles an hour and a half-hour at 30 miles an hour, and she did not.

Choice D was a trap: Jim Braswell included it among the answer choices because he knew that it would *seem* right to the average student. He put a trap among the choices because he wanted this problem to be a *hard* problem, not an *easy* one.

Could Jim Have Made This an Easy Question Instead?

Yes, by writing different answer choices.

Here's the same question with choices we have substituted to make the correct answer obvious:

1. A woman drove to work at an average speed of 40 miles per hour and returned along the same route at 30 miles per hour. If her total traveling time was 1 hour, what was the total number of miles in the round trip?

(A) 1 million (B) 1 billion (C) $34\frac{2}{7}$
(D) 1 trillion (E) 1 zillion

When the problem is written this way, Joe Bloggs can easily see that Jim's answer has to be C. It *seems* right to Joe because all the other answers seem obviously wrong.

Remember:

1. An SAT question is easy if the correct answer *seems* correct to the average person—to Joe Bloggs.
2. An SAT question is hard if the correct answer *seems* correct to almost no one.

The Joe Bloggs Principle

When you take the SAT a few weeks or months from now, you'll have to take it on your own, of course. But suppose for a moment that ETS allowed you to take it with Joe Bloggs as your partner. Would Joe be any help to you on the SAT?

You Probably Don't Think So

After all, Joe is wrong as often as he is right. He knows the answers to the easy questions, but so do you. You'd like to do better than average on the SAT, and Joe only earns an average score (he's the average person, remember). All things considered, you'd probably prefer to have someone else for your partner.

But Joe might turn out to be a pretty helpful partner, after all. Since his hunches are *always* wrong on difficult questions, couldn't you improve your chances on those questions simply by finding out what Joe wanted to pick, and then picking something else?

If you could use the Joe Bloggs principle to *eliminate* one, two or even three obviously incorrect choices on a hard problem, couldn't you improve your score by *guessing* among the remaining choices?

How to Navigate with a Broken Compass

If you were lost in the woods, would it do you any good to have a broken compass? You probably don't think so. But it would depend on *how* the compass was broken. Suppose you had a compass that always pointed south instead of north. Would you throw it away? Of course not. If you wanted to go north, you'd simply see which way the compass was pointing and then walk in the opposite direction.

Joe Bloggs Is Like That Broken Compass

On difficult SAT questions, he always points in the wrong direction. If Joe Bloggs were your partner on the test, you could improve your chances dramatically just by looking to see where he was pointing, and then going a different way.

We're going to teach you to make Joe Bloggs your partner on the SAT. When you come to difficult questions on the test, you're going to stop and ask yourself, "How would Joe Bloggs answer this question?" And when you see what *he* would do, *you* are going to do something else. Why? Because you know that on hard questions Joe Bloggs is *always* wrong.

What If Joe Bloggs Is Right?

Remember what we said about Joe Bloggs at the beginning. He is the average person. He thinks the way most people do. If the right answer to a hard question *seemed right* to *most people*, the question wouldn't be hard, would it?

Joe Bloggs *is* right on some questions: the easy ones. But he's *always* wrong on the hard questions.

Should You Always Just Eliminate Any Answer That Seems To Be Correct?

No!

Remember what we said about Joe Bloggs:

1. His hunches are *correct* on easy questions.
2. His hunches are *sometimes correct* and *sometimes incorrect* on medium questions.
3. His hunches are *always wrong* on difficult questions.

On easy questions, you want to *pick* the choice that Joe Bloggs would pick. On hard questions, you want to *eliminate* the choices that Joe Bloggs would pick.

Putting Joe Bloggs to Work for You

In the chapters that follow, we're going to teach you many specific problem solving techniques based on the Joe Bloggs principle. The Joe Bloggs principle will help you

1. use POE to eliminate incorrect answer choices
2. make up your mind when you have to guess
3. avoid careless mistakes

The more you learn about Joe Bloggs, the more help he'll be on the test. If you make him your partner on the SAT, he'll help you find Pam's and Jim's answers on problems you never dreamed you'd be able to solve.

Summary

1. The questions in every group of questions on the SAT start out easy and gradually get harder. The first question in a group is often so easy that virtually everyone can find Pam's or Jim's answer. The last question is so hard that almost no one can.

2. Because this is true, you should never waste time trying to figure out the answer to a *hard* question if there are still *easy* questions that you haven't tried. All questions are worth the same number of points. Why not do the easy ones first?

3. Every group of questions on the SAT can be divided into thirds by difficulty, as follows:
   - On the easy third of each group of questions, the average person gets all the answers right. The answers that *seem* right to the average person actually *are* right on these questions.
   - On the medium third of each group, though, the average person's hunches are right only some of the time. Sometimes the answers that *seem* right to the average person really *are* right; sometimes they are wrong.
   - Finally, on the difficult third, the average person's hunches are always wrong. The average person only picks the correct answer on the hardest questions by accident. The answers that *seem* right to the average person on these questions invariably turn out to be wrong.

4. Almost everyone approaches the SAT by choosing the answer that *seems* correct, all things considered.

5. Joe Bloggs is the average student. He earns an average score on the SAT. On easy SAT questions, the answers that *seem* correct to him are always correct. On medium questions, they're sometimes correct and sometimes not. On hard questions, they're always wrong.

6. The correct answer to a hard question could never *seem right* to *most people*. If it did, the question would be easy, not hard.

Summary

(1) The questions ... a majority ... questions on the ... [illegible]
[illegible]
[illegible]
[illegible]

[illegible] ... on the ... question
[illegible]
points. [illegible]

(2) The group ... [illegible] ... is as follows:
In the ... [illegible]
... all the ... [illegible]
[illegible]
On the ... [illegible] ... the average
[illegible]
[illegible]
[illegible]
[illegible]
[illegible]
[illegible]
[illegible]

[illegible]
[illegible]

[illegible]
[illegible]
[illegible]
correct ... [illegible]
[illegible]

The correct ... [illegible]
[illegible]

PART TWO

HOW TO CRACK THE VERBAL SAT

A Few Words about Words

The SAT contains six 30-minute sections. Two of these will be verbal, or "English," sections. There may be a third verbal section on your test, but it will be experimental and so won't count toward your score.

Each of the two scored verbal sections on the SAT contains groups of questions drawn from the following four categories:

1. analogies
2. reading comprehensions
3. antonyms
4. sentence completions

One verbal section contains 45 questions, the other contains 40. These questions are arranged as follows:

TYPE I (45 questions)	TYPE II (40 questions)
15 antonyms	10 antonyms
10 sentence completions	5 sentence completions
10 reading comprehensions	10 analogies
10 analogies	15 reading comprehensions

That's 85 questions altogether. Notice that you will have less than a minute to answer each one.

Every once in a while, the 45-question section has a slightly different format:

TYPE I (possible)
15 antonyms
5 sentence completions
10 reading comprehensions
5 sentence completions
10 analogies

ETS says that the verbal SAT tests "verbal reasoning abilities" or "higher-order reasoning abilities" (whatever *that* means). But this is not true. *The verbal SAT is almost entirely a test of your vocabulary.* Even reading comprehension questions often test nothing more than your familiarity with certain words. If you have a big vocabulary, you'll probably do well on the exam. If you have a small vocabulary, you're going to be in trouble no matter how many techniques we teach you.

For this reason, it's absolutely essential that you get to work on your vocabulary *now*! The best way to improve your vocabulary is by reading. Any well-written book is better than television. Even certain periodicals—the *New York Times*, the *Wall Street Journal*, the *New Yorker*, the *Atlantic*—can improve your verbal performance if you read them regularly. Always keep a notebook and a dictionary by your side as you read. When you encounter words whose meanings you don't know, write them down, look them up, and try to incorporate them into your life. The dinner table is a good place to throw around new words.

Building a vocabulary this way can be slow and painful. Most of us have to encounter new words many times before we develop a firm sense of what they mean. You can speed up this process a great deal by taking advantage of the vocabulary section (Part Five) in the back of this book. That section is self-explanatory. It contains a relatively short list of words that are highly likely to turn up on the SAT, a section on roots, and some general guidelines about learning new words. If you work through it carefully between now and the time you take the test, you'll have a much easier time on the verbal SAT. The more SAT words you know, the more help our techniques will be.

Before you go on, turn to Part Five for a few minutes. Read through it quickly and sketch out a vocabulary-building program for yourself. You should follow this program every day, at the same time as you are working through the other chapters of this book.

The techniques described in the four verbal chapters that follow are intended to help you take full advantage of your growing vocabulary by using partial information to attack hard questions. You will also learn to increase your problem-solving speed. In a sense, we are going to teach you how to get the maximum possible mileage out of the words you do know. Almost all students miss SAT questions that they could have answered correctly if they had used POE (the process of elimination) to extend their knowledge.

Study our approach carefully and practice it in the drills we provide. If possible, you should also purchase a copy of *10 SATs*, which is available in bookstores, or *5 SATs*, which must be ordered from the College Board (see page 271). If you can't find your own copy, check your public library, school library, or guidance counselor's office. Both of these books contain real SATs that were actually given to students in recent years. You can never get too much practice on real SATs.

CHAPTER FOUR

Analogies

This chapter is about analogies, the first of the four types of verbal SAT questions. There will be two groups of analogy questions on the SAT you take, one in each verbal section. Each group will contain ten questions.

Before we begin, take a moment to read the following instructions and to answer the sample question that comes after it. Both appear here exactly as they do on real SATs. Be certain that you know and understand these instructions before you take the SAT. If you learn them ahead of time, you won't have to waste valuable seconds reading them on the day you take the test.

> Each question below consists of a related pair of words or phrases, followed by five lettered pairs of words or phrases. Select the lettered pair that *best* expresses a relationship similar to that expressed in the original pair.
>
> Example:
> YAWN:BOREDOM ::
>
> (A) dream:sleep (B) anger:madness
> (C) smile:amusement (D) face:expression
> (E) impatience:rebellion

Pam's answer to this sample question is choice C. A smile is a sign of amusement just as a yawn is a sign of boredom. The two pairs of words are related in the same way.

SAT Analogies: Cracking the System

It's important to know the instructions printed before each analogy group on the SAT, but it's vastly more important to understand what those instructions mean. ETS's instructions don't tell you everything you need to know about SAT analogies. The rest of this chapter will teach you what you do need to know.

Each group of ten analogies on the SAT is arranged in order of increasing difficulty, from very easy to very hard.

In each group of analogies:

1. the first three or four questions will be easy
2. the middle three or four questions will be medium
3. the final three or four questions will be difficult

Because our techniques vary depending on the difficulty of the question, the examples we use in this chapter will always be numbered. A number 1 will always be easy; a number 10 will always be hard. *Always pay attention to the question number in answering SAT questions.*

Our techniques work very well on SAT analogies. For this reason, you must *never* leave an analogy question blank on the SAT. If you learn our techniques, you should be able to eliminate at least one obviously incorrect choice, even on the hardest questions. On some hard questions, you will be able to find Pam's answer even though you don't know several of the words. Every time you leave an analogy blank you'll be throwing away points.

What Is an Analogy?

Every analogy question on the SAT begins with a pair of capitalized words. Your task is to determine how these words are related to each other and then select another pair of words that are related to each other in the same way.

There is only one kind of word relationship that counts on SAT analogy questions. We call this kind of relationship *a clear and necessary* one. What is a clear and necessary relationship? It is a tight, solid, logical relationship that is based on the meanings of the words. To put it somewhat differently: *A clear and necessary relationship is the kind of relationship that exists between a word and its dictionary definition*. The easiest way to understand what we mean is to look at an example.

Take the words *dog* and *kennel*. Is there a clear and necessary relationship between them? Yes, there is. A kennel is a shelter for a dog. If you look up *kennel* in the dictionary, that's exactly what you'll find. The relationship between the two words is *clear* (you don't have to rack your brain to think of a way in which you can sort of make it work, sort of). It is also *necessary*—dogs and kennels have to go together.

Want an example of an *un*clear and *un*necessary relationship? How about *dog* and *garage*. You have a dog, let's say, and it always sleeps in the garage. For your dog, the garage is a shelter. But you can easily see that the two words don't *necessarily* have anything to do with each other. Garages are for cars, not dogs. If you look up *garage* in the dictionary, you won't find it defined as "a structure where cars are parked; also, some people's dogs sleep there." You might be able to come up with a complicated justification for your answer, but it wouldn't win you any points with Pam. Remember, your job on the SAT is to find Pam's answer, not yours. And Pam's dog sleeps in a kennel.

The SAT is a little bit like the television show *Family Feud*. On *Family Feud*, contestants don't get any points for clever or funny answers; they only get points for the answers that were given by "the 100 people in our survey." The SAT works the same way. The only "good answer" on the SAT is Pam's answer.

The Basic Approach

How can you determine what the clear and necessary relationship is between the two words in capital letters? The best way is to construct a brief sentence using them. This sentence must use both words and it must state their relationship clearly. You will make it easier on yourself if you keep your sentence as short and specific as possible. In other words, no creative writing.

First, Form a Sentence

Let's try this approach on an easy question.

1. COMPANY:PRESIDENT :: (A) team:athlete
(B) hospital:patient (C) airline:passenger
(D) library:reader (E) army:general

Here's how to crack it: First we form a sentence: "A president is the head of a company." Then we plug in the answer choices:

(A) Is an athlete the head of a team? Well, an athlete is a part of a team, but the head of a team would be a captain. Eliminate. This could not be Pam's answer.

(B) Is a patient the head of a hospital? No. Eliminate.

(C) Is a passenger the head of an airline? No. Eliminate.

(D) Is a reader the head of a library? No. A reader might use a library, but a library's head would be called something like chief librarian. Eliminate.

(E) Is a general the head of an army? Yes. That's exactly what a general is. This is Pam's answer.

Let's try another one.

2. APPLE:FRUIT :: (A) meal:restaurant
(B) macaroni:cheese (C) dessert:vegetable
(D) beef:meat (E) crust:pizza

Here's how to crack it: First, we form a sentence: "An apple is a kind of fruit." Now we plug in the choices.

(A) Is a meal a kind of restaurant? No. These two words are related, but not like this. Eliminate.

(B) Is macaroni a kind of cheese? No. Eliminate.

(C) Is dessert a kind of vegetable? No. Eliminate.

(D) Is beef a kind of meat? Yes. A possibility.

(E) Is crust a kind of pizza? No. Eliminate.

Pam's answer has to be choice D. It's the only one we weren't able to eliminate.

Notice that even though D looked good immediately, we still checked choice E. You should always do this on the SAT. If you answer too quickly, you may end up with a choice that sounds all right to you but didn't sound good to Pam. *You can never be certain of your answer on an analogy until you have considered all the choices.*

Sometimes, after plugging the choices into your sentence, you may find yourself with two or more answers that seem possible. In such cases, you'll have to go back and make your sentence more specific, then try again.

Here's an example:

3. TIGER:ANIMAL :: (A) eagle:hawk
(B) dinosaur:fossil (C) shark:fish
(D) colt:horse (E) tulip:flower

Suppose that, in approaching this question for the first time, we form our sentence as "A tiger is a kind of animal." Now we plug in the choices:

(A) Is an eagle a kind of hawk? No. Eliminate.

(B) Is a dinosaur a kind of fossil? Not really, although some people might think so. We won't eliminate it yet, although it isn't a very good possibility.

(C) Is a shark a kind of fish? Yes, a possibility.

(D) Is a colt a kind of horse? Yes, in a way. Another possibility.

(E) Is a tulip a kind of flower? Yes. Yet another possibility.

Our problem is that we have made our sentence too loose and vague.

Here's how to crack it: We need to make our sentence more specific. How do we do that? By keeping in mind what the words really *mean*. The important fact about a tiger is not simply that it is a certain kind of animal, but that it is a ferocious one, or a dangerous one, or a meat-eating one. The only answer choice that fulfills this requirement is C.

The very best sentence is a *short* and *specific* one that *defines* one word in terms of the other. Pam only selects one answer on each question. If you come up with more than one, you've done something wrong. And always keep in mind that the verbal SAT is a vocabulary test. Virtually all the relationships tested on SAT analogies are between the *definitions* of words.

DRILL 1

The following drill will give you a better idea of what sort of relationship is tested on the SAT. Link each of the following pairs of words in a short, specific sentence that emphasizes the clear and necessary relationship (if any) between the two words. The best such sentence is one that defines one of the words in terms of the other. If you aren't *absolutely* certain of the meaning of any word, look it up, add it to your word list, and make sure you know it before you take the SAT. Warning: Some of these pairs are unrelated. If you find such a pair, don't try to turn it into a sentence; just put an X beside it. We've answered the first three questions for you. Be sure to check your answers against the key on pages 279-80. (Note: These pairs are *not* presented in order of difficulty.)

1. sorrow:happiness — Sorrow is the opposite of happiness.
2. chemist:laboratory — A chemist works in a laboratory.
3. bed:river — A bed is the bottom of a river.
4. incensed:annoyed
5. babble:speak
6. convict:sentence
7. cynicism:falsehood
8. fuel:motion
9. sprint:speed
10. lunatic:violence
11. vacillate:modest
12. strike:work
13. foundation:building
14. mutter:listener
15. knife:sharpen
16. battle:victory
17. honorary:admiration
18. bow:cello
19. minute:time
20. snack:meal
21. concert:audience
22. eavesdrop:listen
23. emotion:fervor
24. emend:text
25. pacifism:war
26. tirade:speech
27. fear:shame
28. rebel:defiance
29. habitable:occupants
30. fade:disappear
31. forestry:trees
32. focus:image
33. defame:reputation
34. bill:payment
35. annoy:abuse
36. dwindle:size

37. acquit:defendant ______
38. skeptical:doubt ______
39. baffled:angry ______
40. illicit:legality ______
41. casino:gambling ______
42. deface:destroy ______
43. carol:song ______
44. boundary:territory ______
45. drink:guzzle ______
46. courageous:defeat ______
47. dance:leap ______
48. pony:stable ______
49. ointment:painful ______
50. gallery:painter ______

Some Important Facts to Remember about Clear and Necessary Relationships

As you try to determine the clear and necessary relationships in SAT analogies keep the following rules in mind:

PART OF SPEECH

1. Roughly half of all SAT analogies have to do with the relationships between nouns:

NOUN:NOUN ::
(A) noun:noun (B) noun:noun
(C) noun:noun (D) noun:noun (E) noun:noun

2. Other analogies have to do with the relationships between adjectives and nouns (ADJECTIVE:NOUN or NOUN:ADJECTIVE), verbs and nouns (VERB:NOUN or NOUN:VERB), or, less frequently, verbs and adjectives (VERB:ADJECTIVE or ADJECTIVE:VERB). Adverbs are almost never used in SAT analogies.

3. Parts of speech are always consistent within individual analogies. If the words in capital letters are ADJECTIVE:NOUN, then *all* the choices will be adjective:noun. ETS *never* violates this rule. For example:

ADJECTIVE:NOUN :: (A) adjective:noun
(B) adjective:noun (C) adjective:noun
(D) adjective:noun (E) adjective:noun

DON'T GET CONFUSED

4. Some words (such as *run*, *laugh, jump*, and many others) can be used as both verbs and nouns. Don't get confused. If the first word in choice E is *laugh*, and all the other first words are nouns, then you know that *laugh* is being used as a noun.

5. When it is not immediately obvious whether one of the words in capital letters is being tested as a noun, an adjective, or a verb, ETS will almost always "establish the part of speech" in choice A. If you can't tell which category a word in capital letters belongs to, look at the first answer choice. It should clear up your confusion:

CLASP:TIE :: (A) shoe:foot

Although *clasp* could be used as either a verb or a noun, you can tell from choice A that it is being tested as a noun.

BEWARE

6. Beware of answer choices that are catch phrases or words that are often used together such as *fleeting:thought*, *risky:business*, *happy:birthday*, *good:morning*. Because such pairs of words sound so familiar, you may be led to think that they contain a clear and necessary relationship. But they almost never do. When you encounter such a pair of words, split it apart, define each word separately, and make certain they are really related in a clear and necessary way. Virtually all such pairs can be eliminated.

Finding Pam's Answer with Your Eyes Closed

You should now have a good understanding of the sort of relationship that must exist between the words in capital letters in SAT analogy items. You just used this understanding to write sentences in Drill 1. Now we're going to show you how to use this same concept to eliminate incorrect answer choices, and thus improve your guessing odds, *even if you don't know the meaning of the words in capital letters.*

Sound Impossible?

You may think this is impossible. But it's not. Here's how it works:

You already know two important facts about SAT analogy items:

1. The words in capital letters are always related to each other in a clear and necessary way.

2. The words in Pam's answer must be related to each other in exactly the same way as the words in capital letters.

From these two rules we can easily deduce a third:

3. The words in Pam's answer must be related to each other in a clear and necessary way.

This is a very simple idea. Since the relationship between the words in Pam's answer has to be exactly the same as the relationship between the words in capital letters, the relationship between the words in Pam's answer must also be clear and necessary. From this we can deduce a fourth rule—the most important rule of all:

4. Any answer choice containing words that are *not* related to each other in a clear and necessary way could not possibly be ETS's answer and can therefore be eliminated.

This rule will enable you to eliminate incorrect choices even when you don't know the words in capital letters.

Eliminating Unrelated Pairs

Keeping in mind Rule 4, try your hand at the following analogy. Notice that we've left out the words in the stem:

5. _____:_____ :: (A) plentiful:resource
(B) wealthy:money (C) voluntary:result
(D) neutral:activity (E) humorous:movie

Here's how to crack it: We have no idea what the words in capital letters are, so we ignore them and study the choices. Let's look at them one at a time:

(A) Is there a clear and necessary relationship between plentiful and resource? No. A resource might be plentiful, but it also might be scarce. The two words don't necessarily go together.

(B) Is there a clear and necessary relationship between wealthy and money? Yes. Wealthy means something like "having a lot of money." A possibility.

(C) Is there a clear and necessary relationship between voluntary and result? No. Eliminate.

(D) Is there a clear and necessary relationship between neutral and activity? No. Eliminate.

(E) Is there a clear and necessary relationship between humorous and movie? No. Movies don't have to be humorous.

We've eliminated everything but B. That means B has to be Pam's answer. We were able to find it even if we didn't know the words in capital letters. (The missing words were TALL:HEIGHT)

Don't make the mistake of being too clever on analogies. Pam isn't trying to see how ingenious you are. You won't win any points with her for coming up with a brilliant justification for an incorrect answer. Pam thinks of the analogy section as being fairly straightforward. If you can't find the relationship between two words after looking at them for five seconds (assuming you know the meanings of both words), then you should probably assume that there is no relationship.

Working Backward from the Choices

You won't find many SAT analogy items in which it is possible to eliminate all four incorrect choices. On any item where eliminating unrelated pairs doesn't take you all the way to Pam's answer, you'll need to use other techniques. Perhaps the most powerful of these other techniques is working backward.

Working backward is most useful when you are uncertain about the meaning of one of the words in capital letters. It is a method of testing an answer choice by determining whether the relationship between the words in it could possibly be the same as the relationship between the words in capital letters.

How does this work? Remember that when you knew both words in capital letters, you looked for Pam's answer by constructing a sentence and then plugging in the words from each choice. Since you now know only one of the words in capital letters, you cannot construct a sentence using them. However, you may be able to construct a sentence from a choice and then apply it to the words in capital letters.

Here's an example. Assume that you don't know the first word in capital letters and that you have already eliminated three unrelated pairs from among the choices. You are left with two choices that contain clear and necessary relationships. You must decide which one is Pam's answer.

5. ——— : YEAST :: (A) lubricant:oil
(B) [eliminated] (C) detergent:dirt (D) [eliminated]
(E) [eliminated]

Here's how to crack it: Is there a clear and necessary relationship between *lubricant* and *oil*? Of course there is. "Oil is a kind of lubricant." Now go back to the words in capital letters. Could yeast be a kind of ———? Yes, that's possible. Yeast could certainly be a kind of something. You don't have to think of an actual word to go in the blank. All you have to do is decide whether such a word is likely to exist.

Now try the same thing on choice C. Is there a clear and necessary relationship between *detergent* and *dirt*? Yes, definitely. "Detergent cleans away dirt." Now go back to the words in capital letters. Could ——— clean away yeast? No, that doesn't seem plausible. Even though you don't know what the first word in capital letters means, you can see that it probably couldn't mean what it would have to mean in order for C to be Pam's answer. Therefore, you can eliminate it. Pam's answer must be A. (It is. The missing word is *leaven.* Leaven is a substance that makes dough rise, and yeast is a kind of leaven, just as oil is a kind of lubricant.)

When you're trying to figure out whether there is a clear and necessary relationship between the words in an analogy choice, you'll often find it useful to ask yourself, "Could either of these words appear in the dictionary definition of the other?" Sometimes Pam's answers on analogy questions won't quite pass this test. But keeping the dictionary in mind will always help you. Remember, the verbal SAT is a vocabulary test. Pam uses analogy questions to test your understanding of the meanings of words. She isn't interested in whether you know that Shakespeare wrote *The Tempest*. All she cares about is whether you know that a *tempest* is a violent *windstorm*.

Improving the Effectiveness of Working Backward: Decoding the Words in Capital Letters

Working backward is a powerful technique. It becomes even more powerful when it is used in combination with *decoding*, which is a technique for zeroing in on the meaning of an unknown word in capital letters.

Like working backward and eliminating unrelated pairs, decoding is based on the fact that the words in SAT analogies must be related in a clear and necessary way. You can be certain, therefore, that the word you don't know must have something to do with the word you do know. The words may be directly connected in meaning, or they may be opposites, or they may differ only in degree, but there must be a clear and necessary relationship between them.

Let's look at a specific example:

5. ENTOMOLOGIST:INSECTS

Entomologist is a hard word, but there are only so many things it can mean. It couldn't have anything to do with baseball, television, or English literature, because baseball, television, and English literature don't have anything to do with insects. Whatever on earth it really is, *entomologist* must have something to do with bugs. It may mean someone who likes insects, catches insects, studies insects, eats insects—you may not be *exactly* sure, but you can be certain that insects are involved.

Of course, if you realize that the suffix *-ologist* means "one who studies," then you'll be able to figure out exactly what *entomologist* means. Since there has to be a clear and necessary relationship between the two words, an entomologist can only be one who studies insects. ETS would never use two unrelated words—PSYCHOLOGIST:INSECT, for example—in the capitalized pair, so you can guess with confidence.

Decoding analogy words is easiest when the words in capital letters are arranged ADJECTIVE:NOUN or NOUN:ADJECTIVE, because there are usually only two ways in which nouns and adjectives are clearly and necessarily related on the SAT: (1) the adjective may describe the noun, as in DISHONEST: LIAR, or (2) the adjective may describe the *opposite* of the noun, as in HONEST:LIAR. For example:

8. AMORPHOUS:SHAPE

Amorphous is a hard word, but you can probably see that it must be an adjective. (Remember, if you can't tell what part of speech a word in capital letters is, look at the corresponding word in each answer choice.) You also know that it must have something to do with *shape*, an easy noun. Perhaps it describes some kind of shape. Maybe it means something like "shapely"; perhaps it means "shapeless" (it does). Make your best guess, form a sentence, and plug in the choices. If you can't find an answer that satisfies you, make another guess and try again. You won't be right every time, but you should be able to eliminate at least one choice that couldn't possibly be correct.

When You Don't Know Words in the Answer Choices

Decoding words in the answer choices can be tricky, since you can't be certain that the words in a choice are clearly and necessarily related. Assuming you know both words in capital letters, you can still ask yourself whether *any* word could create a relationship in the choice identical to the relationship between the words in capital letters. If not, you can eliminate the choice. Here's an example:

5. INNOVATOR:CREATE :: (A) patient:cure
(B) ——— :give (C) scientist:describe
(D) president:elect (E) prisoner:confess

Here's how to crack it: Let's say we don't know the meaning of the first word in choice B. What should we do? We should simply follow our usual procedure. First we form a sentence: "An innovator is someone who creates." Then we plug in the choices.

(A) Is a patient someone who cures? No. A patient is someone who is (or is not) cured. Eliminate.

(B) Could ——— mean someone who gives? Possibly. We don't know the word, so we have to hang on to choice.

(C) Is a scientist someone who describes? Well a scientist might describe something, but this isn't a good definition of *scientist.* Eliminate. There is no clear and necessary relationship between these two words.

(D) Is a president someone who elects? No. A president is someone who is elected. Eliminate.

(E) Is a prisoner someone who confesses? No. A prisoner might have made a confession, but many prisoners don't confess, and many people who confess aren't prisoners. There is no clear and necessary relationship. Eliminate.

We've eliminated everything except choice B, so it must be Pam's answer. We pick it even though we don't know what one of the words is. (The missing word is *benefactor*, a benefactor is someone who gives.)

Joe Bloggs and SAT Analogies

As is always true on the SAT, Joe Bloggs finds some answer choices much more appealing than others on analogy items. Most of all, Joe is attracted to choices containing words that

1. remind him of one or both of the words in capital letters
2. "just seem to go with" the words in capital letters
3. are easy to understand

Eliminating Joe's Answers on the Difficult Third

The Joe Bloggs principle is most useful in helping you eliminate incorrect answer choices on the difficult third. To do this you first have to know how to spot choices that seem right to Joe.

What makes a choice *seem* right to Joe on an analogy question? Almost always an answer choice will seem right to Joe if one of the words in it reminds him of one of the words in the question. If a word in a choice "just seems to go with" one of the words in capital letter, Joe will be attracted to that choice. Here's an example:

1. SONG:VERSES :: (A) moon:phases
(B) tree:roots (C) battle:soldiers
(D) poem:stanzas (E) newspaper:reporters

Here's how to crack it: Which choice attracts Joe Bloggs on this question? Choice D. Songs and verses just seem to go with poems and stanzas. Does that mean choice D is wrong? *No!* Look at the number of this question. It's a number 1, the easiest in its group. Joe Bloggs gets the easy ones right, and D is Pam's answer.

But Joe's impulse to pick answers that "just seem to go with" the words in capital letters will get him in trouble on *hard* questions. After all, if Joe knew the answer to a hard analogy, it wouldn't be hard, would it? On the hardest analogy questions, therefore, you can safely eliminate choices that you know would seem attractive to Joe Bloggs. *Before you do anything else on a hard question, look for Joe's answers and cross them out.* Here's an example:

9. INFINITESIMAL:SIZE ::
(A) trifling:significance
(B) distant:galaxy (C) cacophonous:music
(D) lucid:behavior (E) enormous:mountain

Here's how to crack it: Which choices attract Joe on this question? Choice E definitely does, because enormous and mountain "just seem to go with" size. What does that mean? It means that E is wrong, because this is a hard question and Joe doesn't get the hard ones right.

Joe is probably also attracted to choice B: galaxies are large, which makes that choice "just seem to go with" the words in capital letters. You can also eliminate choice B.

(Pam's answer on this question is A. *Infinitesimal* means extremely small, or lacking in size; *trifling* means lacking in significance.)

Once you've learned to eliminate choices containing words that attract Joe Bloggs, we'll teach you other techniques for eliminating even more incorrect choices.

The Joe Bloggs Principle: Eliminating "Attractors"

We have a name for answers that seem right to Joe Bloggs. We call them "attractors." You must look at hard analogy questions—the last three or four questions in a ten-analogy group—through Joe's eyes, find the attractors, and eliminate them.

Here's another example:

9. DESTITUTION:MONEY :: (A) budget:options
(B) sobriety:inebriation (C) opulence:wealth
(D) deficit:finance (E) pollution:factory

Here's how to crack it: This is the next to last question in its group, which means it's the second hardest. Joe Bloggs will definitely get it wrong.

Destitution is a very hard word. Most people, including Joe Bloggs, don't know what it means. *Money*, however, is an easy word. Joe looks through the choices for a word that seems to go with *money*. He finds three attractors: *budget* in choice A, *wealth* in choice C, and *finance* in choice D. Joe will weigh these three choices and then pick one of them.

Once again, since this is an extremely difficult question, we know that Joe must certainly be wrong. *We can therefore eliminate all three choices.* If Joe's hunch were correct, this would be an easy question, not a hard one.

(Pam's answer on this question is B. If you guessed blindly after eliminating the three Joe Bloggs answers, you would have a fifty-fifty chance of picking it—good odds! Later in this chapter, you'll learn other techniques that may enable you to eliminate the other incorrect choice.)

Now What?

Your first step in approaching the *hardest* three or four questions in each analogy group should always be to eliminate Joe's attractors. You'll seldom find three, and you sometimes find none, but you'll usually find at least one. When you find it, cross it out in your test booklet. If it's Joe's answer, it can't be Pam's.

When you eliminate an incorrect choice on an analogy or any other SAT question, draw a line through it in your test booklet. On harder questions, you may have to *go back* several times before you settle on an answer. If you cross out choices you've eliminated, you won't waste time looking at them over and over again.

Hard Questions, Hard Answers

Joe Bloggs is lazy. He doesn't like problems that look too hard, and he doesn't like complicated solutions. This means that he has a very strong tendency to select choices containing words that he understands. He is very unlikely to select a choice if it contains words he's never heard of (unless there is something else about that choice that attracts him, such as an easy word that reminds him of one of the words in capital letters). When Joe takes a stab at a question, he picks something easy and familiar.

This can be a big help for you. Because Joe is so irresistibly drawn to *easy* choices, one of the best places to look for Pam's answer on a hard analogy question is in a *hard* choice— a choice containing words that Joe doesn't understand. When you find yourself stumped on a hard analogy item, simply eliminate what you can and then select the remaining choice that contains the hardest words.

This same principle can help you on easy items as well. Since Joe gets the easy analogy items right, and since he avoids choices containing hard words, you don't need to worry about hard choices, either. On easy items, trust your hunches instead.

How easy is easy? How hard is hard? The following drill should help give you a sense of the range of difficulty in the vocabulary tested on the SAT.

DRILL 2

Each group contains five pairs of words. Rearrange the pairs in increasing order of difficulty. The easiest way to do this might be to look for the easiest pair in each group and mark a 1 beside it; then look for the hardest pair and mark a 5 beside it; then look for the easiest pair of the remaining three and mark a 2 beside it; and so on. (The answers are on page 280.)

Remember: You must gauge difficulty from Joe Bloggs' point of view. A word isn't necessarily easy just because *you* know what it means. A word is only easy if *Joe* knows what it means.

GROUP A	GROUP B
scribble:penmanship	taste:connoisseur
banality:bore	mural:painting
urban:city	trees:forest
striped:lines	mendicant:beggar
preamble:statute	finale:opera

GROUP C	GROUP D
word:sentence	threadbare:clothing
arson:conflagration	novel:literature
garrulous:speaker	fins:aquatic
reflex:involuntary	loyal:devotion
mirror:reflection	insurrectionist:docile

Summary: Strategies by Thirds

As we have said several times, you need to use different techniques for the easy, medium, and hard thirds of each analogy group. The following lists should help you remember how to approach each third, as well as the order in which you should apply the techniques.

EASY THIRD
(The first three or four analogies)

1. Remember: Joe Bloggs gets these questions right. The choices that *seem* right *are* right. Trust your hunches, but be careful to consider *all* the choices.

2. Don't worry too much about hard words among the choices (Joe doesn't know them either). If you get stuck, go with something obvious.

3. Form a short, specific sentence that expresses the clear and necessary relationship between the two words in capital letters. The best such sentence is one that *defines* one of the words in terms of the other.

4. Plug each answer choice into your sentence. If you find more than one choice that works, go back and make your sentence more specific.

5. Eliminate unrelated pairs.

MIDDLE THIRD
(The middle three or four analogies)

1. Remember: Joe Bloggs gets some of these questions right, and some of these questions wrong. Don't automatically distrust your hunches, but be very careful about selecting an answer. Be especially careful to consider *all* the choices.

2. Form a short, specific sentence that expresses the clear and necessary relationship between the two words in capital letters. The best such sentence is one that *defines* one of the words in terms of the other.

3. Eliminate unrelated pairs.

4. If you don't know one of the words in capital letters, work backwards from the choices.

DIFFICULT THIRD
(The last three or four analogies)

1. Remember: Joe Bloggs gets these questions wrong. Before you do anything else, eliminate answers that would appeal to Joe Bloggs. Answers that *seem* right to Joe Bloggs in this third can't possibly be right.

2. If you know the words in the stem, form a sentence and plug it in.

3. Eliminate unrelated pairs.

4. If you don't know one of the words in capital letters, work backwards from the choices.

5. When all else fails, pick the choice with the hardest words.

CHAPTER FIVE

Reading Comprehensions

This chapter is about reading comprehensions, the second of the four item types used on the verbal SAT. The verbal SAT contains six reading passages. Each passage is followed by two, three, four, or five questions. One verbal section contains two passages; the other section contains four. Passages vary in length from 250 to 500 words. Together, the two verbal sections contain a total of 25 reading comprehension questions.

Before we begin, take a moment to read the following set of instructions, which appears exactly as it does on real SATs.

> Each passage below is followed by questions based on its content. Answer all questions following a passage on the basis of what is *stated* or *implied* in that passage.

Be sure you know and understand these instruction before you take the SAT. If you learn them ahead of time, you won't have to waste valuable seconds reading them on the day you take the test.

SAT Reading Comprehensions: Cracking the System

It's important to know the instructions printed before each group of reading comprehension passages on the SAT, but it's vastly more important to understand what those instructions mean. ETS's instructions don't tell you everything you need to know about SAT reading comprehensions. The rest of this chapter will teach you what you do need to know.

Our techniques will enable you to

1. gain time on the rest of the test by skipping (in some cases) one or two difficult passages
2. read quickly and efficiently
3. eliminate answer choices that could not possibly be correct
4. take advantage of outside knowledge
5. take advantage of inside knowledge (about how Pam thinks)
6. use proven strategies to find Pam's answers
7. find Pam's answers in some cases *without reading the passages*

Basic Passage Types

There are three basic types of reading passages on the SAT:

1. Factual passages: These are passages that discuss serious topics like science, economics, history, sociology, and philosophy. Or they might present factual information about artists, novelists, historical figures, or other real people. Your SAT will probably contain three factual passages, as follows:

A. one passage about a physical science, such as physics, chemistry, or astronomy
B. one passage about a biological science, such as biology, medicine, botany, or zoology
C. one passage about history, economics, sociology, or politics *or* one passage about an artist, novelist, historical figure, or some other real person

2. Opinion passages: These are passages that express a writer's beliefs and opinions about a topic (such as politics) or a person (such as an artist or an author). An opinion passage is like a book review or a newspaper editorial. It gives one person's opinion. Your SAT will probably contain two opinion passages, as follows:

A. an argumentative passage in which an author expresses a point of view
B. an excerpt from an essay about art, literature, music, philosophy, or folklore

3. *Fiction/humor passage:* This is usually a narrative excerpted from a novel or essay. (We have yet to see a poem on the SAT.) Your SAT will contain one fiction/humor passage.

One of the six passages on your SAT will deal with the members of an ethnic or minority group. This *ethnic passage*, as we call it, will usually be either the history/economics/sociology/politics passage or the art/literature/music/philosophy/folklore passage. The ethnic passage has its own techniques and rules, so we will deal with it separately.

Order of Difficulty

Reading comprehension questions are the only questions on the SAT that are not presented in order of difficulty. Reading comprehension *passages*, however, *are* generally presented in order of difficulty. In the verbal section containing two passages, both will usually be moderate to hard, and each will be followed by five questions. In the verbal section containing four passages, the passages will progress from fairly easy to very difficult. Each will be followed by two, three, four, or five questions.

Save Reading Comprehensions for Last

The most important fact to remember about SAT reading comprehension passages is that they are extraordinarily time-consuming. Reading comprehensions are worth the same number of points as analogies, but they take much, much longer to answer. For this reason, reading comprehension passages should be the *last thing you get to* in each section of the verbal SAT. In other words, do all analogies, antonyms, and sentence completions *before* you do the passages. (If you were offered a job that paid $10 an hour and another that paid $10 a minute, which one would you choose?)

Answering three hard reading comprehension questions could easily take longer than answering all 15 antonym questions. *Don't sacrifice 150 points in the hope of earning 30.*

It May Even Make Sense for You to Skip Some Reading Comprehensions Entirely

Unless you score in the 700s on the SAT verbal or have an unusual knack for answering SAT reading comprehensions, you should probably consider simply ignoring one or more of the passages on your test. This will save you valuable time that you can use to earn easy points elsewhere in each verbal.

Here are the passages you can skip:

1. If you are aiming for a verbal score of less than 700, you should skip either the third or fourth (very hard) passage in the verbal section containing four passages. Simply cross out the harder-looking of these two passages in your test booklet and forget about it.

2. If you are aiming for a verbal score below 600, you should also skip either of the two (fairly hard) passages in the verbal section containing two passages.

3. If you are aiming for a verbal score below 550, you should skip both the third and fourth passages in the section containing four passages and the harder passage in the section containing two passages.

Our experience has shown that skipping these passages can be doubly beneficial to most students. Since these passages are so difficult, most students who try to read them *end up answering virtually all the questions wrong anyway.* They spend a lot of valuable time and then have nothing to show for it.

Please note that we advise skipping *entire passages* rather than one question on this passage and one question on that passage. It makes no sense to spend time reading entire passages and then leave isolated questions blank.

SAT Reading Comprehensions Have Nothing to Do with Comprehending Reading

If you actually tried to *comprehend* the reading passages on the SAT—by reading and rereading them until you understood each one thoroughly—you wouldn't have any time left for the rest of the test.

You will never do well on SAT reading comprehensions unless you keep one central fact in mind: *Your goal is to earn points, not to understand the passage.* The questions cover no more than 10 or 20 percent of the material in each passage. We'll teach you how to identify the important 10 or 20 percent and ignore most of the rest. The less time you spend reading the passage, the more time you'll have for earning points.

Think of Reading Comprehensions as a Treasure Hunt

If we told you that we had hidden $50,000 somewhere in your hometown, and then handed you on envelope filled with clues, would you search every inch of your hometown before you opened the envelope and looked at the clues?

Of course not.

You'd look at the clues first and use them to help you eliminate places where the treasure could not possibly be hidden.

The Same Is True with the SAT

Every reading passage contains a hidden treasure of 20 to 50 points. Your job is to find the treasure. There are a number of clues that will help you. Some of these clues are located in the passage; others are in the questions and answers. In this chapter, we will help you learn to identify these clues and use them to earn a higher SAT score.

Basic Principles: How to Read

A team of psychologists once performed a reading experiment with two groups of students. The students in both groups were asked to read several passages and answer questions about them. All students were given the same instructions, with one important difference—the ones in the second group were told to read each passage as *quickly as possible* while keeping in mind that questions would follow.

What happened?

You may be surprised: The students who read quickly earned the same scores as the students who read slowly. *The only difference was that reading the passages took them just half as long as it took the "careful" readers.* The researchers concluded that most people can push themselves to read much faster if they worry less about details and concentrate on general ideas.

Don't Get Bogged Down

If you read too carefully, underlining every other word and trying to understand every detail, you will discover at the end of the passage that you have understood nothing. Did you ever "finish" a passage only to look up and ask yourself, "What did I just read?" Since the questions will only test a tiny fraction of what you have read, you don't want to waste a lot of time memorizing details that you won't need to know.

Sample Passage and Questions

In the discussion that follows we will refer again and again to the sample passage and questions below.

The subject of my study is women who are initiating social change in a small region in Texas. The women are Mexican Americans who are, or were, migrant agricultural workers. There is more than one kind of innovation at work in the region, of course, but I have chosen to focus on three related patterns of family behavior.

The pattern I life-style represents how migrant farm workers of all nationalities lived in the past and how many continue to live. I treat this pattern as a baseline with which to compare the changes represented by patterns II and III. Families in pattern I work on farms year round, migrating for as many as ten months each year. They work and travel in extended kin units, with the eldest male occupying the position of authority. Families are large—eight or nine children are not unusual—and all members are economic contributors in this strategy of family migration.

Families in pattern II manifest some differences in behavior while still maintaining aspects of pattern I. They continue to migrate but on a reduced scale, often modifying their schedules of migration to allow children to finish the school year. Parents in this pattern often find temporary local jobs as checkers or clerks to offset lost farming income. Pattern II families usually have fewer children than do pattern I families.

The greatest amount of change from pattern I, however, is found in pattern III families, who no longer migrate at all. Both parents work full time in the area and have an average of three children. Children attend school for the entire year. In pattern III, the women in particular create new roles for themselves for which no local models exist. They not only work full time but may, in addition, return to school. They also assume a greater responsibility in family decisions than do women in the other patterns. Although these women are in the minority among residents of the region, they serve as role models for others, causing ripples of change to spread in their communities.

New opportunities have continued to be determined by preexisting values. When federal jobs became available in the region, most involved working under the direction of female professionals such as teachers or nurses. Such positions were unacceptable to many men in the area because they were not accustomed to being subordinate to women. Women therefore took the jobs, at first, because the income was desperately needed. But some of the women decided to stay at their jobs after the family's distress was over. These women enjoyed their work, its responsibility, and the companionship of fellow women workers. The steady, relatively high income allowed their families to stop migrating. And, as the efficaciousness of these women became increasingly apparent, they and their families became even more willing to consider changes in their lives that they would not have considered before.

33. Which of the following titles best reflects the main focus of the passage?

    (A) A Study of Three Mexican-American Families at Work in Texas
    (B) Innovative Career Women: Effects on Family Unity
    (C) Changes in the Life-styles of Migrant Mexican-American Families
    (D) Farming or Family: The Unavoidable Choice for Migrant Farm Workers
    (E) Recent Changes in Methods of Farming in Texas

34. According to the passage, pattern I families are characterized by which of the following?

    (A) Small numbers of children
    (B) Brief periods of migrant labor
    (C) Female figures of family authority
    (D) Commercial as well as agricultural sources of income
    (E) Parents and children working and traveling together

35. All of the following statements about pattern II children express differences between them and pattern I children EXCEPT:

    (A) They migrate for part of each year.
    (B) They have fewer siblings.
    (C) They spend less time contributing to family income.
    (D) They spend more months in school.
    (E) Their parents sometimes work at jobs other than farming.

36. According to the passage, which of the following is NOT true of women in pattern III families?

    (A) They earn a reliable and comparatively high income.
    (B) They continue to work solely to meet the urgent needs of their family.
    (C) They are more involved in the deciding of family issues than they once were.
    (D) They enjoy the fellowship involved in working with other women.
    (E) They serve as models of behavior for others in the region.

37. The author's attitude toward the three patterns of behavior mentioned in the passage is best described as one of

(A) great admiration
(B) grudging respect
(C) unbiased objectivity
(D) dissatisfaction
(E) indifference

Here's Our Step-by-Step Game Plan for Reading SAT Reading Passages

We have a step-by-step game plan for reading SAT reading passages and answering the questions about them. We'll outline the plan first and then discuss each step in detail. Here's the outline:

Step 1: Every passage has a main idea or central theme. Your first task in reading a passage is to find this main idea. Often it will be revealed in the first few lines of the very first paragraph. Read these lines *carefully* until you have a good sense of what the author is up to.

Step 2: Every paragraph also has a main idea or central theme, usually revealed in the first or last sentence. Your goal in reading each paragraph is to find this main idea and then move on.

Step 3: Don't worry about details at this point. Move quickly from paragraph to paragraph, summarizing the main idea and skimming over the rest. You will come back for the details later, when you know which ones you need. (You won't be able to remember the details anyway; why waste time trying to memorize them now?)

Step 4: As you skim, circle *trigger* words and underline the sentences in which they appear. A sentence that contains a trigger word will usually contain the answer to a question. (We'll tell you about trigger words soon.)

Step 5: Go to the questions. Attack them *one at a time*, beginning with the general questions and saving the specific questions for last.

Step 1: Find the Main Idea of the Passage

Every SAT reading passage has the same basic structure: The author has a main idea. Her primary purpose is to develop or explain this idea. She does this by stating her main idea and then supporting it with details, fact, examples, metaphors, and *secondary* ideas. The author also has an attitude toward her subject (she is either for something, against something, or objective), which she conveys in her tone or style.

The main idea of the passage is often expressed in the first few lines of the very first paragraph. Knowing this idea will make it easier for you to keep the general structure of the passage in your mind. It will also make it easier for you to determine the main idea of each paragraph and to find Pam's answers later on. You should read the first few lines of the passage *carefully* until you have a good sense of what the author is up to.

Think of an SAT reading passage as a house. The main idea of the passage is like the overall plan of the house; the main idea of each paragraph is like the plan of each room. Reading the passage is like walking through the house. As you walk, you don't want to waste your time memorizing every detail of every room; you want to develop a *general sense* of the layout of the rooms and of the house as a whole. If you tried to memorize every detail, you'd never get through the house. Later on, when Pam asks you what was sitting on the table beside the chair in the master bedroom, you won't know the answer off the top of you head, *but you will know exactly where to look for it.* And you'll be able to answer *more* questions in *less* time than someone who has tried to memorize every detail.

Step 2: Find the Main Idea of Each Paragraph

Almost every paragraph in an SAT reading passage will have a main idea or central theme that is developed over the course of the paragraph. *This main idea is often revealed in the first or last sentence of the paragraph.* As soon as you can summarize the main idea of a paragraph, make a brief note in the margin and move quickly to the next paragraph.

To see how this works, take a look at the first paragraph from the reading comprehension passage on pages 64-65. (In the rest of this chapter, we'll be referring repeatedly to this passage and the questions that follow it.)

> The subject of my study is women who are initiating social change in a small region in Texas. The women are Mexican Americans who are, or were, migrant agricultural workers. There is more than one kind of innovation at work in the region, of course, but I have chosen to focus on three related patterns of the family behavior.

Here's how to crack it: This paragraph is short and straightforward. The passage is taken from a "study" of some kind; perhaps it is a doctoral thesis or some other academic paper. Since the author says that he or she has chosen to "focus on" three patterns of family behavior, you should focus on them, too. In the margin you might write "3 patterns." (Note that the main idea of this paragraph will probably also be the main idea of the entire passage. Keep this in mind as you continue to read.)

You may have been told that you should underline key words and phrases as you read an SAT reading passage. This is a very *bad* idea. If you start underlining key words and phrases, you'll soon up underlining almost everything. Besides, you won't really know which words are "key" until you know what the questions are. (This doesn't apply to trigger words, which we haven't explained yet.)

Now that you've found the main idea of the first paragraph, you should move immediately to the second paragraph.

Step 3: Skim over Examples and Details

With each new paragraph, read the first sentence and then skim to the last sentence, which you should also read. By skim we don't mean speed-read. Once you can see which direction a paragraph is going, you can ignore the details.

There are surprisingly few things that an author can do in a paragraph to develop her main idea. She can list examples, give descriptions, add details, make comparisons. Once you've seen what the main idea is, you can skip over the examples, description, details, and comparisons. You won't be able to remember them anyway, so don't waste time reading them carefully.

Here's the second paragraph from the passage on pages 64-65:

> The pattern I life-style represents how migrant farm workers of all nationalities lived in the past and how many continue to live. I treat this pattern as a baseline with which to compare the changes represented by patterns II and III. Families in pattern I work on farms year round, migrating for as many as ten months each year. They work and travel in extended kin units, with the eldest male occupying the position of authority. Families are large—eight or nine children are not unusual—and all members are economic contributors in this strategy of family migration.

The theme of this paragraph, as you can see from the first sentence, is "the pattern I life-style." By skimming you can see that the rest of the paragraph simply adds descriptive details about these families. *Do not bother even to read these details; you can come back for them later if you need them to answer questions.* In the margin you should write "pattern I" or simply "I."

Skimming is not reading every tenth word; it's knowing what's worth reading and what's only worth summarizing. Ideas are worth reading; details should always be skimmed and summarized. Once you know that the next few lines are going to describe, say, a nuclear fission reaction, make a note in the margin like "nuc. reac." Then skim the description. It's only going to confuse you anyway!

Now look at the third and fourth paragraphs of the passage. Find the theme of each and skim over the details. Then make a note in the margin.

> Families in pattern II manifest some differences in behavior while still maintaining aspects of pattern I. They continue to migrate but on a reduced scale, often modifying their schedules of migration to allow children to finish the school year. Parents in this pattern often find temporary local jobs as checkers or clerks to offset lost farming income. Pattern II families usually have fewer children than do pattern I families.
>
> The greatest amount of change from pattern I, however, is found in pattern III families, who no longer migrate at all. Both parents work full time in the area and have an average of three children. Children attend school for the entire year. In pattern III, the women in particular create new roles for themselves for which no local models exist. They not only work full time but may, in addition, return to school. They also assume a greater responsibility in family decisions than do women in the other patterns. Although these women are in the minority among residents of the region, they serve as role models for others, causing ripples of change to spread in their communities.

Here's how to crack it: Did you write "II" in the margin of the third paragraph and "III" in the margin of the fourth? If not, go back and look at the paragraphs again. You should have read the first sentence of each and then skimmed quickly over the rest. Each paragraph contains a main idea followed by descriptive details. The third paragraph describes pattern II families; the fourth paragraph describes pattern III families.

Here's the last paragraph of the passage. Read it in the same way you've read the others.

> New opportunities have continued to be determined by preexisting values. When federal jobs became available in the region, most involved working under the direction of female professionals such as teachers or nurses. Such positions were unacceptable to many men in the area because they were not accustomed to being subordinate to women. Women therefore took the jobs, at first, because the income was desperately needed. But some of the women decided to stay at their jobs after the family's distress was over. These women enjoyed their work, its responsibility, and the companionship of fellow women workers. The steady, relatively high income allowed their families to stop migrating. And, as the efficaciousness of these women became increasingly apparent, they and their families became even more willing to consider changes in their lives that they would not have considered before.

Here's how to crack it: This paragraph is ideal for skimming. It is a further description of pattern III women. In the margin you should make a simple note like "III—new changes." If a question asks you for details, you can come back for them.

In reading the paragraphs this way, your ultimate goal is to develop a general sense of the main idea or central theme of the entire passage. You should not attempt to understand the passage too thoroughly—in other words, you should not try to "comprehend" it. An understanding of the minithemes of each paragraph will illuminate the main theme of the entire passage.

Step 4: Find the Trigger Words

As we have already said, reading comprehension questions test only a tiny percentage of the material contained in the passages. Some of your most useful clues as to what these questions will cover are provided by what we call *trigger words.* Sentences that contain trigger words usually contain the author's *secondary* ideas. *They also contain answers to questions nearly 70 percent of the time.* As you skim through a passage, you should always stop to circle trigger words and underline the sentences in which they appear.

You shouldn't focus on trigger-word sentences as you skim the passage. Rather, when you come to a hard question and are stuck among several choices, you should go back to those underlined sentences. They will help you make up your mind.

Here are the trigger words. You *must* memorize this list.

but
although (while, even though)
however
yet
despite (in spite of)
nevertheless
nonetheless
notwithstanding
except (unless)

How do trigger words work?

Trigger words are words that *signal a change in the meaning* of a sentence, paragraph, or passage. Here's a simple example:

> **Sentence:** Mr. Jones loves insects, but he doesn't think much of ants.
>
> **Question:** Which of the following statements is true?
>
> (A) Mr. Jones loves all insects.
> (B) Mr. Jones is not particularly fond of some insects.

Analysis: The trigger word in the sentence is *but*. It signals that the meaning of the sentence is about to change. When Joe Bloggs looks at the sentence to find the answer to the question, he doesn't read past the *but*. He reads the words "Mr. Jones loves insect" and chooses answer choice A. *But choice A is incorrect*. Mr. Jones does not love *all* insects. Ants are a kind of insect, and Mr. Jones doesn't like ants; therefore, he is not particularly fond of *some* insects. The correct answer to the question is choice B.

The answer to the question, in effect, was "hiding behind" the trigger word.

Pam uses reading comprehensions to determine how carefully you read. She will try to trip you up by asking questions that seem to have one answer but actually have another. Very often the real answer will be hiding behind a trigger word. In writing her questions, Pam looks for places in the passage where the meaning changes. She thinks of each of these changes as a trap for a careless reader—as a trap for Joe Bloggs. If you learn to pay attention to the trigger words, you will be able to avoid many of Pam's traps.

Later on, we will teach you how to use trigger words in finding specific answers. For now it is enough that you understand how to find the trigger words themselves. The following drill will give you practice.

DRILL 1

Go back to the reading passage on pages 64-65. Skim through it looking for trigger words. When you find one, circle it and then underline the sentence in which it appears. You'll find answers on pages 281.

Important Notes on Trigger Words, Summarizing, and Skimming

1. Trigger words are most important in *opinion* passages and *ethnic* passages. They still help, but are less important, in *factual* passages, and they are only occasionally helpful in *fiction* passages.

2. Not all passages can be read by the summarize-and-skim method. Sometimes the very hardest passage on the test will be a short, one-paragraph *factual* passage about some scientific or philosophical subject. In a short, difficult passage like this, *every sentence* may have a different theme. On this kind of passage, you should get to the questions as quickly as possible and then *look back* for the answers. Don't be frightened by the hard words in such passages, and don't try to *understand* the passage before you go to the questions.

3. There is one type of SAT reading passage that can *never* be skimmed and summarized: a *fiction* passage. You will have to read fiction passages *slowly*, from beginning to end. Instead of reading for main ideas or general structure, look for the motivations and interrelationships of the characters. The tone of such passages is often "ironic" or "satirical." The author's attitude is often one of "detached sympathy."

4. In *opinion* passages, the author often plays the devil's advocate by describing the opinions of his opponents (in order to refute them). Be careful to disentangle the opinions of the author from the opinions of his opponents.

5. The *ethnic* passage will be the easiest passage on your test, no matter where it's located. *You must never skip this passage*. For specific advice about how to approach it, see the first "Advanced Principles" section later in this chapter.

Step 5: Attack the Questions

Once you have grasped the main ideas of the paragraphs and of the passage, you can attack the questions aggressively. As we noted earlier, each passage is followed by two to five questions of varying difficulty. These questions generally follow the organization of the passage. In other words, a question about the first paragraph will usually come before a question about the second paragraph.

There are two types of reading comprehension questions on the SAT:

1. General questions: These are questions about the passage *as a whole*. An example would be a question asking you about the author's attitude or the passage's main idea. The first and/or last questions are often general questions.

2. Specific questions: These are questions about *specific parts* of the passage, or questions whose answers can be found in specific places (such as a particular line or paragraph). The order of these questions usually follows the organization of the passage.

Here is the strategy you should follow in attacking SAT reading comprehension questions:

1. Find and answer the first *general* question. The very first question asked is often a general question. General questions are usually the easiest; answering them first also makes the specific questions easier. Especially if you don't have time to answer all the questions following a passage, answer the general questions first. Remember POE, the process of elimination.

2. After you have answered the general questions, find the first *specific* one. See if any of the answer choices can be eliminated immediately. When you find a choice that can be eliminated, cross it out. *POE is very important on reading comprehension questions.* We'll talk about this more in a minute.

3. Go to the passage and find Pam's answer. If you don't know immediately where to find the answer, skim quickly until you find it. Remember POE and trigger words.

4. When you have answered the first specific question, move on to the second. *Look for the answer to one question at a time. If you try to keep more than one question in your mind, you will get bogged down and waste valuable time. Don't think about the second question until you have answered the first.*

5. Don't waste time. If you find yourself getting into a rut on a hard question, quickly eliminate as many choices as you can, guess, and move on.

An Important Note on ETS's Terminology

ETS calls some reading comprehension questions *explicit* and others *inferential*. Here's the difference:

1. Explicit questions: These are questions about information *directly stated* in the passage. Questions 34-36 in the sample passage are explicit.

2. Inferential questions: These are questions that ask you to make an *inference* or *deduction* based on what you have read. Questions 33 and 37 in the sample passage are inferential.

Here is an example:

If an author states that he is a vegetarian, that is *explicit*. We can *infer* from this that he would feel out of place at a traditional Thanksgiving feast. When you *infer* something, you draw an independent conclusion based on the *explicit* information that you have been given.

Putting the Strategy to Work: Basic Principles

Let's try this strategy on the sample reading comprehension passage on pages 64-65. Refer back to the passage as you answer the questions. By now you should have the trigger words circled and the trigger-word sentences underlined, and you should have written brief notes in the margins.

Look at the questions one at a time.

QUESTION 33

This is the first general question, and the one you want to answer first. It is asking you to select a title expressing the passage's main idea.

33. Which of the following titles best reflects the main focus of the passage?

(A) A Study of Three Mexican-American Families at Work in Texas
(B) Innovative Career Women: Effects on Family Unity
(C) Changes in the Life-styles of Migrant Mexican-American Families
(D) Farming or Family: The Unavoidable Choice for Migrant Farm Workers
(E) Recent Changes in Methods of Farming in Texas

Here's how to crack it:

(A) This is a trap for Joe Bloggs. It would be a correct answer if it were worded slightly differently: "A Study of Three *Kinds of* Mexican-American Families at Work in Texas." Don't get careless. Eliminate.

(B) A possibility, perhaps, except that the passage doesn't really mention anything about family unity, and "career women" doesn't describe the women in the paper.

(C) Pam's answer. *Note that Pam's answer to this question is contained partly in a trigger-word sentence.*

(D) Eliminate. The women in the passage don't have to choose one or the other.

(E) For Joe Bloggs only. The passage is not about "farming methods." Now, on to the next *general* question.

QUESTION 37

37. The author's attitude toward the three patterns of behavior mentioned in the passage is best described as one of

(A) great admiration
(B) grudging respect
(C) unbiased objectivity
(D) dissatisfaction
(E) indifference

Questions about the author's attitude are the easiest of all reading comprehension questions to answer.

Here's how to crack it: This is a question about the author's attitude, which, as we have said, means that it is really a question about the author's main purpose. The passage is clearly an excerpt from some sort of serious academic research study. Pam's answer is choice C; scholars are supposed to be unbiased and objective. (We'll tell you more about answering this kind of question in a moment.)

You've answered both general questions, so now you can move on to the *specific* ones. The first specific question is number 34.

QUESTION 34

34. According to the passage, pattern I families are characterized by which of the following?

(A) Small numbers of children
(B) Brief periods of migrant labor
(C) Female figures of family authority
(D) Commercial as well as agricultural sources of income
(E) Parents and children working and traveling together

The question is asking you for specific information about pattern I families. Where will you find this information? Look at your marginal notes: The second paragraph of the passage is *about* pattern I families. This is where you should look for the answer.

Here's how to crack it: You should answer this question by looking at each choice in order and using POE. *Remember: You should always look for just one thing at a time.* Look at each choice, refer to the passage, and either eliminate it or save it.

(A) Eliminate. The paragraph says pattern I families "are large—eight or nine children are not unusual."

(B) Eliminate. Pattern I families migrate "for as many as ten months each year."

(C) Eliminate. In pattern I families, "the eldest male" is the figure of family authority.

(D) Eliminate. Pattern I families "work on farms year round."

(E) This is the answer. The paragraph says that pattern I families "work and travel in extended kin units." (Besides, we've eliminated everything else.)

QUESTION 35

35. All of the following statements about pattern II children express differences between them and pattern I children EXCEPT:

(A) They migrate for part of each year.
(B) They have fewer siblings.
(C) They spend less time contributing to family income.
(D) They spend more months in school.
(E) Their parents sometimes work at jobs other than farming.

This is another specific question. It is asking for information about differences between pattern I and pattern II families. The answer, therefore, can be found in the second and third paragraphs.

Here's how to crack it: This question is confusingly worded. It says that all the choices express differences between pattern II and pattern I families *except* the one that you are supposed to find. Pam's answer, therefore, will be the one choice that does *not* express a difference between the two kinds of families.

(A) Pattern II families migrate for part of each year; so do pattern I families. This must be Pam's answer. *Note that Pam's answer to this question is contained in a trigger-word sentence.*

(B) This is a *difference* between the two kinds of families. Eliminate.

(C) Another difference. Eliminate.

(D) Another difference. Eliminate.

(E) Another difference. Eliminate.

QUESTION 36

36. According to the passage, which of the following is NOT true of women in pattern III families?

(A) They earn a reliable and comparatively high income.
(B) They continue to work solely to meet the urgent needs of their family.
(C) They are more involved in the deciding of family issues than they once were.
(D) They enjoy the fellowship involved in working with other women.
(E) They serve as models of behavior for others in the region.

This specific question is about pattern III families, which are described in the fourth and fifth paragraphs.

Here's how to crack it: Once again, the wording of the question is a little tricky. You are being asked to find an *untrue* statement about pattern III families. You can therefore use POE to *eliminate* any answer choice that is a *true* statement.

(A) According to the fifth paragraph, pattern III women have "steady, relatively high income," so this statement is *true*. Eliminate.

(B) According to the fifth paragraph, pattern III women continued to work "after the family's financial distress was over." This statement, therefore, is *untrue*, which means that it must be Pam's answer. *Note that Pam's answer to this questions is contained in a trigger-word sentence.*

(C) According to the fourth paragraph, pattern III women "assume a greater responsibility in family decisions." Eliminate.

(D) According to the fifth paragraph, pattern III women "enjoyed . . . the companionship of fellow women workers." Eliminate.

(E) According to the fourth paragraph, pattern III women "serve as role models for others." Eliminate.

Attacking the Questions: Specific Techniques

On many reading comprehension questions, simply knowing where to look for answers won't guarantee that you will be able to find them. Pam will try to trick you by laying traps. Since reading comprehension questions, unlike analogies, are not arranged in order of difficulty, Joe Bloggs won't be of much direct help in keeping you out of trouble. *But we have a number of techniques that will help.* These techniques are designed to help you choose Pam's answer from among a number of competing choices. In general, we are going to show you how to use POE to eliminate choices that could not possibly be Pam's answer.

TECHNIQUE 1:
Attack Disputable Statements

The answer to an SAT reading comprehension question must be indisputable. That is, it must be so absolutely correct that no one would want to argue with Pam about it. If even 1 percent of the 1.3 million students who take the SAT each year were able to dispute Pam's answer to a question, Pam would have to spend all her time arguing with students. In order to keep this from happening, she tries to make her answers as *in*disputable as possible.

How does she do that? Let's look at an example:

> **Question:** Which of the following statements is indisputable?
> **Statement A:** The population of the world is 4.734 billion people.
> **Statement B:** The population of the world is quite large.

Analysis: Statement A sounds precise and scientific; statement B sounds vague and general. Which is indisputable?

Statement B, of course! Does anyone know *exactly* what the population of the world is? What if some experts say that the population of the world is 4.732 billion people? Doesn't the population of the world change from minute to minute. It's easy to think of dozens of reasons to *dispute* statement A.

Statement B, on the other hand, is so vague and general no one could argue with it. It is indisputable.

Generally speaking, the more *detailed* and *specific* a statement is, the easier it is to dispute. The more *general* and *vague* a statement is, the harder it will be to dispute.

On the SAT, Pam's answers to reading comprehension questions must be indisputable. In trying to decide between competing choices on a question, you should concentrate on the statement that seems more *specific*, and *attack* that choice. If you can find *any* reason to dispute that choice, you should eliminate it and select the other.

This doesn't mean that specific statements are never correct. On the contrary, if after attacking a specific choice you can find *no* reason to dispute it, you should select it as your answer.

Many students, in trying to decide between two possible answers to a reading comprehension question, will say something like: "Well, choice D is true, but it seems so *vague*. I guess the answer must be B."

This is often wrong. Pam's answer must be indisputably true; it doesn't have to be (and usually isn't) profound. Do *not* look for subtle reasons when deciding between competing choices.

Let's look at an example of what we mean. We'll assume that you've already been able to eliminate some of the choices. You don't need to read the passage.

33. With which of the following statements would the author of the passage probably agree?

(A) No useful purpose is served by examining the achievements of the past.
(B) A fuller understanding of the present can often be gained from the study of history.
(C) [eliminated]
(D) [eliminated]
(E) Nothing new ever occurs.

Here's how to crack it: Which of these statements are the most specific and therefore the most disputable? Choices A and E. Choice A says that studying the past has *no* useful purpose, meaning none at all. This statement is easy to dispute. Therefore, the author of the passage probably wouldn't be any more likely to agree with it than you would be. Choice E says that *nothing* new *ever* occurs. Nothing at all? Not even once in a while? Surely there must be an exception somewhere. This statement is also disputable. Choice B, however, is general and vague enough to be entirely indisputable. It must be Pam's answer.

Here's another example:

40. The author of the passage apparently believes that modern techniques are

(A) totally worthless
(B) [eliminated]
(C) in need of further improvement
(D) [eliminated]
(E) [eliminated]

Here's how to crack it: Choice A is highly specific and therefore highly disputable. *Totally* worthless? Never even the least bit valuable? Surely there must be one case in which they might be *somewhat* useful. You should attack this choice aggressively. Choice C, on the other hand, is quite vague and therefore much less disputable. (It is also Pam's answer.)

Our point is not that the vague choice is always correct, or that the specific one is always incorrect. Rather, the point is that when you are trying to decide between two choices, both of which seem good, the more specific choice will be easier to dispute. And a choice that is easier to dispute will be easier to eliminate.

What Makes a Choice Easy to Dispute

Certain words make choices highly specific and therefore easy to dispute. Here are some of these words:

each	totally
all	must
will	always

If a statement says that something is *always* or *never* true, then you only need to find one exception in order to prove it wrong. The following drill will give you practice in identifying why a statement is easy to dispute.

DRILL 2

Each of the following sentences or phrases is an *incorrect* answer choice. Read each one and circle the word or phrase in it that makes it easy to dispute. Answers can be found on page 281.

(A) leads politicians to place complete reliance upon the results of opinions polls
(B) Baker's ideas had no influence on the outcome.

(C) Foreign languages should never be studied.
(D) All financial resources should be directed toward improving the work environment.
(E) the belief that nature is inscrutable and cannot be described

What Makes a Choice Hard to Dispute?

Certain words make choices very vague and general and therefore hard to dispute. Here are some of these words:

may	sometimes
can	might
some	suggest
most	

If a statement says that something is *sometimes* true, then you only need to find one example in order to prove it correct. The following drill will give you practice in identifying why a statement is hard to dispute.

DRILL 3

Each of the following sentences is a *correct* answer choice. Read each one and circle the word or phrase in it that makes it hard to dispute. Answers can be found on page 281.

(A) New research may lead to improvements in manufacturing technology.
(B) Not all workers respond the same way to instruction.
(C) Improved weather was but one of the many factors that led to the record crop.
(D) Most scientists believe that continued progress is possible.
(E) Everyone cannot expect to be happy all the time.

TECHNIQUE 2:
Beware of Direct Repetitions

Even on explicit questions that ask you to find a specific piece of information in a reading passage, Pam usually changes the wording in the answer somewhat so that it isn't exactly like the wording in the passage. *Pam does this in order to prevent Joe Bloggs from picking a correct answer by accident just because the wording sounds familiar to him.* Here are a few lines from a reading passage, followed by a question:

> The idea was to create a common pool of savings that could then be disbursed, where needed, in the form of loans—more or less on the pattern of an ordinary bank or savings-and-loan association.

27. The author states that the creators of the World Bank and the International Monetary Fund hoped to

(A) eliminate a surplus
(B) modernize the saving-and-loans system
(C) establish a financial resource from which nations could borrow
(D) force banks to inaugurate a common pool of savings
(E) obtain loans without paying them back

Analysis: Pam's answer is choice C. Notice that the wording of her answer is different from the wording of the passage ("create a common pool of savings that could then be disbursed, where needed, in the form of loans"). Pam has paraphrased the wording slightly to keep Joe Bloggs from selecting this answer by accident.

Therefore, You Should Be Very Suspicious of Direct Repetitions

Because Pam changes the wording of her answers in order to trip up Joe Bloggs, you should be very suspicious of any answer choice that exactly reproduces more than a word or two from the passage. When two or more words from the passage (or even one unusual word) are repeated exactly in an answer choice, that choice is almost always wrong.

In the preceding example, answer choices B and D reproduce phrases verbatim from the passage ("savings-and-loans" and "common pool of savings"). Both choices, therefore, can probably be eliminated.

This technique is most useful in questions that ask you to make an *inference* about the passage. When a question says "It can be inferred," or "The author suggests," or "The author's main point," you can almost always be certain that any direct repetition of words from the passage will be *incorrect.*

This rule even applies to questions about numbers. Here's an example:

> In 1980, the average annual grocery bill for a family of four was $484, compared with $624 in 1985.
>
> 35. One can infer from the passage that in 1980 the average annual grocery bill per person was approximately
>
> (A) $121 (B) $156 (C) $484 (D) $624 (E) $2,496

Here's how to crack it: Pam's answer is choice A. Notice that the question asks you to *infer* the grocery bill *per person,* which means that you have to divide the figure in the passage by 4 in order to find the answer. Choices C and D *repeated exactly from the passage*, are traps for Joe Bloggs.

TECHNIQUE 3:
Use Outside Knowledge

ETS says you should never use "outside knowledge" in answering reading comprehensions—that is, you are supposed to answer the questions only on the basis of the material in the reading passages. This is very bad advice. Outside knowledge can be a big help on SAT reading comprehensions. *Pam's answer on a reading comprehension will never contradict an established, objective fact.* In writing this chapter we analyzed some 200 SAT reading passages; *not once* did outside knowledge mislead us. In fact, outside knowledge can enable you to eliminate many choices as absurd or disputable.

Here's an example:

> 32. According to the passage, all of the following are true of living organisms EXCEPT that they
> (A) are able to reproduce themselves
> (B) are past the point of further evolution
> (C) are capable of growth
> (D) respond to stimuli
> (E) are characterized by a capacity for metabolism

Here's how to crack it: If you know even a little about biology, you will probably be able to answer this question without reading the passage. (Remember that on this question you are asked to look for a statement that is *not* true.) Now let's consider each choice in turn.

(A) The ability to reproduce is one of the obvious differences between living things and dead things. Eliminate.

(B) Have living organisms stopped evolving? Of course not. This must be Pam's answer.

(C), (D), and (E) These choices are all part of the standard biological definition of life. Eliminate.

Putting the Strategy to Work: Advanced Principles

So far we have described our general strategy for approaching SAT reading comprehensions. Now we are going to teach you some advance principles that will help you earn even more points. These principles are linked to specific types of passages and specific types of questions that you will encounter on the SAT. Note, though, that not all our techniques are equally useful on all types of passages or questions. And some techniques are designed only for certain ones.

Advance Principles: The Ethnic Passage

For many years members of minority groups have complained—justifiably—that the SAT is unfair to them. Several years ago, ETS responded to this criticism by adding an "ethnic passage" to each SAT. This passage is always one of the six passages on the test. It has to do with blacks, Hispanics, Asian-Americans, or some other ethnic group.

The ethnic passage doesn't make the SAT any fairer to minorities, but it does make the test easier to beat. The tone of the ethnic passage is invariably *positive* or *inspirational*. Answer choices that express negative or unflattering opinions about minorities, therefore, can always be eliminated.

Always do the ethnic passage. It is the most predictable passage on the SAT, and you will be able to answer at least some of the questions on it even if you don't have time to read the passage.

Here is an example. *You don't need to read the passage in order to answer it.*

24. The author views Black literature with

(A) apathy
(B) confusion
(C) despair
(D) distaste
(E) admiration

Here's how to crack it: Pam's answer to this question, E, ought to jump right off the page. The purpose of the ethnic passage is to demonstrate that ETS admires minorities. ETS would never use a passage in which the author expressed *negative* or *unflattering* opinions about minorities. *Apathy, confusion, despair* and *distaste* are all negative words; none of them could be Pam's answer. The only possible answer is *admiration.*

Let's look at another example, from another ethnic passage:

30. The passage implies that Prof. Anderson [a Black man] received less credit than he deserved because

(A) he failed to publish his results
(B) his findings were soon disproven by other scientists
(C) he was a frequent victim of racial discrimination
(D) his work was too complex to be of widespread interest
(E) he had no interest in the accolades of his colleagues

Here's how to crack it: Once again, Pam's answer, C, ought to be obvious. ETS added an ethnic passage to the SAT because it had been accused of racial discrimination. The purpose of the passage is to demonstrate that ETS thinks racial discrimination is a bad thing.

Advanced Principles: Respect for Professionals and Artists

Pam has other predictable attitudes, too. One of them is admiration for doctors, lawyers, scientists, writers, and artists. SAT reading passages treat such people with dignity and respect. You would be exceedingly unlikely to find an SAT reading passage about uncaring doctors, ruthless lawyers, or unscrupulous scientists. Nor would you be likely to find a passage about a bad writer or an untalented artist.

For example:

32. The author views the work of modern astrophysicists with

(A) angry skepticism
(B) apologetic confusion
(C) admiring approval
(D) amused antagonism
(E) ambivalent condescension

Here's how to crack it: Pam believes that astrophysicists, like all scientists, are to be admired. Pam's answer can only be C. All the other choices are at least partly negative.

On the very rare occasion when a passage is somewhat critical of a group of professionals or artists, this criticism will be mild, like a gentle slap on the wrist. In fact, most such criticism is really veiled praise. Here is an example:

36. The author believes that federal judges can sometimes be criticized for

(A) failing to consider the meaning of the law
(B) ignoring the rights of defendants
(C) letting their personal opinions influence the outcomes of trials
(D) slowing the flow of court cases by caring too much about the requirements of justice
(E) forgetting that the Constitution is the foundation of the American legal system

Here's how to crack it: Choices A, B, C, and E all contain very serious criticisms of judges. Pam could never agree with any of them, because in her view judges are honorable. If a judge can be criticized, it can only be for "caring too much," as in choice D. This is Pam's answer.

Advance Principles: No Strong Emotions

ETS avoids strong, unqualified emotions on the SAT. The author of a reading passage may be "admiring" or "somewhat skeptical," but he would never be "irrational" or "wildly enthusiastic." On reading comprehension questions about the *attitude, style,* or *tone* of a passage or its author, you can simply eliminate answer choices containing emotions that are too positive or too negative. For example:

28. As revealed in the passage, the author's attitude toward Parliament is one of

(A) angry consternation
(B) unrestrained amusement
(C) gentle criticism
(D) reluctant agreement
(E) sneering disrespect

Here's how to crack it: Let's consider each choice in turn.

(A) This is much too strong an emotion for ETS. Pam is almost never angry. Eliminate.

(B) Pam is sometimes amused, but her amusement is never *unrestrained.* Eliminate.

(C) A possibility. *Criticism* is a fairly strong word, but it is softened by *gentle*.

(D) This is also a possibility: A positive word and a negative word more or less cancel each other out.

(E) This is much too strong an emotion to be Pam's answer. Eliminate.

We've eliminated choices A, B, and E. If we guess now, we have a fifty-fifty chance of being correct. (Pam's answer is C—the better of the two possible answers.)

ETS only uses reading passages that it believes to be well-written and intelligent. Pam would never select a passage whose tone was hysterical or whose author was stupid. *In answering reading comprehension questions, therefore, you can always eliminate answer choices that describe passages or their authors in clearly negative terms.* For example:

28. The author's approach in this passage can best be described as which of the following?

(A) Condescending to the reader in an effort to strengthen a dubious thesis
(B) Presenting only those points that support the author's personal beliefs
(C) Emphasizing certain details in order to mask the weakness of the central argument
(D) Making a thoughtful case in a confident, objective tone
(E) Neglecting to account for the opinions of distinguished critics

Here's how to crack it: Let's consider each choice in turn.

(A) Eliminate. ETS's favorite authors would never condescend to the reader or put forth a dubious thesis. (To condescend is to talk down to or patronize.)

(B) Eliminate. ETS's favorite authors don't leave out points simply in order to support their personal beliefs.

(C) Eliminate. ETS's favorite authors don't have weak central arguments.

(D) This is the best guess (and Pam's answer).

(E) Eliminate. ETS's favorite authors don't neglect the opinions of their critics (especially their distinguished ones).

Pam almost never uses negative words to describe an author's tone or attitude *unless she is describing the author's attitude toward people who do not agree with the author or with Pam.* An author's attitude toward a famous painter will almost always be positive—it will likely be one of "admiration" or "respect"; but the author will have a *negative* attitude toward people who don't also appreciate the work of that artist. Here is an example:

39. The author's attitude about people who believe that Mandel's paintings "are just pretty pictures" (lines 34–36) can be described best as one of

    (A) apathy
    (B) amusement
    (C) disapproval
    (D) fury
    (E) agreement

Here's how to crack it: The author likes Mandel's paintings; therefore, he must disapprove of people who think they "are just pretty pictures." Choice E is therefore easy to eliminate. Choice D is much too strong an emotion to be a likely ETS answer. Choices A and B should also be easy to eliminate. Pam's answer is C.

Advanced Principles: Questions about Tone, Attitude, or Style

The easiest reading comprehension questions to crack are ones about the tone, attitude, or style of the passage or its author. There are usually one or two of these questions on every SAT. They are short and often easy to answer without doing much more than glancing at the passage. *Even on a hard passage that you intend to skip, you may want to take a stab at a tone, style, or attitude question if there is one.* These questions are simple to spot, because they usually contain very few words.

Following are some general guidelines about answering this kind of question. *Do not try to memorize them.* You should simply get a feel for the principles behind them and then try to apply them as you practice on real SATs.

(If you don't know the meaning of words in the "Good Guesses" columns, be sure to look them up and memorize them. You will see these words repeatedly on the SAT.)

1. You are asked to determine the *style* or *tone* of a reading passage that looks like a factual article about science, history, or some other serious topic.

GOOD GUESSES	BAD GUESSES
explanatory	apologetic
objective	pedantic
unbiased	ironic
analytic	apathetic
	indifferent
	dogmatic
	contradictory
	derogatory
	argumentative
	indignant
	impatient
	whimsical
	enthusiastic
	scholarly
	irrational

2. You are asked to determine the *style* or *tone* of a reading passage that looks like a short story or a humorous essay.

GOOD GUESSES	BAD GUESSES
ironic	apologetic
satirical	explanatory
	scholarly
	objective

3. You are asked to determine the *attitude* of an author toward a minority member, a professional, an artist, or a writer.

GOOD GUESSES	BAD GUESSES
admiration	skepticism
approval	apathy
appreciation	indifference
respect	distaste
	disdain
	puzzlement
	exasperation
	irrationality
	nostalgia
	grudging admiration
	great admiration

"Admiration" is the most common answer to questions having to do with the author's attitude toward these groups, but you should eliminate "admiration" as an answer if it is qualified by another word, as in "grudging admiration" or "great admiration."

4. You are asked to determine the *attitude* of an author toward those who *don't agree* with him and Pam (for example, about the greatness of a painter).

GOOD GUESSES	BAD GUESSES
disapproval	approval
gentle mockery	admiration
respectful disagreement	amusement
	apathy
	indifference
	violent indignation

No matter what a passage is about, the following words will *never* be used to describe the style or tone of the passage or the attitude of the author:

apologetic	ambivalent
indifferent	dogmatic
apathetic	pompous
irrational	condescending
skeptical	sentimental
suspicious	honest

Advanced Principles: Main Idea Questions

The most common SAT reading comprehension question is "What is the main idea of the passage?" This question can be phrased in a number of different ways:

"What is the best title for the passage?"
"The passage is primarily concerned with . . . ?"
"Which of the following best describes the content of the passage?"

Answers to "main idea" questions can often be found in the first or last line of the first or last paragraph, or in trigger-word sentences.

Pam is very predictable in the sorts of answers she chooses on main idea questions:

1. In *factual* passages, the main idea is usually
   "To discuss . . ."
   "To describe . . ."
2. In *opinion* passages, the main idea is usually
   "To argue . . ."
   "To urge . . ."
   "To present . . ."
   "To propose . . ."
3. In *fiction/humor* passages, the main idea is usually
   "To portray . . ."
   "To present . . ."
   "To describe . . ."
4. No matter what category the passage falls into, the main idea is almost never
   "To compare . . ."
   "To criticize . . ."
   "To explain . . ."

Advanced Principles: Line-Number Questions

Some SAT questions will refer you to a specific line or group of lines in the reading passage. *The answer to such a question will rarely be contained in the specific line(s) cited.* If you read only the line(s) cited—as Joe Bloggs does—you will probably be misled. Therefore, you should always *surround* the cited line(s) by also reading a few lines before and a few lines after.

Advanced Principles: Least/Except Questions

Pam will often ask questions that require you to determine which of five choices is *least* likely to be true, or she will offer five choices and say that all are true *except* the "correct" answer. These questions can be confusing, because they require you to find an answer that is, in effect, incorrect. These are good questions for POE, but if you are short of time you should avoid them.

Advanced Principles: Triple True/False Questions

Frequently on the SAT, you will find a question like the following:

29. According to the author, which of the following characteristics are common to both literature and biology?

    I. They are concerned with living creatures.
    II. They enrich human experience.
    III. They are guided by scientific principles.

    (A) I only (B) II only (C) I and II only
    (D) I and III only (E) I, II, and III

We call these "triple true/false questions" because you are really being asked to determine whether each of three separate statements are true or false. You will only receive credit if you answer all three questions correctly, but these questions are excellent for educated guessing, because you can improve your odds dramatically by using POE.

Suppose you know from reading the passage that statement III is false. That means you can eliminate two choices, D and E. Since D and E both contain III, neither can be correct. (Pam's answer, incidentally, is C.) Use POE aggressively on these questions and you will improve your SAT score.

Summary

1. There are six reading passages on the SAT. They are spread among three basic categories: factual, opinion, and fiction/humor. One of the six passages will be what we call the ethnic passage. It has its own special rules.

2. Reading comprehension *questions* are not presented in order of difficulty; reading comprehension *passages*, however, are.

3. You should always save reading comprehensions for last in each verbal section of the SAT. These problems take a great deal of time to read and answer, but the questions aren't worth any more points than ones that can be answered quickly.

4. Unless you are a very high scorer or have an unusual knack for answering reading comprehensions, you could probably increase your SAT score simply by *skipping* one or more of the passages. The chapter explains how to determine which passage(s) to skip.

5. SAT reading comprehensions have nothing to do with comprehending reading. The name of the game is scoring points.

6. Every SAT reading passage and the questions that follow it contain clues that will enable you to eliminate obviously incorrect answers and increase your chances of choosing Pam's answer. Your job is to find these clues.

7. Reading slowly will improve neither your reading comprehension nor your SAT score.

8. Every passage has a main idea or central theme. Your first task is to find this main idea. By the time you get to the end of the first paragraph, you should have a good idea of what the entire passage is about.

9. Every paragraph also has a main idea. Your goal in reading each paragraph is to find this main idea and then move on.

10. Don't worry about details. Move quickly from paragraph to paragraph, summarizing the main idea, making a brief note in the margin, and skimming over the details.

11. As you skim, circle the trigger words and underline the sentences in which they appear. *You must memorize the trigger words.* Trigger-word sentences contain answers to questions fully 70 percent of the time. You should *not* underline other words or "key phrases." You should *not* attempt to "comprehend" the passage. Trigger words are most important in *opinion* and *ethnic* passages.

12. *Fiction* passages and some short *factual* passages cannot be read by the summarize-and-skim method.

13. Approach the questions *one at a time* using our techniques. You should do the general questions first.

14. Attack disputable statements. The answer to an SAT reading comprehension question must be indisputable. In trying to decide between competing choices on a question, you should concentrate on the choice that seems more *specific* and *attack* that choice. If you can find any reason to dispute that choice, you should eliminate it and select another.

15. Particularly on *inferential* questions, you should be extremely suspicious of answer choices containing more than a word or two repeated directly from the passage. Pam's answer is usually a *paraphrase*.

16. Take advantage of outside knowledge in choosing your answers. Pam's answer will never contradict an established, objective fact.

17. The tone of the *ethnic* passage is invariably positive or inspirational.

18. You must never skip the ethnic passage. It is the most predictable passage on the SAT, and you will be able to answer at least some of the questions on it even if you don't have time to read the passage.

19. Another of Pam's predictable attitudes is her respectful admiration for doctors, lawyers, scientists, writers, and artists.

20. ETS avoids strong, unqualified emotions on the SAT. The author of a reading passage may be "admiring" or "somewhat skeptical," but he would never be "irrational" or "wildly enthusiastic." On reading comprehension questions about the *attitude, style,* or *tone* of a passage or its author, you can simply eliminate answer choices containing emotions that are too positive or too negative.

21. Answers to "main idea" questions can often be found in the first or last line of the first or last paragraph, or in trigger-word sentences.

22. The answer to a line-number question will quite often *not* be contained in the specific line(s) cited.

23. Triple true/false questions are time-consuming. Do them last and use POE.

CHAPTER SIX

Antonyms

This chapter is about antonyms, the third of the four item types used on the verbal SAT. There will be two groups of antonyms on the SAT you take, one in each verbal section. One of the groups will contain 15 antonyms; the other will contain 10, for a total of 25.

Before we begin, take a moment to read the following set of instructions and to answer the sample question that comes after it. Both appear here exactly as they do on real SATs. Be certain that you know and understand these instructions before you take the SAT. If you learn them ahead of time, you won't have to waste valuable seconds reading them on the day you take the test.

> Each question below consists of a word in capital letters, followed by five lettered words or phrases. Choose the word or phrase that is most nearly *opposite* in meaning to the word in capital letters. Since some of the questions require you to distinguish fine shades of meaning, consider all the choices before deciding which is the best.
>
> Example:
>
> GOOD: (A) sour (B) bad (C) red (D) hot (E) ugly

Pam's answer to this sample question is choice B. The opposite of *good* is *bad*.

SAT Antonyms: Cracking the System

It's important to know the instructions printed before each antonym group on the SAT, but it's vastly more important to understand what those instructions mean. ETS's instructions don't tell you everything you need to know about SAT antonyms. The rest of this chapter will teach you what you do need to know.

In both of the two groups of antonyms on the SAT verbal sections that count, the questions will be arranged in order of increasing difficulty, from very easy to very hard.

Because our techniques vary depending on the difficulty of the question, the examples we use in this chapter will always be numbered. A number 1 will always be easy; a number 10 will always be hard. *Always pay attention to the question number in answering an SAT antonym questions.*

Work on Your Vocabulary

Of the four kinds of verbal questions on the SAT, antonyms are the hardest to crack. An antonym question is a vocabulary question; if you don't know the word in capital letters, you'll have a very hard time finding its opposite. Our strategies and techniques will help you, but their usefulness will depend directly on the size of your vocabulary. The best way to increase your antonym performance is to increase your SAT vocabulary. If you haven't already started building your SAT vocabulary by following the program outlined in Part Five, than you should begin doing so immediately.

Remember the Joe Bloggs Principle

Any group of SAT antonyms can be divided approximately into thirds according to difficulty:

1. The first third contains easy questions.
2. The middle third contains medium questions.
3. The final third contains difficult questions.

Easy Third: If you have an average vocabulary, the easy third will give you little trouble. Remember that Joe Bloggs gets these questions right. If you aren't sure about the meaning of the word in capital letters but have a hunch about which answer choice is correct, then you should trust your hunch.

Medium Third: In the medium third, Joe Bloggs is sometimes right and sometimes wrong. If you have an average vocabulary, you may be able to improve your score by making educated guesses about the meanings of words. But you should use extreme caution in guessing. **Difficult Third:** In the difficult third, unless you are fairly certain about the meaning of the word in capital letters, you are probably better off not wasting *any* time on the question. Only a small percentage of students know the words in this third.

Everyone tries to figure out the meanings of difficult words—including Joe Bloggs. If Joe figures it out correctly, the word ends up in the easy or medium third. Therefore, you should be aggressive on the easy and medium thirds. If Joe's guess is wrong, the word ends up in the difficult third. Therefore, you should not waste time on words you don't know in the difficult third.

Because of the different characteristics of the levels of difficulty in antonym questions, we will outline principles for each one separately in the rest of the chapter.

Easy Third: General Principles

ALWAYS CONSIDER *EVERY* ANSWER CHOICE, EVEN ON EASY QUESTIONS

If you mark you answer without considering all the alternatives, you may overlook Pam's answer. An SAT antonym will frequently contain an attractive answer choice that is *sort of* opposite to the word in capital letters but isn't quite what Pam is looking for. Joe Bloggs doesn't make mistakes on the easy third *unless he gets careless.* Here's an example:

1. PREMATURE: (A) presentable (B) robust (C) old (D) common (E) overdue

Here's how to crack it: A premature baby would be a very young one. Therefore, Pam's answer must be C, right?

Wrong!!!!

Premature means happening, arriving, existing, or performed before the proper or usual time. A premature baby is one born earlier than it was supposed to be. Pam's answer is E: An overdue baby would be one born later than it was supposed to be. Considering every answer choice will also keep you from making careless errors caused by sloppy thinking. Here's an example:

2. RECOLLECT: (A) disapprove (B) dispense (C) forget (D) pardon (E) defer

Here's how to crack it: To recollect is to remember. Pam's answer is C. If you were careless, though, and confused *recollect* with *collect,* you might have settled for B.

EASY QUESTIONS = EASY ANSWERS

Don't fret about hard answers choices in the easy third. Joe Bloggs avoids answer choices that he doesn't understand. If Pam's answer on an easy question were a hard word, Joe would never pick it and the question would not be easy. Here's an example:

2. SPIRITUAL: (A) effervescent (B) significant
 (C) adaptable (D) felicitous (E) worldly

Here's how to crack it: Pam's answer is choice E. A worldly person is someone who has no use for religion or other spiritual matters. Note: Choices A and D are too hard for this easy a question.

Here's another example:

2. JUVENILE: (A) broken (B) full-grown
 (C) eclectic (D) friendly (E) intransigent

Here's how to crack it: Pam's answer is choice B. *Juvenile* means young or physically immature. Choices C and E are much too hard for this easy a question, so they can easily be eliminated.

Medium Third: General Principles

PECULIAR CHOICES

Pay special attention to answer choices that seem completely out of place. Here's an example:

5. SUPPRESS: (A) air (B) accuse
 (C) initiate (D) perplex (E) astound

Here's how to crack it: Choice A seems strangely out of place on this question. What does air have to do with suppressing something?

As it turns out, *air* has everything to do with *suppress.* To suppress a feeling is to hold it in; to air it is to let it out or reveal it.

SIMPLE WORDS = UNUSUAL MEANINGS

In the medium third, when the word in capital letters seems to be a very simple word, it is almost always being used in a different sense from the one that first comes to mind. When you see a simple word in this third, you should always consider alternate or secondary meanings. Here's an example:

6. DISTANT: (A) cordial (B) graceful
(C) scholarly (D) diligent (E) sizable

Here's how to crack it: *Distant* usually means far away. But that would be too easy a word for the medium third. Does *distant* have any other meanings? Yes. It can also mean "far away" in an emotional sense. If you and your brother are distant in this sense, then you aren't friendly with each other. Pam's answer is A. *Cordial* means friendly—the opposite of what distant means in this secondary sense.

When the word in capital letters looks too easy, you should consider whether Pam might be using it as a different part of speech. If the word you are familiar with is a noun, ask yourself whether it might also be used as a verb or an adjective.

As was true with analogies, Pam always uses the same part of speech for the word in capital letters and every answer choice on an antonym problem. If the word in capital letters is a noun, then every answer choice will always be a noun. If you are uncertain about whether the word in capital letters is being tested as a noun or as a verb, check the first answer choice. As was also true with analogies, Pam uses the first choice to "establish the part of speech."

HUNCHES

When you have a hunch about the meaning of an *unusual* word in the medium third, you should go with your hunch. Pam sometimes uses words that aren't so much difficult as they are unusual. Sometimes she uses words that are almost like slang words. You may very well be able to figure out what these words mean simply by seeing what they make you think of. If you have a hunch, go with it. Here's an example:

7. SLUGGARD: (A) fickle lover
(B) impartial judge (C) intelligent answer
(D) energetic person (E) loud attire

Here's how to crack it: You know what a slug is: It's one of those slimy, slow-moving things that appear on the sidewalk after it rains. A sluggard is a person who moves slowly and lazily, like a slug. Pam's answer is D.

WORKING BACKWARD

When you are a bit uncertain about the meaning of the word in capital letters, you may be able to prod your memory by turning each answer choice into its opposite and then asking yourself whether it means the same thing as the capitalized word. Here's an example:

6. CODDLE: (A) summon (B) clarify (C) abuse
(D) separate (E) confess

Here's how to crack it: You are uncertain about the meaning of *coddle*, so you go through the answer choices, turning each into its opposite. Don't worry if you can't think of an exact opposite. Just getting the general idea is good enough.

(A) To summon someone would be to send for him. The opposite would be to send him away. Does coddle mean to send away? That doesn't sound right.

(B) To clarify is to make clear. Its opposite would be to make unclear. Could coddle mean to make unclear? Maybe.

(C) To abuse someone is to treat her badly. The opposite would be to treat her nicely. Could coddle mean to treat nicely? Maybe.

(D) The opposite of separate would be to join together. Does coddle mean to join together? That doesn't sound right.

(E) The opposite of confess would be not to admit. Does coddle mean not to admit? That doesn't sound right.

You've been able to eliminate three choices, dramatically improving your guessing odds. You should toss a coin in your mind and pick one of the two remaining choices. (Pam's answer is C. *Coddle* means to pamper or treat with extreme care. *Abuse* isn't a very good opposite, but it's the closest of the choices.)

On medium questions, you should usually be able to eliminate at least one or two bad choices by working backward and using POE. Don't spend a lot of time doing this; just eliminate what you can, make a guess, and move on.

PARTIAL KNOWLEDGE

In approaching antonym problems on which you have some knowledge, remember POE. Use your partial knowledge to *eliminate* choices that could not possibly be correct, and then *guess* from among the remaining choices. You may know that a word has positive connotations, or you may have heard the word yesterday in history class, or you may have seen the word in a magazine article and neglected to look it up. You may be able to use these clues to improve your guessing odds.

Suppose that you are unsure of the meaning of the word in capital letters but that you know it has positive connotations—let's say the word is *jubilation*. Since you know the word is positive, that means its opposite will almost certainly be negative. You can therefore go through the answer choices and *eliminate any word that is also positive*.

Here's an example:

8. DEARTH: (A) tedium (B) maliciousness
(C) information (D) antagonism (E) bounty

Here's how to crack it: Let's say that you don't know what *dearth* means, but that you've heard it before and you know that it has negative connotations. You can now go through the answer choices and eliminate any words that are also negative.

(A) *Tedium* is a negative word. It means boredom. Eliminate.

(B) *Maliciousness* is a negative word. It means ill will or malice. Eliminate

(C) *Information* is neither negative nor positive, so do not eliminate just yet.

(D) *Antagonism* means hostility. Eliminate.

(E) *Bounty* is a clearly positive word. It means abundance or plenty. A good choice. In fact, it's Pam's answer. *Dearth* means lack or scarcity, just the opposite of bounty.

Even if you were able to eliminate only one or two answer choices on this problem, you tilted the odds in your favor. On all such problems you should eliminate what you can, guess from among the remaining choices, and move on to the next question.

You will sometimes encounter words whose meanings you don't know but which you have seen or heard before in a specific situation. For example, you may not know the meaning of the word *neologism*, but you may remember having heard it in English class. Since words that are opposites are always related—up and down are opposites, but they both have to do with *direction*—you can eliminate choices that seem *un*related. In this case, you would want to eliminate choices that seem the *least* like words you have heard in English class. Here's the full example:

10. NEOLOGISM: (A) nameless article
(B) foreign object (C) exaggerated movement
(D) impoverished condition (E) obsolete expression

Here's how to crack it: Of the five choices, C and D seem *least* like phrases that would be likely to come up in English class. You should eliminate them. Which choice seems most like such a phrase? How about E? An English class is a language class, and an obsolete expression is a kind of language. (Choice E is Pam's answer. A neologism is a newly coined word. An obsolete expression would be a word no longer used.)

ENDINGS I

In deciding how to guess on a medium question, pay special attention to the *ending* of the word in capital letters. Joe Bloggs tends to pick answers that remind him of the questions. On antonyms, Joe is especially attracted to any answer choice that has the same ending as the word in capital letters. If the word in capital letters is attractive*ness*, Joe will be attracted to choices like incorrect*ness* and unrelated*ness*. You should use the following guidelines in deciding how to guess:

1. On a medium question, if only *one* answer choice has the same ending as the word in capital letters, you should eliminate that choice.
2. On a medium question, if *two or more* answer choices have the same ending as the word in capital letters, you should make your guess from among those choices.

Here's an example:

4. CONVENTIONAL: (A) ornamental
(B) unorthodox (C) misunderstood
(D) widely dispersed (E) rapidly constructed

Here's how to crack it: The word in capital letters ends in *-al*; so does choice A. You should therefore eliminate choice A and, if you have no other clues, guess from among the remaining choices. (Pam's answer is B.)

Of course, if two or more of the choices had ended in *-al*, you would have made your choice from among those.

Here are some examples of other common endings:

disturb*ance* (or conflu*ence*)
vulner*able* (or contempt*ible*)
restrict*ion*
effront*ery*
amelior*ate*
bane*ful*
rhapsod*ize* (or paral*yze*)
pejorat*ive*
mir*ed*
insipid*ness*

Do you know the meanings of these words? You should! Get your dictionary and look them up.

Difficult Third: General Principles

ENDINGS II

With a minor variation, what we just said about endings also applies to the difficult third:

1. On a difficult question, if only *one or two* answer choices have the same ending as the word in capital letters, you should eliminate those choices.
2. On a difficult question, if *three or more* answer choices have the same ending as the word in capital letters, you should make your guess from among those choices.

Here's an example:

10. CAPRICIOUS: (A) listless (B) impartial (C) steadfast (D) truthful (E) malicious

Here's how to crack it: The word in capital letters end in *-ious*; so does choice E. You should therefore eliminate choice E and, if you have no other clues, guess from among the remaining choices. (Pam's answer is C.)

Here's another example:

9. QUALIFIED: (A) underlying (B) disregarded (C) unrestricted (D) predetermined (E) rehabilitated

Here's how to crack it: The word in capital letters ends in *-ed*; so do choices B, C, D, and E. Therefore, you should limit your guess (assuming you have no other information) to these four choices. (Pam's answer is C.)

Important note: *Qualified*, as it usually used, is an easy word—much too easy to be a difficult antonym. Therefore, Pam must be using this word in an alternate meaning. In this question, *qualified* is being used to mean limited or modified. If a group gives qualified support to a political candidate, it is only giving *limited* or *partial* support. Always be on the alert for words that seem too easy for their position in the antonym group. Such words usually have alternate meanings.

On a difficult question, when you don't know the meaning of the word in capital letters, make a quick check to see if any of the answer choices has the same ending, guess accordingly, and move

on. If none of the choices has the same ending and you have no other clues, leave the question blank and move on.

ELIMINATING JOE BLOGGS ATTRACTORS

As we've mentioned already, Joe Bloggs is especially attracted to answer choices that remind him of the word in capital letters. You can turn this fact to your advantage by eliminating choices that would attract Joe Bloggs and then guessing from among the remaining choices. Here is an example:

8. UPSHOT: (A) initial step (B) quick descent
   (C) severe punishment (D) complete silence
   (E) total destruction

Here's how to crack it: When Joe Bloggs sees *upshot*, he thinks of *down*. Which answer attracts him? Choice B, of course. You should eliminate it and guess from among the remaining choices. (Pam's answer is A. Upshot means outcome.)

Here's another example:

9. AMBULATORY: (A) irritable (B) satisfactory
   (C) hospitalized (D) self-propelled
   (E) bedridden

Here's how to crack it: When Joe Bloggs sees *ambulatory*, he thinks of ambulance. Which answer attracts him? Choice C. You should eliminate it and guess from among the remaining choices. (Pam's answer is E. *Ambulatory* means able to walk; a bedridden person would be unable to walk.)

THE HIT PARADE

If, after all else fails, you notice that one of the choices is a word from the Hit Parade, go for that choice. If you don't know what the Hit Parade is, then you haven't been working on your vocabulary. Get to work now! See Part Five.

CALLING IT QUITS

Don't get bogged down on hard antonyms. If the word in capital letters is completely unfamiliar to you, don't waste time trying to figure out what it means. Trying to decode the meaning of hard antonyms—by using roots, associations, or other clues—is likely to lead you to an incorrect choice. Remember, Joe Bloggs tries to figure out the meanings of hard words, too. Don't waste time on hard antonyms. If you can apply a rule, do so quickly and guess. Otherwise, save your time for questions (such as analogies and sentence completions) that are easier to crack.

Summary: Strategies by Thirds

As was true with analogies, you need to use different techniques for the easy, medium, and difficult thirds of each antonym group. The following reminders should help you remember how to approach each third.

GENERAL PRINCIPLES
(All Thirds)

1. Antonym questions are vocabulary questions. Get to work on the vocabulary section, which begins on page 251.

2. Always consider *every* choice, even on easy questions.

3. As was true with analogies, Pam always uses the same part of speech for the word in capital letters and every choice on an antonym problem. If the word in capital letters is a noun, then every answer choice will always be a noun.

EASY THIRD

1. Remember: Joe Bloggs gets these questions right. If you aren't sure about the meaning of the word in capital letters but have a hunch about which answer choice is correct, then you should trust your hunch.

2. Easy questions have easy answers; don't fret about hard choices in the easy third.

MEDIUM THIRD

1. Remember: In the medium third, Joe Bloggs is sometimes right and sometimes wrong. If you have an average vocabulary, you may be able to improve your score by making educated guesses about the meanings of words. But you should use extreme caution in making your guesses.

2. Pay special attention to answer choices that seem peculiar or completely out of place (suppress:air)

3. In the medium third, when the word in capital letters seems to be a very simple word, it is almost always being used in a different sense from the one that first comes to mind.

4. When you have a hunch about an *unusual* word (harebrained, sluggard) in the medium third, you should go with your hunch.

5. When you are somewhat uncertain about the meaning of the word in capital letters, work backward from the answer choices by turning each of them into its opposite.

6. If you have partial knowledge, *use it* in making an educated guess.

7. Pay special attention to endings:
   A. On a medium question, if only *one* answer choice has the same ending as the word in capital letters, *you should eliminate that choice.*
   B. On a medium question, if *two or more* answer choices have the same ending as the word in capital letters, you should make your guess from among those choices.

DIFFICULT THIRD

1. Remember: Joe Bloggs gets difficult questions wrong. Unless you are fairly certain about the meaning of the word in capital letters, you are probably better off not wasting *any* time on it.

2. Pay special attention to endings:
   A. On a difficult question, if only *one* or *two* answer choices have the same ending as the word in capital letters, *you should eliminate those choices.*
   B. On a difficult question, if *three or more* answer choices have the same ending as the word in capital letters, you should make your guess from among those choices.

3. Before guessing, eliminate Joe Bloggs attractors.

4. If, after all else fails, you notice that one of the choices is a word from the Hit Parade, go for that choice.

5. Don't get bogged down on hard antonyms. If the word in capital letters is completely unfamiliar to you, don't waste time trying to figure out what it means.

CHAPTER SEVEN

Sentence Completions

Before we begin, take a moment to read the following set of instructions and to answer the sample question that comes after it. Both appear here exactly as they do on real SATs. Be certain that you know and understand these instructions before you take the SAT. If you learn them ahead of time, you won't have to waste valuable seconds reading them on the day you take the test.

Each sentence below has one or two blanks, each blank indicating that something has been omitted. Beneath the sentence are five lettered words or sets of words. Choose the word or set of words that *best* fits the meaning of the sentence as a whole.

Example:

Although its publicity has been _____, the film itself is intelligent, well-acted, handsomely produced, and altogether _____.

(A) tasteless..respectable (B) extensive..moderate
(C) sophisticated..amateur (D) risqué..crude
(E) perfect..spectacular

Pam's answer to this sample question is A.

SAT Sentence Completions: Cracking the System

It's important to know the instructions printed before each group of sentence completions on the SAT, but it's vastly more important to understand what those instructions mean. ETS's instructions don't tell you everything you need to know about SAT sentence completions. The rest of this chapter will teach you what you do need to know.

One of the two scored verbal sections on your SAT will contain 45 questions; the other will contain 40 questions. The 45-question section will contain 10 sentence completions. The 40-question section will contain 5 sentence completions.

Both groups of sentence completions will be arranged in order of increasing difficulty. In the 10-question group, a number 1 will be relatively easy and a number 10 will be very hard. In the 5-question group, a number 1 will be relatively easy and a number 5 will be relatively hard.

Because our techniques vary depending on the difficulty of the question, the examples we use in this chapter will always be numbered. These examples will be numbered from 1 to 5. A number 1 will always be easy; a number 5 will always be hard. On the actual test, you'll need to make sure you know whether you have 10 sentences in a row or 5 sentences in a row, so you'll know whether the fifth question is medium (in the group of 10) or difficult (in the group of 5). *Always pay attention to the question number in answering SAT questions.*

Your Job Is to Find Clues

Sentence completions are sentences from which one or two words have been removed. Your job is to find what is missing. You will do this by looking for clues among the words you have been given and using those clues to eliminate obviously incorrect choices. Our techniques will enable you to

1. anticipate what is missing by learning to recognize what has been given
2. use contextual clues
3. use structural clues
4. eliminate Joe Bloggs attractors

Think of Yourself as an Archaeologist

Archaeologists sometimes discover stone tablets covered with ancient writing. Very often the tablets are in fragments, with many pieces missing. Yet the archaeologists can sometimes translate the writing on the tablets anyway.

How do they do it? By looking for clues among the words that are there and then using clues to make educated guesses about the words that are missing.

Catch the Drift

When an archaeologist tries to fill in the missing words on a stone tablet, she doesn't merely plug in any word that fits; she plugs in only words that "catch the drift" of the rest of the tablet. If the tablet as a whole is about methods of planting corn, she won't fill in the blanks with words about digging wells.

You must do the same thing on the SAT. It isn't enough to plug in a choice that is merely plausible; you must find the *one* choice that "catches the drift" of the rest of the sentence and completes the thought that Pam was trying to convey. Here is an example:

2. Some developing nations have become remarkably ____, using aid from other countries to build successful industries.

(A) populous (B) dry (C) warlike
(D) prosperous (E) isolated

Here's how to crack it: Every one of the five choices is a word that could plausibly be used to describe a developing nation. Yet only one can be Pam's answer. Which one is it? The clue is in the sentence: *using aid . . .* to build *successful industries.* What kind of countries would build successful industries? *Prosperous* ones. This is Pam's answer.

Look for the Doctor

Consider the following two sentence completions:

I. The banker told the woman, "You're very ____."

(A) rich (B) correct (C) preposterous
(D) cloistered (E) sick

II. The doctor told the woman, "You're very ____."

(A) rich (B) correct (C) preposterous
(D) cloistered (E) sick

Analysis: Questions I and II are identical, with the exception of a single word. And yet that single word makes a great deal of difference. It changes Pam's answer from A in number I to E in number II. *Banker* is the key word in question I; *doctor* is the key word in question II. In each case, it is this key word that determines Pam's answer.

Every SAT sentence completion contains a key word or phrase that will provide the clue to solving it. In approaching a sentence completion, you should always ask yourself, "Where's the doctor? Where's the key to the solution?"

Learn to Anticipate

"Finding the doctor" in each sentence completion will often enable you to develop an idea of Pam's answer before you even look at the answer choices. By looking for the doctor in every sentence, you will learn to *anticipate* what each missing word might be. Here's an example:

4. The people were tired of reform crusades; they wanted no part of an idea that might turn into a ____.

Analysis: If this sentence consisted *only* of the part after the semicolon, you wouldn't have any idea of what the blank might be: "The people wanted no part of an idea that might turn into a ____." The doctor—the important clue—must therefore be in the first part of the sentence. What did the people want no part of? Why, it says right there: *reform crusades*. Those two words are "the doctor." Plugging them into the blank doesn't yield a very well written sentence, but it conveys Pam's general intention. It catches the drift. The answer we are looking for, therefore, will be a word that means (or could mean) something like "reform crusade." Now we can look at the choices:

(A) respite (B) reality (C) necessity (D) mistake (E) cause

Here's how to crack it: Go through the choices one by one:

(A) Could a respite be the same thing as a reform crusade? No. *Respite* means *rest*, as in a respite from labor. Eliminate.

(B) Could reality be the same thing as a reform crusade? No. That doesn't make any sense. Eliminate.

(C) Could a necessity be the same thing as a reform crusade? No. This doesn't make sense, either, especially if you try to plug it into the sentence. Eliminate.

(D) Could a mistake mean the same thing as a reform crusade? A reform crusade could be a mistake, but this doesn't make any sense, either. Eliminate. (Be careful! This is a Joe Bloggs attractor. Joe doesn't pay attention to the clue in the first part of the sentence. He just knows he doesn't want any part of an idea that could turn into a mistake, so he selects this answer. This is a hard question—a number 4—so his hunch is incorrect.)

(E) Could a cause be the same thing as a reform crusade? Yes. For example, attempting to reform laws regarding chemical wastes would be a "cause." This is Pam's answer.

The following drill contains sentences from real SATs. We've left out the answer choices, so you'll have to use only the clues in the sentences to help you *anticipate* what the answers might be.

DRILL 1

Look for the doctor in each sentence; when you find it, circle it. Then try to think of three possible choices for each blank. Don't worry if you can't think of a single, perfect word for each blank; you can use a phrase if you need to, *as long as it catches the drift*. When you've finished these questions, go on to Drill 2 and use your notes to help you select answers from among the actual choices. Then check all your answers on page 282.

1. Although the critics agreed that the book was brilliant, so few copies were sold that the work brought the author little _____ reward.

____

____

____

2. Sadly, many tropical rain forests are so _____ by agricultural and industrial overdevelopment that they may _____ by the end of the century.

_______________ _______________

_______________ _______________

_______________ _______________

3. My plea is not for drab and _____ technical writing about music but for pertinent information conveyed with as much _____ as possible.

_______________ _______________

_______________ _______________

_______________ _______________

DRILL 2

Here are the same questions, this time with answer choices provided. Refer to your notes from Drill 1 and make a choice for each question. Remember POE, the process of elimination. Pam's answers are on page 282.

1. Although the critics agreed that the book was brilliant, so few copies were sold that the work brought the author little _____ reward.

   (A) theoretical (B) thoughtful (C) financial
   (D) abstract (E) informative

2. Sadly, many tropical rain forests are so _____ by agricultural and industrial overdevelopment that they may _____ by the end of the century.

   (A) isolated..separate
   (B) threatened..vanish
   (C) consumed..expand
   (D) augmented..diminish
   (E) rejuvenated..disappear

3. My plea is not for drab and _____ technical writing about music but for pertinent information conveyed with as much _____ as possible.

(A) repetitive..redundancy
(B) obscure..felicity
(C) inscrutable..ambivalence
(D) euphonious..harmony
(E) provocative..exhilaration

Beyond the Doctor

"Finding the doctor" and anticipating answers should always be your first steps in solving SAT sentence completions. But on some questions, especially the harder ones, you'll need more help. We have several techniques that should enable you to rule out obviously incorrect answers and zero in on Pam's answer. These techniques will enable you to

1. eliminate Joe Bloggs attractors
2. use the good-word/bad-word method for finding Pam's answers
3. take advantage of the order of difficulty

Technique 1: Eliminate Joe Bloggs Attractors

Your SAT will include three sentence completion groups, each containing five questions. In each group, the last question or two (or even three) will be quite difficult. On these hard questions, you will find it useful to remember the Joe Bloggs principle and eliminate choices that you know would attract Joe. Here's an example:

5. The phenomenon is called viral _____ because the presence of one kind of virus seems to inhibit infection by any other.

(A) proliferation (B) mutation (C) interference
(D) epidemic (E) cooperation

Here's how to crack it: Joe Bloggs is attracted to choices containing easy words that remind him of the subject matter of the sentence. The words in the sentence that Joe notices are *virus* and *infection*—words related to medicine or biology. Which answers attract him? Choices B and D. You can therefore eliminate both.

(Where's the doctor in this sentence? It's the word *inhibit*. By rewording the sentence a little, you can catch the drift and anticipate Pam's answer: "The phenomenon is called viral *inhibition* because ne presence of one kind of virus seems to inhibit infection by any ther." Which answer choice could mean something similar to inhiition? Interference. Pam's answer is C.)

Important note: Eliminating Joe Bloggs attractors should always be the first thing you do in considering answer choices on a hard sentence completion. If you don't eliminate them immediately, you will run a strong risk of falling for them as you consider the various choices.

However: You should never eliminate a choice unless you are dictionary-sure of its meaning.

Eliminating choices without justification is the most common mistake students make when they learn to apply POE to sentence completions. One example of this is eliminating a choice because it "doesn't sound right." Remember that this is *exactly* what Joe Bloggs does. On difficult sentence completions, a choice that "doesn't sound right" may very well be Pam's answer.

Some students prefer to use POE in stages, eliminating first the choices that are obviously incorrect, then eliminating the ones that are doubtful, and finally selecting an answer.

Technique 2: Use the Good-Word/Bad-Word Method for Finding Pam's Answers

On many sentence completions, the wording of the sentence will give you general clues that will enable you to eliminate bad choices and zero in on Pam's answer. An extremely useful technique is to look at each blank and ask yourself whether, based on the context, the missing word is probably a "good" word (that is, one with positive connotations) or a "bad" word (one with negative connotations).

Using this technique is a bit like anticipating Pam's answer, except that all you are trying to do is determine what *sort* of word the missing word is. It's a technique to try when direct anticipation doesn't make you think of anything. Here's an example:

4. Ruskin's vitriolic attack was the climax of the _____ heaped on paintings that today seem amazingly _____.

(A) criticism..unpopular
(B) ridicule..inoffensive
(C) praise..amateurish
(D) indifference..scandalous
(E) acclaim..creditable

Here's how to crack it: A vitriolic attack is something bad (so is just a plain attack, if you don't know what *vitriolic* means). Therefore, the climax of a vitriolic attack must also be bad, and the first blank must be a bad word. Already we can eliminate choices C and E (and possibly also choice D).

Now look at the second blank. The first part of the sentence says that Ruskin thought the paintings were very bad; today, "amazingly," they seem—what? Bad? No! This has to be a good word. If the paintings were still regarded as bad, Ruskin's attack wouldn't seem amazing today. The second blank, therefore, must be a good word. We can now eliminate A, C, and D. The only choice left is B—Pam's answer.

As always on the SAT, your aim should be to eliminate incorrect answers. Get rid of as many bad choices as you can, guess from among the remaining choices, and move on.

Technique 3: Take Advantage of the Order of Difficulty

Let's assume you've tried everything: You've looked for the doctor, you've tried to anticipate Pam's answer, you've eliminated the Joe Bloggs attractors, you've used the good-word/bad-word technique. But you still can't find Pam's answer. What should you do?

In Chapter Four we taught you that easy questions have easy answers and hard questions have hard answers. Joe Bloggs tends to avoid choices containing words whose meaning he doesn't understand. As a result, we can be fairly certain that on easy questions (which Joe gets right) Pam's answer will contain easy words, and on hard questions (which Joe gets wrong) her answer will contain hard words.

What does this mean in terms of strategies for the SAT? It means two things:

1. On easy questions, you should be very suspicious of hard choices.
2. On hard questions, you should be very suspicious of easy choices.

To put it another way, a hard word will usually not be Pam's answer on an easy question. And an easy word will usually not be Pam's answer on a hard question.

How easy is easy? How hard is hard? The following drill should help give you a sense of the range of difficulty in the vocabulary tested on the SAT.

DRILL 3

Each group contains three sentence completion answer choices. Rearrange each group in increasing order of difficulty. Just put a 1 beside the easiest choice, a 2 beside the medium choice, and a 3 beside the most difficult choice. You can check your answers on page 282.

GROUP A	GROUP B
interrupted	postulate..explore
inevitable..mitigates	detect..overlook
force..lacking	paradigm

GROUP C	GROUP D
certitudes..elusive	gullible..distant
vague..traditions	parsimony..chary of
represent..diversity	increased..inadequate

Summary

1. Catch the drift of every sentence by figuring out the point that Pam is trying to make.

2. Look for the doctor—the key word or words that give you the most important clue you need to catch the drift.

3. Learn to anticipate Pam's answer by mentally filling in each blank before you look at the answer choices.

4. Eliminate Joe Bloggs attractors. On difficult questions, Joe is attracted to answers containing easy words that remind him of the subject matter of the sentence. Learn to recognize these words, and be extremely suspicious of the answer choices in which they appear.

5. On difficult questions, eliminating the Joe Bloggs attractors should always be the first thing you do in considering the answer choices. If you don't eliminate them immediately, you will run a very strong risk of falling for them as you consider the various choices.

6. You should never eliminate a choice unless you are dictionary-sure of its meaning.

7. When you have trouble finding the doctor or anticipating Pam's answer in a hard sentence completion, use the good-word/bad-word method of catching the general drift of the sentence and then use POE to eliminate obviously incorrect choices.

8. Take advantage of the order of difficulty. As with analogies and antonyms, easy sentence completions tend to have easy answers; hard ones have hard answers. Remember to verify whether you have five sentences in a row or ten in a row so you will know whether the fifth question is medium or difficult.

PART THREE

HOW TO CRACK THE MATH SAT

A Few Words about Numbers

The SAT contains six 30-minute sections. Two of these will be math sections. There may be a third math section on your test, but it won't count toward your score.

Each of the two scored math sections on the SAT contains groups of questions drawn from the following four categories:

1. arithmetic
2. basic algebra
3. geometry
4. quantitative comparisons

Quantitative comparison is really a format rather than a kind of question. The quantitative comparisons on your test will be arithmetic, algebra, or geometry problems. But because the format has special characteristics, we will treat it separately.

What Does the Math SAT Measure?

ETS says that the math SAT measures "mathematical reasoning abilities" or "higher-order reasoning abilities." But this is not true. The math SAT is merely a brief test of arithmetic, first-year algebra, and a bit of geometry. By a "bit" we mean just that. You won't have to know how to figure the volume of a sphere or the cross section of a cone. You also won't have to know calculus, trigonometry, or the quadratic formula. The principles you'll need to know are few and simple. We'll show you which ones are important.

Basic Organization

One of your scored math sections will contain 25 questions; the other will contain 35. The questions are not divided into subject-matter groups the way they were on the verbal SAT. You could have an algebra question followed by a geometry question followed by another algebra question. Quantitative comparisons, however, are grouped together. There will be one group of 20 of them right in the middle of your 35-question math section.

Order of Difficulty

As was true on the verbal SAT, questions on the math SAT are arranged in order of difficulty. On the 25-question math section:

1. the first third of the section is easy
2. the middle third of the section is medium
3. the final third of the section is difficult

On the 35-question math section:

1. the first seven questions increase in difficulty from easy to medium
2. questions 8 through 27 are quantitative comparisons divided into easy, medium, and difficult thirds
3. the last eight question increase in difficulty from medium to difficult

Here's a chart that should help you envision the order of difficulty on the math SAT:

TYPE I (25 questions)		TYPE II (35 questions)	
1–8	easy	1–7	easy, medium
9–17	medium	8–14	easy quant comps
18–25	difficult	15–22	medium quant comps
		23–27	difficult quant comps
		28–35	medium, difficult

The Princeton Review Approach

The average student will have little trouble with easy math questions, a fair amount of trouble with medium ones, and very little luck at all with difficult ones. For this reason, the focus of our approach is on techniques that are most useful in solving medium problems. This is where most students stand to benefit the most. If you learn to handle these problems well, you can expect a score of 600 or so.

This doesn't mean that the average student should not attempt the difficult problems; nor does it mean that we have no techniques for these problems. All we mean is that unless you expect to score above 600 or so, concentrating on easy and medium questions will be the best use of your time. If you finish these satisfactorily and have time remaining, you can turn your attention to the hardest problems, focusing on the types that are most susceptible to our techniques or that are familiar to you from math class.

Generally speaking, each chapter in this part will begin with the basics and then gradually move into more advanced principles and techniques. If you find yourself getting lost toward the end of a chapter, don't worry. Concentrate your efforts on principles you can understand but have yet to master.

Don't Throw Away Your Math Book

Although we will show you which mathematical principles are most important to know for the SAT, this book cannot take the place of a basic foundation in math. For example, if you discover as you read this book that you have trouble adding fractions, you'll want to go back and review the appropriate chapter in your math book or ask your math teacher for an explanation. Our drills and examples will refresh your memory if you've gotten rusty, but if you have serious difficulties with the following chapters, you should consider getting extra help. This book will enable you to see where you need the most work. Always keep in mind, though, that the math tested on the SAT is different from the math taught in class. If you want to raise your score, don't waste time studying math that ETS never tests.

Basic Information

Before moving on to the rest of this part, you should be certain that you are familiar with some basic terms and concepts that you'll need to know for the math SAT. This material isn't at all difficult, but you must know it cold. If you don't, you'll waste valuable time on the test and lose points that you easily could have earned.

INTEGERS

Integers are the numbers that most of us are accustomed to thinking of simply as "numbers." They can be either positive or negative. The positive integers are

1, 2, 3, 4, 5, 6, 7, and so on

The negative integers are

–1, –2, –3, –4, –5, –6, –7, and so on

Zero (0) is also an integer, *but it is neither positive nor negative.*

Note that positive integers get *bigger* as they move away from 0, while negative integers get *smaller*. In other words, 2 is bigger than 1, but –2 is smaller than –1.

DIGITS

There are ten digits:

0, 1, 2, 3, 4, 5, 6, 7, 8, 9

All integers are made up of digits. In the integer 3,476, the digits are 3, 4, 7, and 6. *Digits are to numbers what letters are to words.*

The integer 645 is called a "three-digit number" for obvious reasons. Each of its digits has a different name:

5 is called the units digit
4 is called the tens digit
6 is called the hundreds digit

Thus, the value of any number depends on which digits are in which places. The number 645 could be rewritten as follows:

$$\begin{array}{rrcr} & 6 \times 100 & & 600 \\ & 4 \times 10 & = & 40 \\ + & 5 \times 1 & & \underline{+\ \ 5} \\ & & & 645 \end{array}$$

POSITIVE AND NEGATIVE

There are three rules regarding the multiplication of positive and negative numbers:

1. pos × pos = pos
2. neg × neg = pos
3. pos × neg = neg

ODD OR EVEN

Even numbers are integers that can be divided evenly by 2. Here are some examples of even numbers:

–4, –2, 0, 2, 4, 6, 8, 10, and so on

You can always tell at a glance whether a number is even: *It is even if its final digit is even.* Thus 999,999,999,992 is an even number because 2, the final digit, is an even number.

Odd numbers are integers that *cannot* be divided evenly by 2. Here are some examples of odd numbers:

–5, –3, –1, 1, 3, 5, 7, 9, and so on

You can always tell at a glance whether a number is odd: *It is odd if its final digit is odd*. Thus, 222,222,222,229 is an odd number because 9, the final digit, is an odd number.

Several rules always hold true with odd and even numbers:

even + even = even	even × even = even
odd + odd = even	odd × odd = odd
even + odd = odd	even × odd = even

REMAINDERS

If a number cannot be divided evenly by another number, the number left over at the end of the division is called the remainder. For example, 25 cannot be divided evenly by 3. Twenty-five divided by 3 is 8 with 1 left over. The 1 is the remainder.

CONSECUTIVE INTEGERS

Consecutive integers are integers listed in increasing order of size without any integers missing in between. For example, –1, 0, 1, 2, 3, 4, and 5 are consecutive integers; 2, 4, 5, 7, and 8 are not. Nor are –1, –2, –3, and –4 consecutive integers, because they are *decreasing* in size. The formula for consecutive integers is n, $n + 1$, $n + 2$, $n + 3$, and so on, where n is an integer.

PRIME NUMBERS

A prime number is a number that can be divided evenly only by itself and by 1. For example, the following are *all* the prime numbers less than 30: 2, 3, 5, 7, 11, 13, 17, 19, 23, 29. *Note: 0 and 1 are not prime numbers.*

DIVISIBILITY RULES

1. An integer can be divided evenly by 2 if its final digit can be divided evenly by 2.
2. An integer can be divided evenly by 3 if the sum of its digits can be divided evenly by 3.
3. An integer can be divided evenly by 5 if its final digit is either 0 or 5.

STANDARD SYMBOLS

The following standard symbols are used frequently on the SAT:

SYMBOL	MEANING
$=$	is equal to
$\neq$	is not equal to
$<$	is less than
$>$	is greater than
$\leq$	is less than or equal to
$\geq$	is greater than or equal to

FINALLY, THE INSTRUCTION

Each of the two scored math sections on your SAT will begin with the same set of instructions. These instructions include a few formulas and other information that you may need to answer some of the questions. Much of the mathematical information in them is repeated from the basic principles we just discussed. You must learn these instructions ahead of time. *You should never have to waste valuable time by referring to them during the test.* Following are the instructions exactly as they will appear on your test.

In this section solve each problem, using any available space on the page for scratchwork. Then decide which is the best of the choices given and blacken the corresponding space on the answer sheet.

The following information is for your reference in solving some of the problems.

Circle of radius r: Area $= \pi r^2$;
Circumference $= 2\pi r$
The number of degrees of arc in a circle is 360.
The measure in degrees of a straight angle is 180.

Definitions of symbols:

$=$ is equal to	$\leq$ is less than or equal to
$\neq$ is unequal to	$\geq$ is greater than or equal to
$<$ is less than	$\parallel$ is parallel to
$>$ is greater than	$\perp$ is perpendicular to

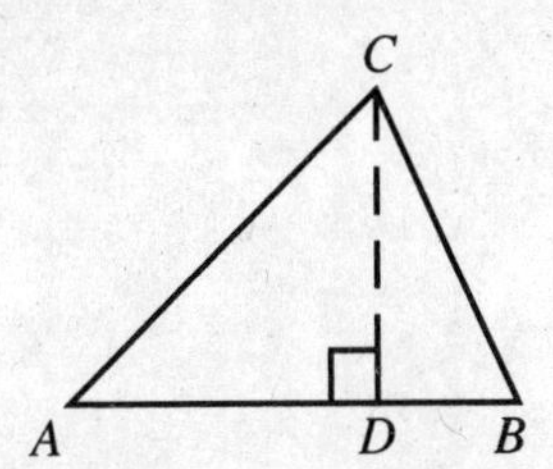

Triangle: The sum of the measures in degrees of the angles of a triangle is 180.
If $\angle CDA$ is a right angle, then

(1) area of $\Delta ABC = \frac{AB \times CD}{2}$

(2) $AC^2 = AD^2 + DC^2$

Note: Figures which accompany problems in this test are intended to provide information useful in solving the problems. They are drawn as accurately as possible EXCEPT when it is stated in a specific problem that its figure is not drawn to scale. All figures lie in a plane unless otherwise indicated. All numbers used are real numbers.

(Quantitative comparison questions have their own set of instructions. We'll discuss those in Chapter Twelve.)

CHAPTER EIGHT

Joe Bloggs and the Math SAT

Yo, Joe!

Joe Bloggs should have been a big help to you on the verbal SAT questions. By learning to anticipate which answer choices would attract Joe on difficult questions, you taught yourself to avoid careless mistakes and eliminate obviously incorrect answers.

You can do the same thing on the math SAT. In fact, Joe Bloggs attractors are often easier to spot on math questions. Jim is quite predictable in the way he writes incorrect answer choices, and this predictability will make it possible for you to zero in on his answers to questions that would have seemed impossible to you before.

Joe Bloggs and the Order of Difficulty

As was true on the verbal SAT, Joe gets the easy questions right and the hard questions wrong. The following chart will show you how that general principle will translate into actual problems on the two scored math sections of your SAT:

TYPE I SECTION
(25 questions)
1–8 easy—Joe gets these questions right
9–17 medium—Joe gets some right, some wrong
18–25 difficult—Joe gets these questions wrong

TYPE II SECTION
(35 questions)
1–7 easy, medium—Joe gets most of these right
8–14 easy quant comps—Joe gets these right
15–22 medium quant comps—Joe gets some right, some wrong
23–27 difficult quant comps—Joe gets these wrong
28–35 medium, difficult—Joe gets most of these wrong

How Joe Thinks

In Chapter Three, we introduced Joe Bloggs by showing you how he approached a particular math problem. That problem, you may remember, involved the calculation of an average speed. Here it is again:

25. A woman drove to work at an average speed of 40 miles per hour and returned along the same route at 30 miles per hour. If her total traveling time was 1 hour, what was the total number of miles in the round trip?

(A) 30 (B) $30\frac{1}{7}$ (C) $34\frac{2}{7}$ (D) 35 (E) 40

When we showed this problem the first time, you were just learning about Joe Bloggs. Now that you've made him your invisible partner on the SAT, you ought to know a great deal about how he thinks, at least on the verbal SAT. What you need to do now is extend your knowledge of Joe's thought processes to include math.

Here's how to crack it: This problem was the last in a 25-item math section. Therefore, it was the hardest problem in that section. Therefore, Joe got it wrong.

The answer choice most attractive to Joe on this problem is D. The question obviously involves an average of some kind, and 35 is the average of 30 and 40, so Joe picked it. Choice D just *seemed* like the right answer to Joe. (Of course, it *wasn't* the right answer; Joe gets the hard ones wrong.) From this fact we can derive a general rule:

On difficult math problems, Joe Bloggs is attracted to easy solutions arrived at through methods that he understands.

Because this is true, we know which answers we should *avoid* on hard questions: answers that *seem obvious* or that can be arrived at *simply and quickly*. If the answer really were obvious, and if finding it really were simple, the question would be easy, not hard.

Joe Bloggs is also attracted to answer choices that simply repeat numbers from the problem. On reading comprehensions, you remember, Joe likes to pick choices that repeat phrases from the passages. Something similar holds true on the math SAT. From this fact we can derive a second general rule:

On difficult math problems, Joe Bloggs is attracted to answer choices that simply repeat numbers from the problem.

This means, of course, that you should avoid all such choices. In the problem about the woman traveling to work, it means that you can also eliminate choices A and E, because 30 and 40 are numbers repeated directly from the problem. Therefore, they are extremely unlikely to be Jim's answer.

Having now eliminated three of the five choices, you shouldn't have much trouble in seeing that Jim's answer has to be C. (If you can't choose between the two remaining choices, guess and go on; you'll have a fifty-fifty chance of being right—heads you win a dollar, tails you lose a quarter.)

Putting Joe to Work on the Math SAT

Generally speaking, the Joe Bloggs principle teaches you to

1. trust your hunches on easy questions
2. double-check your hunches on medium questions
3. eliminate Joe Bloggs attractors on difficult questions

The rest of this chapter will be devoted to using Joe Bloggs to zero in on Jim's answers on difficult questions. The other math chapters will help you deal with medium questions, and you're on your own with the easy ones. (Quantitative comparisons will be treated separately in Chapter Twelve; there are special Joe Bloggs rules for those.)

Basic Techniques

HARD QUESTIONS = HARD ANSWERS

As we've just explained, hard questions on the SAT simply don't have answers that are obvious to the average person. Avoiding the "obvious" choices will take some discipline on your part, but you'll lose points if you don't. Even if you're a math whiz, the Joe Bloggs principle will keep you from making careless mistakes.

Here's an example:

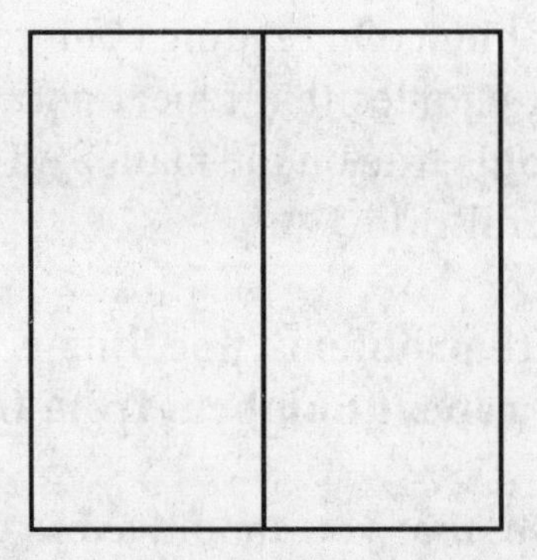

25. The figure above is a square divided into two non-overlapping regions. What is the greatest number of non-overlapping regions that can be obtained by drawing any two additional straight lines?

(A) 4 (B) 5 (C) 6 (D) 7 (E) 8

Here's how to crack it: This is the last question from a 25-item section. Therefore, it's extremely difficult. One reason it's so difficult is that it is badly and confusingly written. (Jim's strengths are mathematical, not verbal.) Here's a clearer way to think of it: The drawing is a pizza cut in half; what's the greatest number of pieces you could end up with if you make just two more cuts with a knife?

The *most obvious* way to cut the pizza would to make cuts perpendicular to the center cut, dividing the pizza into six pieces, like this:

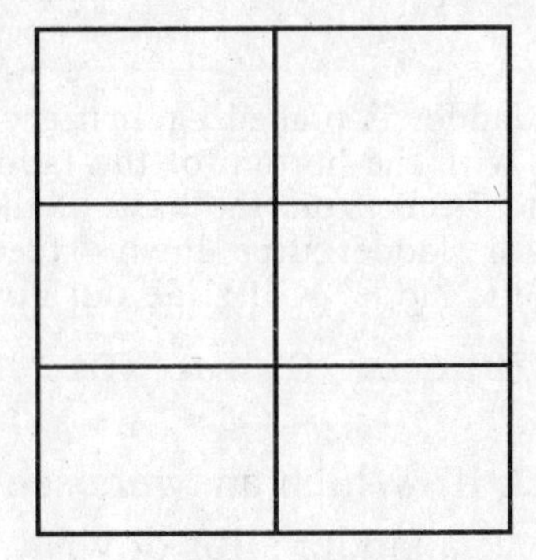

There, that was easy. Which means? Which means that 6 can't possibly be correct and that choice C can be eliminated. If finding Jim's answer were that simple, Joe Bloggs would have gotten this question right and it would have been an easy question, not a difficult one.

Will this fact help you eliminate any other choices? Yes. Because you know that if you can divide the pizza into at least *six* pieces, neither *five* nor *four* could be the *greatest* number of pieces into which it can be divided. Six is a greater number than either 5 or 4; if you can get six pieces you can also get five or four. You can thus eliminate choices A and B as well.

Now you've narrowed it down to two choices. Which will you pick? You shouldn't waste time trying to find the exact answer to a question like this. It isn't testing any mathematical principle, and you won't figure out the trick unless you get lucky. If you can't use another of our techniques to eliminate the remaining wrong answer, you should just guess and go on. Heads you win a dollar, tails you lose a quarter. (Jim's answer is D. Our third technique, incidentally, will enable you to zero in on it exactly. Keep reading.)

In case you're wondering, here's how Jim divides the pizza:

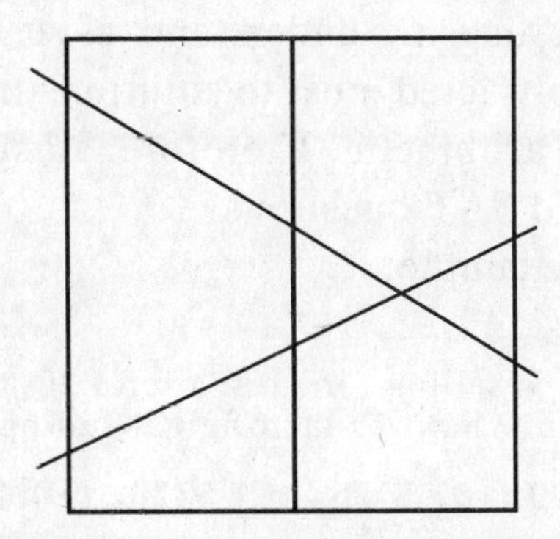

Here's another example:

24. A 25-foot ladder is placed against a vertical wall of a building with the bottom of the ladder standing on concrete 7 feet from the base of the building. If the top of the ladder slips down 4 feet, then the bottom of the ladder will slide out how many feet?

(A) 4 ft (B) 5 ft (C) 6 ft (D) 7 ft (E) 8 ft

Here's how to crack it: Which answers seems simple and obvious? Choice A, of course. If a ladder slips down 4 feet on one end, it *seems* obvious that it would slip down 4 feet on the other.

What does that mean? It means that we can eliminate choice A. If 4 feet were Jim's answer, Joe Bloggs would get this problem right and it would be an easy one, not among the hardest in its section.

Choice A also repeats a number from the problem, which means we can be doubly certain that it's wrong. Which other choice repeats a number? Choice D. So we can eliminate that one, too.

If you don't know how to do this problem, working on it further probably won't get you anywhere. You've eliminated two choices; you should guess and move on. (Jim's answer is E. Finding it would require you to use the Pythagorean theorem—see Chapter Eleven.)

No matter how thoroughly you prepare yourself, when you actually take the SAT you may find that you are irresistibly attracted to an "obvious" choice on a hard SAT math question. You'll look at the problem and see no other possible solution. If this happens, you will probably say to yourself, "Aha! I've found an exception to the Joe Bloggs rule!" Trust us: Don't be tempted. Eliminate and guess.

SIMPLE OPERATIONS = WRONG ANSWERS ON HARD QUESTIONS

Since Joe Bloggs doesn't understand most difficult mathematical operations, he is attracted most to solutions that can be arrived at by using very simple arithmetic. Therefore, all such solutions should be eliminated on hard SAT questions.

Here's an example:

20. A dress is selling for $100 after a 20 percent discount. What was the original selling price?

(A) $200 (B) $125 (C) $120 (D) $80 (E) $75

Here's how to crack it: When Joe Bloggs looks at this problem he sees "20 percent less than $100" and is attracted to choice D. Therefore, you must eliminate it. If finding the answer were that easy, Joe Bloggs would be on his way to Harvard. Joe is also attracted to choice C, which is 20 percent *more* than $100. Again, eliminate.

With two attractors out of the way, you ought to be able to solve this problem quickly. The dress is on sale, which means that its original price must have been *more* than its current price. That means that Jim's answer has to be greater than $100. Two of the remaining choices, A and B, fulfill this requirement. Now you can ask yourself:

(A) Is $100 20 percent less than $200? No. Eliminate.

(B) Is $100 20 percent less than $125? Could be. This must be Jim's answer. (It is.)

Once you have eliminated the Joe Bloggs attractor(s), look at the problem again. With the attractors out of the way, you can often find Jim's answer quickly by using common sense to eliminate less attractive but equally obvious incorrect choices. Eliminating an attractor is like getting rid of a temptation. Once it's gone, the correct answer is often apparent.

LEAST/GREATEST

Hard SAT math problems will sometimes ask you to find the *least* (or *greatest*) number that fulfills certain conditions. *On such problems, Joe Bloggs is attracted to the answer choice containing the* least *(or* greatest*) number*. You can therefore eliminate such choices. (ETS sometimes uses similar words that mean the same thing: *most, maximum, fewest,* and so on. The same rules apply to problems containing all such terms.)

Look back at the square problem on page 134. The question asks you for the *greatest* number of regions into which the square can be divided. Which choice will therefore attract Joe Bloggs? Choice E. Eight is the *greatest* number among the choices offered, so, it will *seem* right to Joe. Therefore, you can eliminate it.

Here's another example:

17. If 3 parallel lines are cut by 3 nonparallel lines, what is the maximum number of intersections possible?

(A) 9 (B) 10 (C) 11 (D) 12 (E) 13

Here's how to crack it: The problem asks you for the "maximum," or greatest number. What is thc maximum number among the choices? It is 13; therefore you can eliminate choice E.

By the simple operations = wrong answers rule that we just discussed, you can also eliminate choice A. Joe's preference for simple arithmetic makes him tend to think that the answer to this problem can be found by multiplying 3 times 3. The simple operation leads quickly to an answer of 9, which must therefore be wrong.

Jim's answer is D. Here's how he gets it:

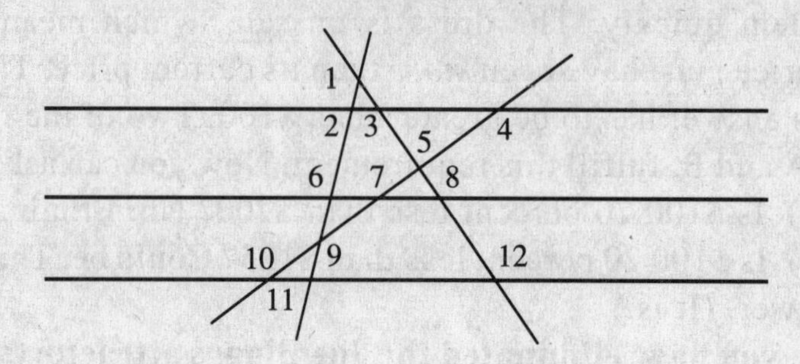

"IT CANNOT BE DETERMINED"

Once or twice on every math SAT, the fifth answer choice on a problem will be

(E) It cannot be determined from the information given.

The Joe Bloggs principle makes these questions easy to crack. Here's why:

Joe Bloggs can *never* determine the correct answer on *difficult* SAT problems. Therefore, when Joe sees this answer choice on a difficult problem, he is greatly attracted to it.

What does this mean?

It means that if "cannot be determined" is offered as an answer choice on a difficult problem, it is almost certainly wrong. In fact, *if "cannot be determined" is offered as an answer choice on one of the last* five *problems in the 25-item section or one of the last* eight *problems in a 35-item section, you should eliminate it*. (There is one exception to this rule; read on.)

Here's an example:

24. If the average of x, y, and 80 is 6 more than the average of y, z, and 80, what is the value of $x - z$?

(A) 2 (B) 3 (C) 6 (D) 18
(E) It cannot be determined from the information given.

Here's how to crack it: This problem is next to last in a 25-item section. It looks absolutely impossible to Joe. Therefore, he assumes that it is impossible for *everyone*, and he selects E as his answer. Naturally, he is wrong. Choice E should be eliminated. If it were Jim's answer, Joe would be right and this would be an easy problem.

Choice C simply repeats a number from the problem, so you can also eliminate that.

Jim's answer is D. The problem can be restated as follows:

$$\frac{x+y+80}{3} - 6 = \frac{x+z+80}{3}, \text{ which means that}$$

$$\frac{x}{3} + \frac{y}{3} + \frac{80}{3} - 6 = \frac{y}{3} + \frac{z}{3} + \frac{80}{3}$$

Subtracting common terms from both sides of the equation yields

$$\frac{x}{3} - 6 = \frac{z}{3}$$

Multiplying both sides by 3 to eliminate the fractions yields

$$x - 18 = z, \text{ or}$$
$$x - z = 18$$

Should "cannot be determined" always be eliminated as an answer choice?

No!!!

On easy and medium problems, "cannot be determined" has a very good chance of being Jim's answer. Specifically, "cannot be determined" has about one chance in two of being Jim's answer if it is offered as a choice in

1. questions 1–19 on the 25-item math section
2. questions 1–7 on the 35-item math section

What this means is that if you are stuck on an easy or medium problem and "cannot be determined" is one of the choices, you should pick it and move on. You will have one chance in two of being correct.

Quantitative comparisons (which offer "cannot be determined" as a choice on every problem) are a special case and will be dealt with separately in Chapter Twelve.

Summary

1. Joe Bloggs gets the easy math SAT questions right and the hard ones wrong.

2. On difficult problems, Joe Bloggs is attracted to easy solutions arrived at through methods he understands. Therefore, you should eliminate obvious, simple answers on difficult questions.

3. On difficult problems, Joe Bloggs is also attracted to answer choices that simply repeat numbers from the problem. Therefore, you should eliminate any such choices.

4. On difficult problems that ask you to find the *least* (or *greatest*) number that fulfills certain conditions, you can eliminate the answer choice containing the *least* (or *greatest*) number.

5. On difficult problems, you can eliminate any answer choice that says, "It cannot be determined from the information given."

CHAPTER NINE

Arithmetic

SAT Arithmetic: Cracking the System

About a third of the math problems on your SAT will involve basic arithmetic. This category includes seven separate topics:

1. arithmetic operations
2. fractions
3. decimals
4. ratios
5. percentages
6. averages
7. exponents and radicals

If you're like most students, you probably haven't paid much serious attention to these topics since junior high school. You'll need to learn about them again if you want to do well on the SAT. By the time you take the test, using them should be automatic. All the arithmetic concepts are fairly basic, but you'll have to know them cold.

In this chapter, we'll deal with each of these seven topics.

Arithmetic Operations

THERE ARE ONLY SIX OPERATIONS

There are only six arithmetic operations that you will ever need to perform on the SAT:

1. addition $(3 + 3)$
2. subtraction $(3 - 3)$
3. multiplication $(3 \times 3$ or $3 \cdot 3)$
4. division $(3 \div 3)$
5. raising to a power (3^3)
6. finding a square root or a cube root $(\sqrt{3}$ or $\sqrt[3]{3})$

What Do You Get?

You should know the following arithmetic terms:

1. The result of addition is *sum* or *total.*
2. The result of subtraction is a *difference.*
3. The result of multiplication is a *product.*
4. The result of division is a *quotient.*
5. In the expression 5^2, the little 2 is called an *exponent.* The entire expression is an example of *exponential notation.*

The Six Operations Must Be Performed in the Proper Order

Very often solving an equation on the SAT will require you to perform several different operations one after another. These operations must be performed in the proper order. In general, the problems are written in such a way that you won't have trouble deciding what comes first. In cases where you are uncertain, you only need to remember the following sentence:

Please **E**xcuse **M**y **D**ear **A**unt **S**ally

That's **PEMDAS**, for short. The acronym PEMDAS stands for **P**arentheses, **E**xponents, **M**ultiplication, **D**ivision, **A**ddition, **S**ubtraction. First you clear the parentheses; then you take care of the exponents; then you multiply, divide, add, and subtract. (We'll have more to say about exponents in a little while.)

The following drill will help you learn the order in which to perform the six operations.

DRILL 1

Solve each of the following problems by performing the indicated operations in the proper order. Answers can be found on page 283.

1. $107 + (109 - 107) =$
2. $(7 \times 5) + 3 =$
3. $6 - 3(6 - 3) =$
4. $2 \times [7 - (6 \div 3)] =$
5. $10 - (9 - 8 - 6) =$

PARENTHESES CAN HELP YOU SOLVE EQUATIONS

Using parentheses to regroup information in SAT arithmetic problems can be very helpful. In order to do this you need to understand two basic laws that you may have forgotten since the days when you last took arithmetic: the associative law and the distributive law. You don't need to remember the name of either law, but you do need to know how each works. Let's look at them one at a time.

The associative law: There are really two associative laws, one for addition and one for multiplication. But both laws say basically the same thing, so we can combine them into one: *When you are adding or multiplying a series of numbers, you can group or regroup the numbers any way you like.* For example:

$$a + (b + c) = (a + b) + c = b + (a + c)$$
$$a(bc) = (ab)c = b(ac)$$

The distributive law: This is one of the most important principles on the SAT. You must be absolutely certain that you know it:

$$a(b + c) = ab + ac$$
$$a(b - c) = ab - ac$$

This law is so important that you must *always* apply it *whenever* you have a chance. If a problem gives you information in "factored form"—$a(b + c)$—then you should multiply through or *distribute* the first variable before you do anything else. If you are given information that has already been distributed—$ab + ac$—then you should factor out the common term, putting the information back in factored form. *Very often on the SAT, simply doing this will enable you to spot Jim's answer.*

Note: Earlier we told you that you should perform all operations within parentheses first. The distributive law is something of an exception to that rule. It gives you a different route to the same result. For example:

Distributive: $2(3 + 4) = 2(3) + 2(4) = 6 + 8 = 14$

Parentheses first: $2(3 + 4) = 2(7) = 14$

You get the same answer each way. But whenever you see a chance to apply the distributive law, you should do it.

The following drill illustrates the distributive law.

DRILL 2

Don't bother to calculate the actual result. Simply rewrite each problem by either distributing or factoring, whichever is called for. Answers can be found on page 283.

1. $6(57 + 18) =$
2. $51(52) + 51(53) + 51(54) =$
3. $a(b + c - d) =$
4. $xy - xz =$
5. $abc + xyc =$

Fractions

A FRACTION IS JUST ANOTHER WAY OF EXPRESSING DIVISION

The expression $\frac{x}{y}$ is exactly the same thing as $x \div y$. The expression $\frac{1}{2}$ means nothing more than $1 \div 2$. In the fraction $\frac{x}{y}$, x is known as the *numerator* and y is known as the *denominator*. (You won't need to know these terms on the SAT, but you will need to know them to follow the explanations in this book.)

ADDING AND SUBTRACTING FRACTIONS WITH THE SAME DENOMINATOR

To add two or more fractions that *all* have the *same* denominator, simply add up the numerators and put the sum over one of the denominators. For example:

$$\frac{1}{100} + \frac{4}{100} = \frac{1+4}{100} = \frac{5}{100}$$

Subtraction works exactly the same way:

$$\frac{4}{100} - \frac{1}{100} = \frac{4-1}{100} = \frac{3}{100}$$

MULTIPLYING ALL FRACTIONS

Multiplying fractions is easy. Just multiply the numerators and put their product over the product of the denominators. Here's an example:

$$\frac{4}{5} \times \frac{5}{6} = \frac{20}{30}$$

When you multiply fractions, all you are really doing is performing one multiplication on top of another.

REDUCING FRACTIONS

When you add or multiply fractions, you will very often end up with a big fraction that is hard to work with. You can almost always *reduce* such fraction into one that is easier to handle.

To reduce a fraction all you have to do is express the numerator and the denominator as the products of their factors and then eliminate, or "cancel," factors that are common to both. **Note that we aren't actually cancelling factors, but *dividing* them and replacing them with 1's.** For example:

$$\frac{12}{60} = \frac{2 \times 2 \times 3}{2 \times 2 \times 3 \times 5}$$

$$= \frac{\cancel{2}^1 \times \cancel{2}^1 \times \cancel{3}^1}{\cancel{2}^1 \times \cancel{2}^1 \times \cancel{3}^1 \times 5}$$

$$= \frac{1}{5}$$

Another way to do this is to divide both the numerator and the denominator by the largest number that is a factor of both. In the preceding example, 12 is a factor of both 12 or 60. Dividing numerator and denominator by 12 also yields the reduced fraction $\frac{1}{5}$.

In any problem involving large or confusing fractions, try to reduce the fractions first. For example, you should never multiply two fractions before looking to see if you can reduce either or both. Your multiplication will be much easier if you can put the fractions in simpler form, and you will be much less likely to make a computational error. And if you reduce first, you may find that you don't need to multiply at all.

ADDING AND SUBTRACTING FRACTIONS WITH DIFFERENT DENOMINATORS

Before you can add or subtract two or more fractions that don't all have the same denominator, you have to give them the same denominator. The way to do this is to multiply each fraction by a number that will change its denominator without changing the value of the fraction. What number will do this? *The number 1, when it is expressed as the denominator of the other fraction over itself.* That's a mouthful, but it's easy to see with an example:

$$\frac{1}{3} + \frac{1}{2} =$$

$$\left(\frac{1}{3}\right)\left(\frac{2}{2}\right) + \left(\frac{1}{2}\right)\left(\frac{3}{3}\right) =$$

$$\frac{2}{6} + \frac{3}{6} =$$

$$\frac{5}{6}$$

Analysis: All we've done here is multiply both fractions by 1 ($\frac{2}{2}$ and $\frac{3}{3}$ both equal 1). This doesn't change the value of either fraction, but it does change the form of both.

DIVIDING ALL FRACTIONS

To divide one fraction by another, invert the second fraction and multiply. To *invert* a fraction is to stand it on its head—to put its denominator over its numerator. Doing this is extremely easy, as long as you remember how it works. Here's an example:

$$\frac{2}{3} \div \frac{3}{4} =$$

$$\frac{2}{3} \times \frac{4}{3} =$$

$$\frac{8}{9}$$

You can even do the same thing with fractions whose numerators and/or denominators are fractions. These problems look quite frightening but they're actually easy if you keep your cool. Here's an example:

$$\frac{4}{\frac{4}{3}} =$$

$$\frac{\frac{4}{1}}{\frac{4}{3}} =$$

$$\frac{4}{1} \div \frac{4}{3} =$$

$$\frac{4}{1} \times \frac{3}{4} =$$

$$\frac{12}{4} =$$

$$3$$

CONVERTING MIXED NUMBERS TO FRACTIONS

A mixed number is a number like $2\frac{3}{4}$. It is the sum of an integer and a fraction. When you see mixed numbers on the SAT, you should usually convert them to ordinary fractions. You can do this easily by using a combination of the techniques we've just outlined. Here's how:

1. Convert the integer to a fraction with the same denominator as the fraction in the mixed number. With $2\frac{3}{4}$, in other words, you would convert the 2 to the fraction $\frac{8}{4}$. Note that $\frac{8}{4}$ equals 2 and has the same denominator as $\frac{3}{4}$.

2. Now that you have two fractions with the same denominator, you can simply add them:

$$\frac{8}{4} + \frac{3}{4} = \frac{11}{4}$$

Analysis: The mixed number $2\frac{3}{4}$ is exactly the same as the fraction $\frac{11}{4}$. We converted the one to the other because fractions are easier to work with than mixed numbers.

COMPARING TWO FRACTIONS

The SAT often contains problems that require you to compare one fraction with another and determine which is larger. Many students have trouble with these problems, but there's nothing really difficult about them—as long as you keep in mind the fundamental rules we've already described.

For example, suppose an SAT problem required you to compare the fractions $\frac{1}{2}$ and $\frac{4}{9}$. How would you determine which is larger? Here's how:

1. Find a common denominator. The easiest to work with is 18 (2×9).
2. Convert each fraction. $\frac{1}{2} = \frac{9}{18}$; $\frac{4}{9} = \frac{8}{18}$.

Analysis: Now the answer is obvious; $\frac{9}{18}$ is clearly larger than $\frac{8}{18}$.

You can obtain the same result by *cross-multiplying*:

$$9 \leftarrow \frac{1}{2} \times \frac{4}{9} \rightarrow 8$$

$$9 > 8;\text{ therefore, } \frac{1}{2} > \frac{4}{9}$$

COMPARING MORE THAN TWO FRACTIONS

If you are asked to compare more than two fractions, don't bother trying to find a common denominator for all of them. It could take all day! Simply hold a "tournament" and eliminate the losers.

Suppose you are given five fractions and asked to determine which is the least. Here's how to do it:

1. Compare the *first two* fractions by the method just described, and eliminate the greater one.
2. Take the remaining fraction (the "winner") and compare it with the next fraction in line.
3. Repeat until you have found Jim's answer.

FRACTIONS BEHAVE IN PECULIAR WAYS

Joe Bloggs has trouble with fractions because they don't always behave the way he thinks they ought to. For example, because 4 is obviously greater than 2, Joe Bloggs sometimes forgets that $\frac{1}{4}$ is *less than* $\frac{1}{2}$. He becomes especially confused when the numerator is some number other than 1. For example, $\frac{2}{6}$ is *less than* $\frac{2}{5}$.

Joe also has a hard time understanding that when you multiply one fraction by another, you will get a fraction that is *smaller than* either of the first two. For example:

$$\frac{1}{2} \times \frac{1}{4} = \frac{1}{8}$$

$$\frac{1}{8} < \frac{1}{2}$$

$$\frac{1}{8} < \frac{1}{4}$$

REMEMBERING EVERYTHING AT ONCE

Very often on problems dealing with fractions, you will have to apply several of the rules we've just given you in order to find an answer. For example, you may have to convert a mixed number to a fraction, then reduce that fraction, then find a common denominator with another fraction, and so on. Your goal in doing all this is to express the problem in the simplest form possible. The simpler a problem is, the less likely you will be to make an error.

The most common source of mistakes on word problems involving fractions is misreading. Read fraction word problems carefully.

The following drill will give you practice with handling fractions.

DRILL 3

If you have trouble on any of these problems, go back and review the information just outlined. Answers can be found on page 283.

1. Reduce $\frac{18}{6}$ as far as you can.
2. Convert $6\frac{1}{5}$ to a fraction.
3. $2\frac{1}{3} - 3\frac{3}{5} =$
4. $\frac{5}{18} \times \frac{6}{25} =$

5. $\frac{3}{4} \div \frac{7}{8} =$

6. $\dfrac{\frac{2}{5}}{5} =$

7. $\dfrac{\frac{1}{3}}{\frac{3}{4}} =$

Decimals

A DECIMAL IS JUST ANOTHER WAY OF EXPRESSING A FRACTION

Every fraction can be expressed as a decimal. To find a fraction's decimal equivalent, simply divide the numerator by the denominator. For example:

$\frac{3}{5} =$

$3 \div 5 =$

$$\begin{array}{r} 0.6 \\ 5\overline{)3.0} \\ \underline{3.0} \end{array}$$

$= 0.6$

NOT ALL DECIMALS HAVE (VISIBLE) DECIMAL POINTS

How many of these number are decimals?

0.6 56 –12

Answer: They all are. It's just that we usually don't bother to note the decimal point on a number like 56 or –12. But these numbers could easily be written with decimal points, like this:

56.0
–12.0

Keep this in mind as you read what follows.

THE POSITION OF THE DECIMAL POINT DETERMINES THE VALUE OF THE DIGITS.

The following table will show you how the value of a number is determined by the placement of the decimal point:

$$1{,}420 = 1{,}000 + 400 + 20 + 0$$

$$142.0 = 142 = 100 + 40 + 2$$

$$14.20 = 14.2 = 10 + 4 + \frac{2}{10}$$

$$1.420 = 1.42 = 1 + \frac{4}{10} + \frac{2}{100}$$

$$0.1420 = 0.142 = \frac{1}{10} + \frac{4}{100} + \frac{2}{1{,}000}$$

$$0.01420 = 0.0142 = \frac{0}{10} + \frac{1}{100} + \frac{4}{1{,}000} + \frac{2}{10{,}000}$$

ADDING AND SUBTRACTING DECIMALS

There's nothing tricky about adding and subtracting decimals. All you have to do is line up the decimal points and then proceed exactly as you would with integers. If you want to, you can add 0's to the *right* of the *final* digit to keep from confusing yourself. For example:

Problem: Add 3.7, 14.23, and 9

Solution:

$$\begin{array}{r} 3.70 \\ 14.23 \\ +\ 9.00 \\ \hline 26.93 \end{array}$$

Analysis: In adding these three numbers, you did exactly what you would have done in adding 370, 1,423, and 900. All you had to remember to do was keep the decimal points in line.

Subtraction works exactly the same way:

$$\begin{array}{r} 4.25 \\ -\ 3.50 \\ \hline 0.75 \end{array}$$

MULTIPLYING DECIMALS

Multiplying decimals is also easy. You multiply them exactly as you would integers. The only tricky part is putting the decimal point in the right spot in your answer. A simple two-step rule tells you how to do this:

1. Count the *total* number of digits located to the *right* of the decimal points in the numbers you are multiplying (ignoring any final zeroes).
2. Place the decimal point in your answer so that there are the *same* number of digits to the right of it.

A few examples will make this easier to understand:

$$\begin{array}{r} 0.4 \\ \underline{\times\, 0.4} \\ 0.16 \end{array} \qquad \begin{array}{r} 2.3 \\ \underline{\times\ \ 3} \\ 6.9 \end{array} \qquad \begin{array}{r} 1.23 \\ \underline{\times\ \ 0.4} \\ 0.492 \end{array}$$

Analysis: In the first problem, a total of two digits are located to the right of the decimal points in the numbers being multiplied; therefore, there must be two digits to the right of the decimal point in the answer.

In the second problem, only one digit is located to the right of a decimal point in the numbers being multiplied (the .3 in 2.3); therefore, there must be one digit to the right of the decimal point in the answer.

In the third problem, a total of three digits are located to the right of the decimal points in the numbers being multiplied (.23 and .4); therefore, there must be three digits to the right of the decimal point in the answer.

DIVIDING DECIMALS

To divide one decimal by another, you must first convert the divisor to a whole number. (In the division problem $\frac{4}{8}$, 8 is called the divisor and 4 is called the dividend.) How will you do that? Easy. *By moving the decimal point in the divisor*. You can do this as long as you move the decimal point in the dividend the same number of spaces. Here's an example:

Problem: Divide 6 by 0.48.
Solution: The first step is to set this up like an ordinary division problem:

$$\frac{6}{0.48}$$

Now we have to turn the divisor (0.48) into a whole number. To do this, we simply move the decimal point two places to the right. At the same time, we also move the decimal point in the dividend two places to the right. Here's what we end up with:

$$\frac{600}{48}$$

Now we simply work out the problem as though we were dividing 48 into 600. All we have to remember to do is put the decimal point in our answer. It goes directly above the decimal point in the dividend.

```
      12.5
48 | 600.0
     48
     120
      96
      240
      240
```

COMPARING DECIMALS

Some SAT problems will ask you to determine whether one decimal is larger or smaller than another. Many students have trouble doing this. It isn't difficult, though, and you will do fine as long as you *remember to line up the decimal points and fill in missing zeros.* Here's an example:

Problem: Which is larger, 0.0099, or 0.01?
Solution: Simply place one decimal over the other with the decimal points lined up, like this:

0.0099
0.01

To make the solution seem clearer, you can add two zeros *to the right* of 0.01. (You can always add zeros to the right of a decimal without changing its value.) Now you have this:

0.0099
0.0100

Which decimal is larger? Clearly, 0.0100 is, just as 100 is larger than 99. (Remember that $0.0099 = \frac{99}{10{,}000}$, while $0.0100 = \frac{100}{10{,}000}$. Now the answer seems obvious, doesn't it?)

Analysis: Joe Bloggs has a terrible time on this problem. Because 99 is obviously larger than 1, he tends to think that 0.0099 must be larger than 0.01. But it isn't. Don't get sloppy on problems like this! Jim loves to trip up Joe Bloggs with decimals. In fact, any time you encounter a problem involving the comparison of decimals, you should stop and ask yourself whether you are just about to make a Joe Bloggs mistake.

STAY OUT OF TROUBLE BY CONVERTING DECIMALS TO FRACTIONS

Confusion about decimal points causes more errors on the SAT than confusion about fractions. Therefore:

Whenever you can conveniently convert a decimal to a fraction, you should do so, especially when the answer choices are fractions.

Which did you learn about first in grade school, fractions or decimals? Fractions, of course. And for a good reason: Fractions are easier to work with. If you don't believe this, which would you prefer to square, $\frac{1}{4}$ or 0.25?

MONEY!

If you get confused about decimals, remember dollars and cents. \$3.35 is a decimal. It means 3 dollars plus $\frac{35}{100}$ of a dollar. \$4.20 equals 4 dollars plus $\frac{2}{10}$ of a dollar. \$0.50 equals half of a dollar.

When you get stuck on a decimal problem, convert the decimal into its money equivalent to clear your head and remind yourself what decimals are all about.

The following drill will give you practice working with decimals.

DRILL 4

Work the following problems. If you have trouble with any of them, go back and review the material just outlined. Answers can be found on page 283.

1. $\begin{array}{r} 7.931 \\ -\ 6.1 \\ \hline \end{array}$

2. $\begin{array}{r} 3.24 \\ \times\ 4.5 \\ \hline \end{array}$

3. $\dfrac{22.5}{1.5}$

4. $\dfrac{0.00025}{0.05}$

Ratios

A RATIO IS A FRACTION

Many students get extremely nervous when they are asked to work with ratios. But there's no need to be nervous. In fact, you just finished working with some ratios: Every fraction is a ratio. Furthermore, every ratio can be expressed as a fraction. The fraction $\frac{1}{2}$ is just another way of expressing "the ratio of 1 to 2" or, in the customary ratio notation, 1:2. Thus, there are three ways of denoting a ratio:

1. $\frac{x}{y}$
2. the ratio of x to y
3. $x{:}y$

IF YOU CAN DO IT TO A FRACTION, YOU CAN DO IT TO A RATIO

Since a ratio is a fraction, it can be converted to a decimal or a percentage. All the following are methods of expressing the ratio of 1 to 2:

1. $\frac{1}{2}$
2. 1:2
3. 0.5
4. 50 percent

The ratio of 2 to 1 can be expressed as follows:

1. $\frac{2}{1}$
2. 2:1
3. 2
4. 200 percent

You can also do everything else that you've learned to do with fractions: cross-multiply, find common denominators, reduce, and so on.

THINK OF A RATIO AS A NUMBER OF PARTS

If a class contains 3 students and the ratio of boys to girls in that class is 2:1, how many boys and how many girls are there in the class? Of course: There are 2 boys and 1 girl.

Now, suppose a class contains 24 students and the ratio of boys to girls is still 2:1. How many boys and how many girls are there in the class? This is a little harder, but the answer is easy to find if you think about it. There are 16 boys and 8 girls.

How did we get the answer? We added up the number of "parts" in the ratio (2 parts boys plus 1 part girls, or 3 parts altogether) and divided it into the total number of students. In other words, we divided 24 by 3. This told us that the class contained 3 equal parts of 8 students each. From the given ratio (2:1), we knew that two of these parts consisted of boys and one of them consisted of girls.

Here's another example:

18. In a jar of red and green jelly beans, the ratio of green jelly beans to red jelly beans is 5:3. If the jar contains a total of 160 jelly beans, how many of them are red?

(A) 20 (B) 36 (C) 45 (D) 60 (E) 100

Here's how to crack it: The ratio is 5:3, which means there are 8 parts altogether. How many jelly beans are in a part? To find out all we have to do is *divide the total number of jelly beans by the total number of parts:* 160 divided by 8 equals 20. That means each part consists of 20 jelly beans. How many parts contain red jelly beans? Three. That means there are 60 red jelly beans and Jim's answer is D.

PROPORTIONS ARE EQUAL RATIOS

Very often on SAT math problems you will be given a problem containing two proportional, or equal, ratios from which one piece of information is missing. Here's an example:

7. If 2 packages contain a total of 12 donuts, how many donuts are there in 5 packages?

(A) 12 (B) 24 (C) 30 (D) 36 (E) 60

Here's how to crack it: This problem simply describes two equal ratios, one of which is missing a single piece of information. Here's the given information represented as two equal ratios:

$$\frac{2 \text{ (packages)}}{12 \text{ (donuts)}} = \frac{5 \text{ (packages)}}{x \text{ (donuts)}}$$

Since ratios are fractions, we can treat them exactly like fractions. To find the answer all you have to do is figure out what you could plug in for x that would make $\frac{2}{12} = \frac{5}{x}$. One way to do this is to cross-multiply:

$$\frac{2}{12} \quad \frac{5}{x}$$

so, $2x = 60$

$x = 30$

Jim's answer is thus C.

Percentages

PERCENTAGES AREN'T SCARY

There should be nothing frightening about a percentage. It's just a convenient way of expressing a fraction whose denominator is 100.

Percent means "per 100" or "out of 100." If there are 100 questions on your math test and you answer 50 of them, you will have answered 50 out of 100, or $\frac{50}{100}$, or 50 percent. Or, to think of it another way:

$$\frac{part}{whole} = \frac{x}{100} = x \text{ percent}$$

Memorize These Percentage-Decimal-Fraction Equivalents

$0.01 = \frac{1}{100} = 1$ percent $\qquad 0.25 = \frac{1}{4} = 25$ percent

$0.1 = \frac{1}{10} = 10$ percent $\qquad 0.5 = \frac{1}{2} = 50$ percent

$0.2 = \frac{1}{5} = 20$ percent $\qquad 0.75 = \frac{3}{4} = 75$ percent

CONVERTING PERCENTAGES TO FRACTIONS

To convert a percentage to a fraction, simply put the percentage over a denominator of 100 and reduce. For example 80 percent $= \frac{80}{100} = \frac{8}{10} = \frac{4}{5}$.

CONVERTING FRACTIONS TO PERCENTAGES

Since a percentage is just another way of expressing a certain kind of fraction, you shouldn't be surprised that it is easy to convert a fraction to a percentage. To do so, simply divide the numerator by the denominator and move the decimal point in the result two places to the *right*. Here's an example:

Problem: Express $\frac{3}{4}$ as a percentage.

Solution: $\frac{3}{4} = 4\overline{)3.00}$ with quotient 0.75 $= 0.75$ or 75 percent

$$\begin{array}{r} 0.75 \\ 4\overline{)3.00} \\ \underline{28} \\ 20 \\ \underline{20} \end{array}$$

CONVERTING PERCENTAGES TO DECIMALS

To convert a percentage to a decimal, simply move the decimal point two places to the *left*. For example: 25 percent can be expressed as the decimal 0.25; 50 percent is the same as 0.50 or 0.5; 100 percent is the same as 1.00 or 1.

CONVERTING DECIMALS TO PERCENTAGES

To convert a decimal to a percentage just do the opposite of what you did in the preceding instruction. All you have to do is move the decimal point two places to the *right*. Thus, 0.5 = 50 percent; 0.375 = 37.5 percent; 2 = 200 percent.

The following drill will give you practice working with fractions, decimals, and percentages.

DRILL 5

Fill in the missing information in the following table. Answers can be found on page 283.

	Fraction	*Decimal*	*Percentage*
1.	$\frac{1}{2}$		
2.		3.0	
3.			0.5 percent
4.	$\frac{1}{3}$		

WHAT PERCENT OF WHAT?

Problem: What number is 10 percent greater than 20?

Solution: We know that 10 percent of 20 is 2. So the question really reads: What is 2 greater than 20? The answer is 22.

Analysis: Joe Bloggs gets confused on questions like this. You won't if you take them slowly, and solve them one step at a time. The same holds true for problems that ask you what number is a certain percentage *less* than another number. What number is 10 percent less than 500? Well, 10 percent of 500 is 50. The number that is 10 percent less than 500, therefore, is 500 – 50, or 450.

WHAT PERCENT OF WHAT PERCENT OF WHAT?

On harder SAT questions, you may be asked to determine the effect of a *series* of percentage increases or reductions. The key point to remember on such problems is that each *successive* increase or reduction is performed on the result of the *previous* one. Here's an example:

18. A business paid $300 to rent a piece of office equipment for one year. The rent was then increased by 10 percent each year thereafter. How much will the company pay for the first three years it rents the equipment?

(A) $920 (B) $960 (C) $990 (D) $993 (E) $999

Here's how to crack it: You are being asked to find a business's total rent for a piece of equipment for three years. The easiest way to keep from getting confused on a problem like this is to take it *one step at a time*. First, make a sort of outline of exactly what you have to find out:

Year 1:
Year 2:
Year 3:

Actually write this down in the margin of your test booklet. There's one slot for each year's rent; Jim's answer will be the total.

You already know the number that goes in the first slot: 300, because that is what the problem says will be paid for the first year.

What number goes in the second slot? 330, because 330 equals 300 plus 10 percent of 300.

Now, here's where you have to pay attention. What number goes in the third slot? *Not 360!* The rent goes up 10 percent each year. This increase is calculated from the *previous* year's rent. That means that the rent for the third year is $363, because 363 equals 330 plus 10 percent of 330.

Now you are ready to find Jim's answer:

Year 1:	300
Year 2:	330
Year 3:	363
	993

Jim's answer is thus choice D, $993.

***Never* try to solve a problem like this by rewriting it as an equation: $x = y + (y + 0.1y) + [(y + 0.1y) + 0.1(y + 0.1y)]$ or something like that. You may eventually end up with the right answer, but you'll spend too much time doing it and you'll stop enjoying life.**

WHAT PERCENT OF WHAT PERCENT OF YIKES!

Sometimes you may find successive-percentage problems in which you aren't given actual numbers to work with. In such cases you need to *plug in* some numbers. Here's an example:

21. A number is increased by 25 percent and then decreased by 20 percent. The result is what percent of the original number?

(A) 80 (B) 100 (C) 105 (D) 120 (E) 125

Here's how to crack it: Using the Joe Bloggs principle, you ought to be able to eliminate three choices right off the bat: A, D, and E. Joe loves easy answers. Choices A, D, and E are all equal to 100 plus or minus 20 or 25. All three choices *seem* right to Joe for different reasons. This is a difficult question, so answers that seem right to Joe must be eliminated. Get rid of them.

A somewhat more subtle Joe Bloggs attractor is choice C. Joe thinks that if you increase a number by 25 percent and then decrease by 20 percent, you end up with a net increase of 5 percent. He has forgotten that in a series of percentage changes (which is what we have here), each successive change is based on the result of the previous one.

We've now eliminated everything but choice B, which is Jim's answer. Could we have found it without Joe's help? Yes. Here's how:

You aren't given a particular number to work with in this problem—just "a number." Rather than trying to deal with the problem in the abstract, you should immediately plug in a number to work with. What number would be easiest to work with in a *percentage* problem? Why, 100, of course:

1. 25 percent of 100 is 25, so 100 increased by 25 percent is 125.
2. Now you have to decrease *125* by 20 percent, 20 percent of 125 is 25, so 125 decreased by 20 percent is 100.
3. 100 (our result) is 100 percent of 100 (the number you plugged in), so Jim's answer, once again, is B.

Beware of percentage-change problems in the difficult third. The answers to these problems almost always defy common sense. Unless you are careful, you may fall for a Joe Bloggs attractor.

Averages

WHAT IS AN AVERAGE?

The average (arithmetic mean) of a set of *n* numbers is simply the total of the numbers divided by *n*. In other words, if you want to find the average of three numbers, you add them up and divide by 3. For example, the average of 1, 2, and 3 is $\frac{(1 + 2 + 3)}{3}$, or $\frac{6}{3}$, or 2. Here are some other examples:

The average of –4 and 2 is $\frac{(-4 + 2)}{2}$, or –1.

The average of $\frac{1}{2}$ and $\frac{1}{4}$ is $\frac{\left(\frac{1}{2} + \frac{1}{4}\right)}{2}$, or $\frac{3}{8}$.

The average of 0.1 and 0.2 is $\frac{(0.1 + 0.2)}{2}$, or 0.15.

ALGEBRAIC AVERAGES

Algebraic averages work just like the averages described previously, except that there are letters in place of some or all of the numbers. The same basic formula still applies. The average of x, y, and z, for example, is $\frac{(x + y + z)}{3}$.

WHAT DOES MEAN MEAN?

When ETS asks you to find an average, it will always ask you to find an "average (arithmetic mean)." Don't worry about those words in parentheses. They're only there for students of statistics who know that there are several other kinds of averages (medians and modes, for example). These other kinds of averages are never tested on the SAT.

AVERAGES, TOTALLY

The key to solving any problem involving an average is to find the total *of the items before you do anything else.* This is absolutely crucial. For example, if a problem states that the *average* of 3 test scores is 70, the first thing for you to note is that the *total* of the three scores is 210 (70 × 3). If you are then told that one of the three scores is 100, you know that the *total* of the remaining scores is 110 (210 – 100) and that their average is 55 $\left(\frac{110}{2}\right)$.

ONE ITEM, ONE VOTE

Averages are democratic. Every item counts the same as every other, even if there are repeats. For example, the average of 10, 10, 10, and 50 is $\frac{(10 + 10 + 10 + 50)}{4}$, *not* $\frac{(10 + 50)}{4}$ or $\frac{(10 + 50)}{2}$.

Suppose a student takes 2 tests and scores an 80 on one and a 50 on the other. His average score is $\frac{(80 + 50)}{2}$, or 65. Now, suppose he takes a third test and scores another 50. Does his average stay the same? No. His new average is $\frac{(80 + 50 + 50)}{3}$, or 60.

Every item is always counted equally with every other. *This is true even if the item is 0.* For example, the average of 4, 0, 0, and 0 is $\frac{(4 + 0 + 0 + 0)}{4}$, or 1. It is *not* 4.

THE BEHAVIOR OF AVERAGES

You should know automatically what happens to averages in certain situations. Suppose you have taken 3 tests and earned an average score of 80. Now you take a fourth test:

1. If your average *goes up* as a result, then you know that your score on the fourth test was greater than 80.
2. If your average *stays the same*, then your fourth score was exactly 80.
3. If your average *goes down*, then your fourth score was less than 80.

Averages: Advanced Principles

Difficult average problems are often difficult only because some of the information is missing. Here's an example:

Problem: A group of students has an average score of 80. If 40 percent of the students have an average score of 70, what is the average score of the remaining 60 percent?

Solution: How many students are in "a group"? The number 10 is easy to work with, so let's say there are 10. Simply plug in 10 for the number of students.

The first thing you must always do on average problems is find the total. This is easy now that we know how many students we're talking about. If 10 students have an average score of 80, their total score is 80×10, or 800.

We've also been told that 40 percent of the students have an average score of 70. Forty percent of 10 is 4, so the total score of these 4 students is 4×70, or 280. We aren't interested in these 4 students, though; we're interested in the other 6. What's the total of their scores? It has to be $800 - 280$, or 520. To find *their* average score—

which is what the problem asks for —all we have to do is divide 520 by 6, which equals $86\frac{2}{3}$. This is Jim's answer.

Analysis: Finding the total is always important on problems involving averages, but it is especially important on difficult problems where you're given only partial information.

Exponents and Radicals

EXPONENTS ARE A KIND OF SHORTHAND

Many numbers are the product of the same factor multiplied over and over again. For example, $32 = 2 \times 2 \times 2 \times 2 \times 2$. Another way to write this would be : $32 = 2^5$, or "thirty-two equals two to the fifth power." The little number, or *exponent*, denotes the number of times that 2 is to be used as a factor. In the same way, $10^3 = 10 \times 10 \times 10$, or 1,000, or "ten to the third power," or "ten cubed." In this example, the 10 is called the *base* and the little 3 is called the *exponent*. (You won't need to know these terms on the SAT, but you will need to know them to follow our explanations.)

MULTIPLYING NUMBERS WITH EXPONENTS

When you multiply two numbers with the same base, you simply add the exponents. For example, $2^3 \times 2^5 = 2^{3+5} = 2^8$.

Warning: Don't get careless with this rule; it applies to *multiplication*, not to *addition*. $2^3 + 2^5$ does *not* equal 2^8.

DIVIDING NUMBERS WITH EXPONENTS

When you divide two numbers with the same base, you simply subtract the exponents. For example, $\frac{2^5}{2^3} = 2^{5-3} = 2^2$.

Warning: Don't get careless with this rule; it applies to *division*, not to *subtraction*. $2^5 - 2^3$ does *not* equal 2^2.

RAISING A POWER TO A POWER

When you raise a power to a power, you multiply the exponents. For example, $(2^3)^4 = 2^{3 \times 4} = 2^{12}$.

Warning: Parentheses are very important with exponents, because you must remember to *distribute* powers to everything within them. For example: $(3x)^2 = 9x^2$, not $3x^2$. Many students

carelessly forget that they must also square the 3. Similarly, $\left(\frac{3}{2}\right)^2 = \frac{9}{4}$, not $\frac{9}{2}$.

THE PECULIAR BEHAVIOR OF EXPONENTS

Raising a number to a power can have quite peculiar and unexpected results, depending on what sort of number you start out with. Here are some examples:

1. If you square or cube a number greater than 1, it becomes *larger*. For example, $2^3 = 8$.
2. If you square or cube a fraction, it becomes *smaller*. For example $\left(\frac{1}{2}\right)^3 = \frac{1}{8}$.
3. A negative number raised to an even power becomes *positive*. For example, $(-2)^2 = 4$.
4. A negative number raised to an odd power remains *negative*. For example, $(-2)^3 = -8$.

You should also have a feel for relative sizes of exponential numbers without calculating them. For example 2^{10} is much larger than 10^2. ($2^{10} = 1{,}024$; $10^2 = 100$.) To take another example, 2^5 is twice as large as 2^4, even though 5 only seems a bit larger than 4.

RADICALS

The sign $\sqrt{}$ indicates the square root of a number. For example, $\sqrt{25} = 5$.

Important note: When you are asked for $\sqrt{x}$, or the square root of any number, you are being asked for a *positive* root only. Although 5^2 and $(-5)^2$ both equal 25, only 5 is a square root of 25.

The sign $\sqrt[3]{}$ indicates the cube root of a number. Thus, $\sqrt[3]{8} = 2$, since $2^3 = 8$.

THE ONLY RULES YOU NEED TO KNOW

Here are the only rules regarding radicals that you need to know for the SAT:

1. $\sqrt{x}\sqrt{y} = \sqrt{xy}$. For example, $\sqrt{3}\sqrt{3} = \sqrt{9} = 3$.
2. $\sqrt{\frac{x}{y}} = \frac{\sqrt{x}}{\sqrt{y}}$. For example, $\sqrt{\frac{5}{4}} = \frac{\sqrt{5}}{\sqrt{4}} = \frac{\sqrt{5}}{2}$.

Note that rule 1 works in reverse: $\sqrt{50} = \sqrt{25} \times \sqrt{2} = 5\sqrt{2}$. This is really a kind of factoring. You are using rule 1 to factor a large, clumsy radical into numbers that are easier to work with.

BEWARE OF COMMON SENSE

Don't make careless mistakes. Remember that the square root of a positive fraction less than 1 is *larger* than the fraction. For example, $\sqrt{\frac{1}{4}} = \frac{1}{2}$, and $\frac{1}{2} > \frac{1}{4}$.

Summary

1. There are only six arithmetic operations: addition, subtraction, multiplication, division, raising to a power, and finding a square root or a cube root.

2. These operations must be performed in the proper order, beginning with operations inside parentheses.

3. The associative law states that when you are adding or multiplying a series of numbers, you can group or regroup the numbers any way you like.

4. The distributive law is one of the most important principles on the SAT. You must be absolutely certain that you know it:

   $$a(b + c) = ab + ac$$
   $$a(b - c) = ab - ac$$

   This law is so important that you must *always* apply it *whenever* you have a chance. If a problem gives you information in "factored form"—$a(b + c)$—then you should multiply through or *distribute* the first variable before you do anything else. If you are given information that has already been distributed— $ab + ac$—then you should factor out the common term, putting the information back in factored form. Very often, simply doing this will enable you to spot Jim's answer.

5. A fraction is just another way of expressing division.

6. You must know how to add, subtract, multiply, and divide fractions. You must also know how to raise them to a power and find their roots.

7. In any problem involving large or confusing fractions, try to reduce the fractions first. For example, you should never multiply two fractions before looking to see if you can reduce either or both.

8. The most common source of mistakes on word problems involving fractions is misreading. Read fraction word problems carefully!

9. A decimal is just another way of expressing a fraction.

10. You must know how to add, subtract, multiply, and divide decimals.

11. Stay out of trouble by converting decimals to fractions.

12. If you get confused about decimals, remember dollars and cents.

13. A ratio is a fraction. If you can do it to a fraction, you can do it to a ratio.

14. Always think of a ratio as a number of parts.

15. A percentage is just a convenient way of expressing a fraction whose denominator is 100.

16. To convert a percentage to a fraction, simply put the percentage over a denominator of 100 and reduce.

17. To convert a fraction to a percentage, simply divide the numerator by the denominator and move the decimal point in the result two places to the right.

18. To convert a percentage to a decimal, simply move the decimal point two places to the left. To convert a decimal to a percentage, simply move the decimal point two places to the right.

19. In problems requiring you to determine the effect of series of percentage increases or reductions, remember that each successive increase or reduction is performed on the result of the previous one.

20. To find the average of several values, add up the values and divide the total by the number of values.

21. The key to solving any problem involving an average is to find the *total* of the items before you do anything else.

22. In an average, every item counts the same as every other, even if there are repeats.

23. Exponents are a kind of shorthand for expressing numbers that are the product of the same factor multiplied over and over again.

24. When you multiply two numbers with the same base you simply add the exponents. (This rule applies to *multiplication*, not to *addition*.)

25. When you divide two numbers with the same base, you simply subtract the exponents. (This rule applies to *division*, not to *subtraction*.)

26. When you raise a power to a power, you multiply the exponents.

27. You should know how to write any number in expanded and scientific notations.

28. A positive number greater than 1 raised to a power greater than 1 becomes *larger*. A positive fraction less than 1 raised to an exponent greater than 1 becomes *smaller*. A negative number raised to an even power becomes *positive*. A negative number raised to an odd power remains *negative*.

29. When you asked for $\sqrt{x}$ or the square root of any number, you are being asked for a *positive* root only.

30. Here are the only rules regarding radicals that you need to know for the SAT:

    1. $\sqrt{x}\sqrt{y} = \sqrt{xy}$
    2. $\sqrt{\frac{x}{y}} = \frac{\sqrt{x}}{\sqrt{y}}$

CHAPTER TEN

Algebra

Algebra: Cracking the System

About a third of the math problems on your SAT will involve algebra. Some students are terrified of algebra. Fortunately, we have several techniques that should enable you to solve the most frightening-looking algebra problems—even word problems.

This chapter is divided into three main sections;

1. Working Backward
2. Plugging In
3. Basic Princeton Review Algebra

Princeton Review algebra is our name for the kind of algebra you need to do well on the SAT. It isn't the same as the algebra you were taught in math class. Why did we bother to create our own kind of algebra? *Because math-class algebra takes too much time on the SAT.* If you want big score gains, you're going to have to forget about your algebra class and learn the techniques that work on the SAT. Math-class algebra is slower and riskier than Princeton Review algebra. On the SAT, do it our way instead.

Your biggest scoring gains will come from the next two sections: "Working Backward" and "Plugging In." These are two simple but extremely powerful techniques. You won't need to know much algebra in order to use them, but you'll have to stay on your toes.

The third section of this chapter is a summary of basic Princeton Review algebra. It's a bit dull by comparison with the rest of the chapter, but you should read it carefully, even if you already feel comfortable with algebra. You should think of our summary as a sort of guide to the small handful of algebraic concepts that you'll need to answer problems that can't be solved by working backward or plugging in. If you find that you are confused by some of the concepts, you should go back to your old algebra textbook or to a teacher for a fuller explanation.

Working Backward

Algebra uses letters to stand for numbers, but no one else does. You don't go to the grocery store to buy x eggs or y bottles of milk. Most people think in terms of numbers, not letters that stand for numbers.

You should do the same thing on the SAT as much as possible. On many SAT algebra problems, even very difficult ones, you will be able to find Jim's answer without using any algebra at all. You will do this by working backward from the answer choices instead of trying to solve the problem using math-class algebra.

Working backward is a technique for solving *word problems* whose answer choices are all *numbers*. Many so-called algebra problems on the SAT can be solved simply and quickly by using this powerful technique.

In algebra class at school, you solve word problems by using equations. Then, if you're careful, you check your solution by plugging in your answer to see if it works. But why not avoid equations entirely by simply checking the five solutions ETS offers? One of these has to be correct. You don't have to do any algebra, you will seldom have to try more than three choices, and you will never have to try all five.

Here's an example:

10. The units digit of a 2-digit number is 3 times the tens digit. If the digits are reversed, the resulting number is 36 more than the original number. What is the original number?

    (A) 26 (B) 31 (C) 36 (D) 62 (E) 93

Here's how to crack it: If ETS didn't give you any answer choices on this problem, finding the solution would take a very, very long time. After all, there are 90 two-digit numbers. But ETS has limited your decision to 5 choices—they've already gotten rid of 85 possible answers! Eliminating 4 more ought to be easy.

What you want to do is look at each answer choice to see if it fulfills the *conditions* stated in the problem. If it doesn't, you can use POE, the process of elimination, to get rid of it.

Doing that on this problem is a piece of cake. You simply take the stated conditions *one at a time* and try them out against the answer choices.

The first condition stated in the problem is that the units (or ones) digit of the number you are looking for is three times the tens digit. Now you look at the choices:

(A) Is 6 three times 2? Yes. A possibility.
(B) Is 1 three times 3? No. Eliminate.
(C) Is 6 three times 3? No. Eliminate.
(D) Is 2 three times 6? No. Eliminate.
(E) Is 3 three times 9? No. Eliminate.

Jim's answer is A. You found it without even testing the other conditions stated in the problem. Mark your answer and move on.

Never mark your answer until you have either tested all the conditions or eliminated all but one of the choices. In this problem, if there had been another choice whose units digit was 3 times its tens digit, you would have had to move on to the next condition.

Here's another example:

11. A woman made 5 payments on a loan with each payment being twice the amount of the preceding one. If the total of all 5 payments was $465, how much was the first payment?

(A) $5 (B) $15 (C) $31 (D) $93 (E) $155

Here's how to crack it: To solve this problem in math class, you'd have to set up and solve an equation like this:

$$p + 2p + 4p + 8p + 16p = 465$$

Forget it! That's too much work. Why not just try out the answers?

Numeric answer choices on the SAT are always given in order of size. *Thus, when you are working backward like this, you should always start out with the number in the middle—choice C.* If that number turns out to be too big, you can try a lower number next; if it's too small, you can try a higher one. That way you'll save time.

Let's look at what happens when you try choice C: If the payments double each month, the woman will pay 31 + 62 + 124 + 248 + 496—you can stop right there. *You don't have to add up these numbers* to see clearly that the total is going to be much more than

465; the fifth number alone is more than that. You need to eliminate this choice and try again with a smaller number.

Two of the choices are smaller. Which one should you try? Why not A, the *smaller* of the two? It will be easier and faster to work with. If it works, you'll pick it; if it doesn't, you'll eliminate it and pick B.

Here's what you get when you try choice A: 5 + 10 + 20 + 40 + 80. You don't have to add up these numbers to see clearly that they aren't going to come anywhere near totaling 465. Jim's answer must be B. (It is.)

Working Backward: Advanced Principles

Working backward is the same on difficult problems as it is on easy and medium ones. You just have to watch your step and make certain you don't make any careless mistakes or fall for Joe Bloggs attractors. Here's one of our examples:

18. Out of a total of 154 games played, a ball team won 54 more games than it lost. If there were no ties, how many games did the team win?

    (A) 94 (B) 98 (C) 100 (D) 102 (E) 104

Here's how to crack it: What's the Joe Bloggs attractor here? It is choice C. Be careful!

To solve the problem all you have to do is work backward. You've eliminated choice C already, so start with D. If the team won 102 games, how many games did it lose? It lost 52 (154 – 102 = 52). Is 102 (wins) 54 greater than 52 (losses)? No. 102 – 52 = 50. You need more wins to make the problem come out right. That means that Jim's answer must be E. (It is.)

Here's another example we created:

22. Committee A has 18 members and Committee B has 3 members. How many members from Committee A must switch to Committee B so that Committee A will have twice as many members as Committee B?

    (A) 4 (B) 6 (C) 7 (D) 9 (E) 14

Here's how to crack it: This problem represents one of the most difficult principles tested in the SAT math section. Only a tiny percentage of students get it right. But if you work backward, you won't have any trouble.

This problem is about two committees, so the first thing you should do is quickly draw a picture in your test booklet to keep you from getting confused, like this:

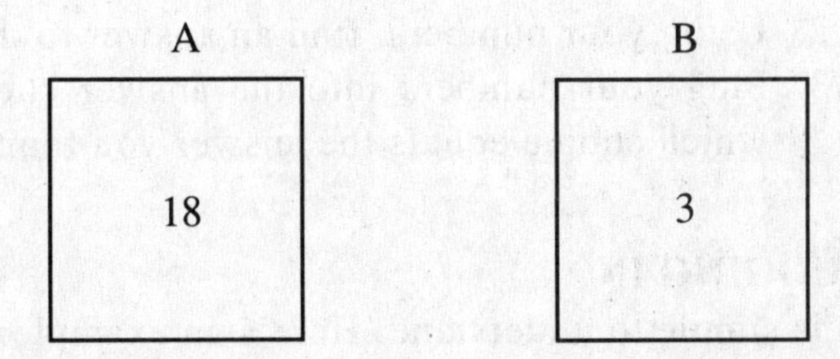

Now work backward, starting with answer choice C. If you move 7 members out of Committee A, there will be 11 members left in A and 10 members in B. Is 11 twice as many as 10? No, eliminate.

As you work through the choices, keep track of them, like this:

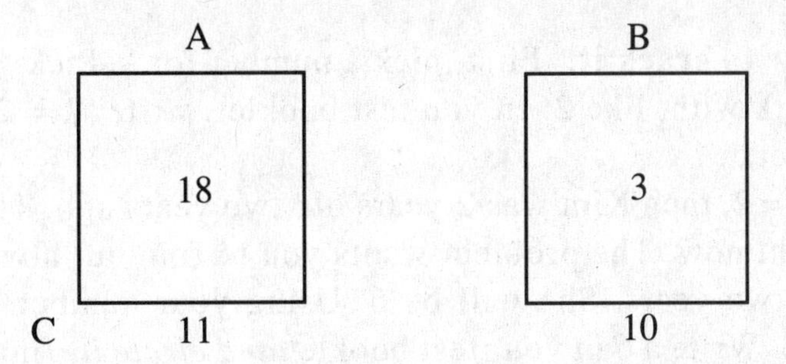

Choice C didn't work. To make the answer come out right, you need more members in Committee A and fewer in Committee B. In other words, you need to try a smaller number. Try the smallest one, choice A. Moving 4 members from Committee A will leave 14 in A and 7 in B. Is 14 twice as many as 7? Yes, of course. This is Jim's answer.

Don't worry if you can't tell whether you should next try a smaller or larger number. If you get confused, just try *all* the choices until you find the answer. And keep track of the ones you've eliminated by crossing them out in your test booklet. You'll end up with Jim's answer.

Plugging In

Working backward enables you to find Jim's answer on problems where all the answer choices are numbers. What about problems whose answer choices contain letters? On these problems, you will usually be ablc to find Jim's answer by plugging in. Plugging in is similar to working backward. And, like working backward, it has very little to do with the algebra you learned in math class.

Plugging in is easy. It has three steps:

1. Pick numbers for the letters in the problem.
2. Using your numbers, find an answer to the problem.
3. Plug your numbers into the answer choices to see which choice equals the answer you found in step 2.

BASIC PLUGGING IN

Plugging in is simple to understand. Here's an example:

3. Kim was k years of age 2 years ago. In terms of k, how old will Kim be 2 years from now?

(A) $k + 4$ (B) $k + 2$ (C) $2k$ (D) k (E) $\frac{k}{2}$

Here's how to crack it: First, pick a number for k. Pick something easy to work with, like 2. In you test booklet, write "$k = 2$," so you won't forget.

If $k = 2$, then Kim was 2 years old two years ago. That means she's 4 right now. The problem wants you to find out how old Kim will be in two years. She will be 6. Using your number for k, the answer is 6. Write a 6 in your test booklet *and circle it*. Jim's answer will be the choice that, when you plug in your k, equals 6.

Now it's time to plug in. (Don't worry about phrases like "in terms of k"; they're for students who solve these problems the math-class way. You don't need to pay attention.)

In working backward, we started with choice C. *In plugging in, we start with choice A. If that doesn't work we go to choice E, then B, then D, then C.* In other words, we work from the outside in.

Plugging in 2 for k in answer choice A, you get 2 + 4, or 6. This is the number you are looking for, so this must be Jim's answer. (It is.)

Don't try to solve problems like this by writing equations and "solving for x" or "solving for y." Plugging in is faster, easier, and less likely to produce errors.

Here's another example:

17. The sum of two positive consecutive integers is x. In terms of x, what is the value of the smaller of these two integers?

(A) $\frac{x}{2} - 1$ (B) $\frac{x-1}{2}$ (C) $\frac{x}{2}$

(D) $\frac{x+1}{2}$ (E) $\frac{x}{2} + 1$

Here's how to crack it: If we pick 2 and 3 for our two positive consecutive integers, then $x = 5$. Write "2," "3," and "$x = 5$" in your test booklet.

The smaller of our two integers is 2. Circle it; we are looking for the choice that equals 2 when we plug in 5. Let's try each choice:

(A) Plugging in 5 gives us $\frac{5}{2} - 1$. You shouldn't have to work that out to see that it doesn't equal 2. Eliminate.

(E) Plugging in 5 gives us $\frac{5}{2} + 1$. Eliminate.

(B) Plugging in 5 gives us $\frac{4}{2}$, which equals 2. This is Jim's answer.

WHICH NUMBERS?

Although you can plug in any number, you can make your life much easier by plugging in "good" numbers—numbers that are simple to work with or that make the problem easier to manipulate. Picking a small number like 2 will usually make finding the answer easier. If the problem asks for a percentage, plug in 10 or 100. If the problem has to do with minutes, try 60. If you plug in wisely, you can sometimes eliminate computation altogether.

You should avoid plugging in 0 and 1; they are special cases and using them may allow you to eliminate only one or two choices at a time.

(Plugging in 0 and 1 is useful, though, on inequalities, as we'll explain in the next section. Later on, in Chapter Twelve, we'll tell you about even more situations in which you should plug in 0 and 1.)

Many times you'll find that there is an advantage to picking a particular number, even a very large one, because it makes solving the problem easier. Here's an example:

17. If 100 equally priced tickets cost a total of d dollars, 5 of these tickets cost how many dollars?

(A) $\frac{d}{20}$ (B) $\frac{d}{5}$ (C) 5d (D) $\frac{5}{d}$ (E) $\frac{20}{d}$

Here's how to crack it: Should you plug in 2 for d, as we did in the two previous problems? You could, but plugging in 100 would make the problem easier. After all, if 100 tickets cost a total of $100, then each ticket costs $1. Write "$d = 100$" in your test booklet.

If each ticket costs a dollar, then 5 tickets cost $5. Write a "5" in your test booklet and circle it. You are looking for the answer choice that works out to 5 when you plug in 100 for d. Let's try each choice:

(A) $\frac{100}{20} = 5$

We don't need to go any further. This is Jim's answer. Here's another example:

25. A watch loses x minutes every y hours. At this rate, how many hours will the watch lose in one week?

(A) $7xy$ (B) $\frac{7y}{x}$ (C) $\frac{x}{7y}$ (D) $\frac{14y}{5x}$ (E) $\frac{14x}{5y}$

Here's how to crack it: This is an extremely difficult problem for students who try to solve it the math-class way. You'll be able to find the answer easily, though, if you plug in carefully.

What should you plug in? As always, you can plug in anything, but if you select wisely you'll make things easier on yourself. There are three units of time in this problem: minutes, hours, and weeks. If we plug in 60 for x, we can get it down to two, because 60 minutes equal an hour. Write "$x = 60$" in your test booklet.

We can also make things easier for ourselves by plugging in 24 for y. There are 24 hours in a day. What we are saying so far is that the watch loses 60 minutes every 24 hours. In other words, it loses an hour a day. Write "$y = 24$" in your test booklet.

At this rate, how many hours will the watch lose in a week? It will lose 7, obviously, because there are 7 days in a week. Write "7" in your test booklet and circle it. We are looking for the answer choice that equals 7 when we plug in 60 for x and 24 for y.

Now let's check each choice, starting from the outside (A and E):

(A) $7xy = (7)(60)(24)$. You don't have to multiply this out to see that it doesn't equal 7! Eliminate.

(E) $\frac{14x}{5y} = \frac{(14)(\cancel{60})^{12}}{(\cancel{5})(\cancel{24})_{2}} = \frac{14}{2} = 7$. More big numbers, so you cancel.

This is Jim's answer.

Never multiply out big numbers if you don't absolutely have to. Sometimes you will be able to tell immediately whether the result would even be close to the number you are looking for. Other times you will be able to get the big number down to a workable size by canceling.

INEQUALITIES

Plugging in works on problems containing inequalities, but you will have to be careful and follow some different rules. Plugging in *one* number is seldom enough; to find Jim's answer you may have to plug in several. For example, on one problem you might have to plug in two or three of the following numbers: -1, 0, 1, $\frac{1}{2}$, and $-\frac{1}{2}$.

The five numbers just mentioned all have special properties. Negatives, fractions, 0, and 1 all behave in peculiar ways when, for example, they are squared. Don't forget about them!

Sometimes you can avoid plugging in altogether by simplifying. Here's an example:

9. If $-3x + 6 \geq 18$, which of the following is true?

(A) $x \leq -4$ (B) $x \leq 6$ (C) $x \geq -4$
(D) $x \geq -6$ (E) $x = 2$

Here's how to crack it: The inequality in the problem can be simplified quite a bit. Do it:

$$-3x + 6 \geq 18$$
$$-3x \geq 12$$
$$-x \geq 4$$

We're close to one of the answer choices, but not quite there yet. Multiply through by -1 to make x positive. (Remember to change the direction of the inequality sign!):

$x \leq -4$

So choice A is Jim's answer.

"IT CANNOT BE DETERMINED"

Two or three times on every SAT, choice E on an algebra problem will be "It cannot be determined from the information given." You have already learned, in Chapter Eight, that this choice is almost *never* Jim's answer in the difficult part of either math section (with the exception of quantitative comparisons). But in the easy and medium parts of the test, "It cannot be determined" is Jim's answer about half the time. If you get stumped on one of these questions, therefore, choice E is a very good guess. But you'd probably like to be right on these problems more than half the time. If you plug in carefully, you can be right all the time.

On an ordinary algebra problem based on an equation, all you need to do is find one answer that works. That's why you plug in. But on a problem in which "It cannot be determined" is one of the choices, you have to be certain that your answer is *always* correct. If it isn't, then a definite answer "cannot be determined," even though the example you chose may have worked.

To see why this is true, look at this simple example:

If $x^2 = 4$, then $x = ?$

(A) 2
(B) It cannot be determined from the information given.

Suppose you try to solve this little problem by working backward from the answer choices. You plug in 2 for x and find that, indeed, $2^2 = 4$. But choice B is "cannot be determined." Are you certain that 2 is the only number that works in the equation $x^2 = 4$?

If you are, you shouldn't be, because -2 also works. The correct answer to this question, therefore, is B, even though working backward and plugging in initially made it appear as though the correct choice was A.

Here's another example:

15. If $x > 0$, which of the following is greatest?

(A) $\frac{1}{x}$ (B) $\sqrt{x}$ (C) x (D) x^2
(E) It cannot be determined from the information given.

Here's how to crack it: First, plug in a number that satisfies the condition ($x > 0$) stated in the problem. How about 2? If $x = 2$, we come up with the following values for the first four answer choices:

(A) $\frac{1}{2}$ (C) 2
(B) 1.4 (D) 4

The greatest number here is 4. Does that mean choice D is correct?

Not necessarily. Because "cannot be determined" is one of the choices, we have to be certain that x^2 will *always* be the greatest, no matter what we plug in for x.

What should we plug in next? One of the numbers with special properties. The problem says that $x > 0$, but it doesn't say that x has to be an integer. Let's try a fraction. Plugging in $\frac{1}{2}$ for x, we come up with the following:

(A) 2 (C) $\frac{1}{2}$
(B) $1\frac{1}{4}$ (D) $\frac{1}{4}$

Choice A is now the greatest. That means that neither choice D nor choice A can *always* be correct. Therefore, Jim's answer has to be E.

Joe Bloggs Alert: On this problem, where you are asked to find the *greatest* number, Joe Bloggs is irresistibly attracted to choice D, x^2. Any number squared must be pretty large, right? Wrong! Joe forgets about *fractions*, which get *smaller* when they are squared. Don't be fooled!

We said earlier that on easy and medium problems where it is offered as a choice, "cannot be determined" is Jim's answer about half the time. But that also means that "cannot be determined" is *wrong* about half the time. Don't assume that it's necessarily your best choice just because it's offered. Here's an example:

16. A certain number n is multiplied by 10. If a number that is 7 less than n is also multiplied by 10, how much greater is the first product than the second?

(A) 7 (B) 10 (C) 17 (D) 70
(E) It cannot be determined from the information given.

Here's how to crack it: First, plug in an easy number. How about 10? Write "$n = 10$" in your test booklet. $10 \times 10 = 100$. This is the first product. Write it in your test booklet, too.

To obtain the second product, multiply $10(10 - 7)$, or 10×3, which equals 30. What is the difference of the two products? It is 70, which is choice D.

Should you select choice D as your answer? Not yet. You have to be certain that the difference between the two products will *always* be 70, no matter what you plug in for n.

Before you do, you should cross out choices A, B, and C in your test booklet. If D can be right at least *some* of the time, then A, B, and C can't be right *all* the time, so you can eliminate all of them. You've narrowed your choices down to D and E. If you guess right now, you'll have a fifty-fifty chance of being correct.

Your job now is to try to find a case in which the difference is *not* 70. To do this, check one of the numbers with special properties that we mentioned earlier. How about 0? If $n = 0$, $n \times 10 = 0$. The number 7 less 0 is –7. $10 \times -7 = -70$, which is 70 less than n. Once again, D works out.

It seems fairly certain now that D is Jim's answer. (It is.)

OTHER SPECIAL CASES

Sometimes SAT algebra problems will require you to determine certain *characteristics* of a number or numbers. Is x odd or even? Is it small or large? Is it positive or negative?

On questions like this, you will probably have to plug in more than one number, just as you do on problems containing inequalities and "cannot be determined." Sometimes ETS's wording will tip you off. If the problem states only that $x > 0$, you know for certain that x is positive but you *don't* know that x is an integer. See what happens when you plug in a fraction.

Here are some other tip-offs you should be aware of:

If the problem asked for this:	*and you plugged in this:*	*also try this, just to be sure:*
an integer	3	1, 0, or –1
a fraction	$\frac{1}{4}$	$-\frac{1}{4}$
two even numbers	2, 4	2, –2
a number	an integer	a fraction
a number	an even number	an odd number
a multiple of 7	7	7,000 or –7
consecutive numbers	odd, even	even, odd
$x^2 = 4$	2	–2
$xy > 0$	(2, 4)	(–2, –4)
$x = 2y$	(4, 2)	(–4, –2) or (0, 0)

ODDS OR EVENS

Here's an example of a problem involving odds and evens:

12. If x is an odd integer and y is an even integer, which of the following could be an even integer?

(A) $x + y$ (B) $x - y$ (C) $\frac{x}{2} + y$ (D) $x + \frac{y}{2}$

(E) $\frac{x}{y} + \frac{x}{2}$

Here's how to crack it: All you have to do to solve this problem is find a single instance in which one of the choices is an even integer. The easiest way to do this is to plug in simple choices for x and y and see what happens.

The easiest odd number to deal with is 1; the easiest even is 2. Plugging in these values for x and y, we discover the following:

(A) $x + y = 1 + 2 = 3$ (not even)

(B) $x - y = 1 - 2 = -1$ (not even)

(C) $\frac{x}{2} + y = \frac{1}{2} + 2 = 2\frac{1}{2}$ (not even)

(D) $x + \frac{y}{2} = 1 + \frac{2}{2} = 1 + 1 = 2$ (even—this is Jim's answer)

(E) We don't even need to check E. All we had to do was find one instance in which the choice *could* be even, and we found it in D.

Plugging In: Advanced Principles

As you have just learned, you should plug in whenever you don't know what a number is. But you can also plug in when you have numbers that are too big, too ugly, or too inconvenient to work with. On such problems you can often find Jim's answer simply by using numbers that aren't as ugly as the ones ETS has given you. Here's an example:

20. On the last day of a one-week sale, customers numbered 149 through 201 were waited on. How many customers were waited on that day?

(A) 51 (B) 52 (C) 53 (D) 152 (E) 153

Here's how to crack it: This is a number 20—a difficult question. Finding Jim's answer *has* to be harder than simply subtracting 149 from 201 to get 52, which means that choice B *has* to be wrong. Cross it out. (You can also immediately eliminate D and E, which are much, much too big.)

One way to find the answer would be to count this out by hand. But to count from 149 to 201 is an awful lot of counting. *You can achieve the same result by using simpler numbers instead.*

It doesn't matter which numbers you use. How about 7 and 11? The difference between 7 and 11 is 4. But if you count out the numbers on your hand—7, 8. 9. 10. 11—you see that there are 5 numbers. In other words, if the store had served customers 7 through 11, the number of customers would have been 1 greater than the difference of 7 and 11. Jim's answer, therefore, will be 1 greater than the difference of 149 and 201. Jim's answer, in other words, is C.

Here's another example:

22. $2^8 - 2^7 =$

(A) 2^1 (B) $2^{\frac{8}{7}}$ (C) 2^7 (D) 2^8 (E) 2^{15}

Here's how to crack it: These are big, ugly, inconvenient exponents. No wonder this item is a number 22. But you'll be able to solve it if you plug in easier numbers.

Instead of 2^8, let's use 2^4. And instead of 2^7, let's use 2^3. Now we can rewrite the problem: $2^4 - 2^3 = 16 - 8 = 8 = 2^3$.

Our answer is the second of the two numbers we started with. Jim's answer, therefore, must be the second number *he* started with, or 2^7, which is choice C. (If you don't believe this always works, try it with 2^2 and 2^3, and with 2^3 and 2^4, or any other similar pair of numbers. By the way, choices A and B are Joe Bloggs attractors.)

Basic Princeton Review Algebra

Working backward and plugging in will be huge helps to you on the math SAT. But they won't be enough to answer every algebra problem. On some problems, you'll have to know a few basic principles of Princeton Review algebra. If the explanations we give you leave you still confused, you should dig out your old algebra textbook or check with your math teacher.

UNIMPORTANT TERMINOLOGY

Here are some words that you won't need to know on the SAT but that you will need to know to follow the rest of this chapter. After you finish reading the chapter, you can forget about them.

Term: If an equation is like a sentence, then a term is the equivalent of a word in that sentence. For example, $9x^2$ is a term in the equation $9x^2 + 3x = 5y$.

Coefficient: In the same equation, the coefficient of the term $9x^2$ is 9 and the coefficient of $3x$ is 3.

Expression: An expression is a combination of terms and mathematical operations. For example, $9x^2 + 3x$ is an expression. If an equation is like a sentence, then an expression is like a phrase or clause.

Binomial: A binomial is an expression that contains two terms. For instance, $12x + 4$ is binomial.

Trinomial: A trinomial is an expression that contains three terms. For example, $2x^2 + 12x + 4$ is a trinomial.

Polynomial: A polynomial is any expression containing two or more terms. Binomials and trinomials are both polynomials.

SIMPLIFYING EXPRESSIONS

If a problem contains an expression that can be factored, you should factor it immediately. For example, if you come upon a problem containing the expression $2x + 2y$, you should factor it immediately to produce the expression $2(x + y)$.

If a problem contains an expression that is already factored, you should multiply it out according to the distributive law to return it to its original unfactored state. For example, if you come upon a problem containing the expression $2(x + y)$, you should *un*factor it by multiplying through to produce the expression $2x + 2y$.

Why should you do this? Because factoring or unfactoring is usually the key to finding Jim's answer on such problems. By learning to recognize expressions that could be either factored or unfactored, you will earn more points.

Here are five worked examples:

1: $4x + 24 = 4(x) + 4(6) = 4(x + 6)$

2: $\frac{10x - 60}{2} = \frac{10(x) - 10(6)}{2} = \frac{10(x - 6)}{2}$
$= 5(x - 6) = 5x - 30$

3: $\frac{x + y}{y} = \frac{x}{y} + \frac{y}{y} = \frac{x}{y} + 1$

4: $2(x + y) + 3(x + y) = (2 + 3)(x + y) = 5(x + y)$

5: $p(r + s) + q(r + s) = (p + q)(r + s)$

MULTIPLYING POLYNOMIALS

Multiplying polynomials is easy. Just be sure that every term in the first polynomial gets multiplied by every term in the second.

$$\begin{aligned}(x + 2)(x + 4) &= (x + 2)(x + 4)\\ &= (x \times x) + (x \times 4) + (2 \times x) + (2 \times 4)\\ &= x^2 + 4x + 2x + 8\\ &= x^2 + 6x + 8\end{aligned}$$

ETS'S FAVORITE QUADRATIC EXPRESSIONS

ETS has two favorite quadratic expressions. They appear over and over again on the SAT. You should train yourself to recognize them instantly in *both factored and unfactored form.* Here they are:

$$x^2 - y^2 = (x + y)(x - y)$$
$$x^2 + 2xy + y^2 = (x + y)^2$$

Here's an example:

Factor the following expression:

$$\frac{3x^2 - 3}{x - 1}$$

Here's how to crack it: First, simply factor out a 3 from the expression in the numerator: $3x^2 - 3 = 3(x^2 - 1)$. Now, because we told you to be on the lookout for it, you should realize instantly that $x^2 - 1 = (x + 1)(x - 1)$, which means that $3(x^2 - 1) = 3(x + 1)(x - 1)$. Doing this gives you the following:

$$\frac{3(x + 1)(x - 1)}{(x - 1)}$$

Since $(x - 1)$ is a common factor in the numerator and the denominator, you can cancel it from both. The final factored form of the original expression is simply $3(x + 1)$.

Here are a few more worked examples:

1. $$\begin{aligned}x^2 - y^2 + 2y(y + x) &= x^2 - y^2 + 2y^2 + 2yx\\ &= x^2 + y^2 + 2yx\\ &= (x + y)^2\end{aligned}$$

2. $(45)^2 + 2(45)(55) + (55)^2 = (45 + 55)^2$
$= 100^2$
$= 10{,}000$

3. $0.84^2 - 0.83^2 = (0.84 + 0.83)(0.84 - 0.83)$
$= (1.67)(0.01)$
$= 0.0167$

One of ETS's favorite problems is based on these rules. It appears in many editions of the SAT. In its typical version, you are given two expressions and asked which is greater. The expressions look something like this:

100^2 $\quad\quad\quad\quad$ 99×101

Notice that the expression on the right is just another way of stating the expression $(100 - 1)(100 + 1)$, which in turn equals $100^2 - 1$. The expression on the right, therefore, is less than than the expression on the left.

For an even simpler solution to problem like this, just plug in smaller numbers:

2^2 $\quad\quad\quad\quad$ 1×3

The value of the first expression is 4; the value of the second is 3. The expression on the right is therefore 1 less than the expression on the left.

COMBINE SIMILAR TERMS FIRST

In manipulating long, complicated algebraic expressions, combine all similar terms before doing anything else. In other words, if one of the terms is $5x$ and another is $-3x$, simply combine them into $2x$. Then you won't have as many terms to work with. Here's a worked example:

$(3x^2 + 3x + 4) + (2 - x) - (6 + 2x) =$
$3x^2 + 3x + 4 + 2 - x - 6 - 2x =$
$3x^2 + (3x - x - 2x) + (4 + 2 - 6) =$
$3x^2$

EVALUATING EXPRESSIONS

Sometimes ETS will give you the value of one of the letters in an algebraic expression and ask you to find the value of the entire expression. All you have to do is plug in the given value and see what

you come up with. Here is an example:
Problem: If $2x = -1$, then $(2x - 3)^2 = ?$
Solution: Don't solve for x; simply plug in -1 for $2x$, like this:

$$\begin{aligned}(2x - 3)^2 &= (-1 - 3)^2 \\ &= (-4)^2 \\ &= 16\end{aligned}$$

SOLVING EQUATIONS

In algebra class you learned to solve equations by "solving for x" or "solving for y." In doing this you isolate x or y on one side of the equal sign and put everything else on the other side. This is a long, laborious process with many steps and many opportunities for mistakes.

On the SAT, you usually won't have time to solve equations this way. You've already learned how to work backward and plug in. On problems where these techniques don't work, you should still hesitate before using math-class algebra. Instead, you should learn to find *direct solutions*. To demonstrate what we mean, we'll show you the same problem solved two different ways.

Problem: If $2x = 5$ and $3y = 6$, then $6xy = ?$
Math-class solution: Your teacher would tell you to:

1. find x
2. find y
3. multiply 6 times x times y

Using this procedure, you find that $x = \frac{5}{2}$ and $y = 2$. Therefore, $6xy = (6)\left(\frac{5}{2}\right)(2)$, or 30.

Princeton Review solution: You notice that $6xy$ equals $(2x)(3y)$. Therefore, $6xy$ equals 5×6, or 30.

Analysis: Finding direct solutions will save you time. ETS never expects you to perform long, complicated calculations on the SAT. You should always stop and think for a moment before beginning such a process. Look for a trick, a shortcut to the answer.

Here's another example:

$$\text{If } x = \frac{y}{5} \text{ and } 10x = 14, \text{ then } y = ?$$

Here's how to crack it: In math class, you would probably proceed by substituting $\frac{y}{5}$ (which equals x) for x in the second equation. This would give you $10\left(\frac{y}{5}\right) = 14$. This will lead you to the correct answer, but you run the risk of making a careless computation error.

It's a much better idea to try for a direct solution. One way to do this is to notice that if you multiply both sides of the first equation by 10, you'll end up with both equations having $10x$ on one side. Multiplying both sides of the first equation by 10, you get:

$$10x = \frac{10y}{5}$$

Simplifying the term on the right, you get:

$$10x = 2y$$

Since $10x$ and $2y$ are equal, you can now substitute $2y$ for $10x$ in the *second* equation. This gives you:

$$2y = 14$$
$$y = 7$$

Here's another example:

> If a, b, c, and d are integers and $ab = 12$, $bc = 20$, $cd = 30$, and $ad = 18$, then $abcd = ?$

Here's how to crack it: If you try to solve this the math-class way, you'll end up fiddling forever with the equations, trying to find individual values for a, b, c, and d. Once again, you may get the correct answer, but you'll spend an eternity doing it.

This problem is much simpler if you look for a direct solution. The first thing to notice is that you have given a lot of information you don't need. For example, the problem would have been much simpler to answer if you had been given only *two* equations: $ab = 12$ and $cd = 30$. You should know that $(ab)(cd) = abcd$, which means that $abcd = (12)(30)$, which means that the answer is 360.

Never let yourself get bogged down looking for a direct solution. But you should always ask yourself if there is a simple way to find the answer. If you train yourself to think in terms of shortcuts, you won't waste a lot of time.

SOLVING INEQUALITIES

In an equation, one side equals the other. In an inequality, one side *does not* equal the other. The following symbols are used in inequalities:

$\neq$ is not equal to	$\geq$ is greater than or equal to
$>$ is greater than	$\leq$ is less than or equal to
$<$ is less than	

Solving inequalities is pretty much like solving equations. You can collect similar terms, and you can simplify by doing the same thing to both sides. *All you have to remember is that if you multiply or divide both sides of an inequality by a negative number, the direction of the inequality symbol changes.* For example, here's a simple inequality:

$$x > y$$

Now, just as you can with an equation, you can multiply both sides of this inequality by the same number. But if the number you multiply by is negative, you have to change the direction of the symbol in the result. For example, if we multiply both sides of the inequality above by –2, we end up with the following:

$$-2x < -2y$$

AVOID MULTIPLICATION IF POSSIBLE

If ETS gives you a problem in which you are supposed to determine, say, whether $9 \times 9 \times 9$ is larger or smaller than 27×27, remind yourself that ETS is *not* testing your ability to multiply big numbers. As in the problems in the preceding section, there must be a shortcut.

What's the shortcut in the problem we just described? It has to do with noticing the following:

$$27 \times 27 = 3 \times 9 \times 3 \times 9$$
$$= 9 \times 9 \times 9$$

The two expressions, therefore, are equal.

SOLVING SIMULTANEOUS EQUATIONS

Sometimes on the SAT you will be asked to find the value of an expression based on two given equations. To find Jim's answer on such problems, simply add or subtract the two equations. Here's an example:

If $4x + y = 14$ and $3x + 2y = 13$, then $x - y = ?$

Here's how to crack it: You've been given two equations here. But instead of being asked to solve for a variable (x or y), you've been asked to solve for an expression ($x - y$). *Why? Because there must be a direct solution.*

In math class, you're taught to multiply one equation by one number and then subtract equations to find the second variable. Or you're taught to solve one equation for one variable in terms of the other and to substitute that value into the second equation to solve for the other variable, and, having found the other variable, to plug it back into the equation to find the value of the first variable.

Whew! Forget it. Fortunately, we have a better way. Just add or subtract the two equations; either addition or subtraction will produce an easy answer. Adding the two equations produces this:

$$\begin{array}{r} 4x + y = 14 \\ +3x + 2y = 13 \\ \hline 7x + 3y = 27 \end{array}$$

This doesn't get us anywhere. So try subtracting:

$$\begin{array}{r} 4x + y = 14 \\ -3x + 2y = 13 \\ \hline x - y = 1 \end{array}$$

The value of $(x - y)$ is precisely what you are looking for, so this must be Jim's answer.

***Never* do this the way you are taught to in school, by multiplying one equation by one coefficient, the other equation by the other coefficient, and then adding or subtracting. We have yet to see an SAT on which simultaneous equations had to be solved this way. Simply add or subtract them as they are written.**

SOLVING QUADRATIC EQUATIONS

To solve quadratic equations, remember everything you've learned so far: Look for direct solutions and either factor or unfactor when possible. Here's an example:

If $(x + 3)^2 = (x - 3)^2$, then $x = ?$

Here's how to crack it: Since both sides of the equation have been factored, you should *un*factor them by multiplying them out:

Left: $(x + 3)(x + 3) = x^2 + 6x + 9$
Right: $(x - 3)(x - 3) = x^2 - 6x + 9$
Therefore: $x^2 + 6x + 9 = x^2 - 6x + 9$

Now you can simplify by eliminating like terms from both sides of the new equations, leaving you with:

$$6x = -6x$$
$$x = -x$$
$$x = 0$$

Here's another example:

If $x^2 - 4 = (18)(14)$, then x could be ?

Here's how to crack it: You should recognize instantly that $x^2 - 4$ is one of ETS's two favorite quadratic expressions in unfactored form and that it can easily be factored. Do so:

$x^2 - 4 = (x + 2)(x - 2)$
Therefore: $(x + 2)(x - 2) = (18)(14)$

Notice that each side of the equation consists of two terms multiplied by each other. Set the corresponding parts equal to each other and see what you get:

$$(x + 2) = 18$$
$$(x - 2) = 14$$

Both equations work if x is 16.

SOLVING QUADRATIC EQUATIONS SET TO ZERO

If $ab = 0$, what do you know about a and b? You know that one or both of them has to equal 0, because if the product of two numbers is 0, then at least one of the numbers *has* to be 0. You can use this fact in solving some quadratic equations. Here's an example:

What are all the values of x for which $x(x - 3) = 0$?

Here's how to crack it: Because the product of x and $(x - 3)$ is 0, you know that x or $(x - 3)$—or both of them—has to equal 0. To solve the problem, simply ask yourself what x would have to be to make either expression equal 0. The answer is obvious: x could be either 0 or 3.

FUNCTIONS

When you learned about functions in algebra class, you probably talked about "f of x," or $f(x)$.

The SAT is different. It tests functions, but in a peculiar way. Instead of using $f(x)$, it uses funny symbols to stand for operations. If you understand functions, just remember them when you see the funny symbols. If you don't understand functions, just follow what we tell you.

In a function problem, an arithmetic operation is defined and then you are asked to perform it on a number, a pair of numbers, or an ordered pair of numbers. All you have to do is keep your wits about you, use your scratch paper, and do as you are told. A function is like a set of instructions: follow it and you'll find Jim's answer.

Here's an example:

18. If $x \# y = \frac{1}{x - y}$, what is the value $\frac{1}{2} \# \frac{1}{3}$?

(A) 6 (B) $\frac{6}{5}$ (C) $\frac{1}{6}$ (D) -1 (E) -6

Here's how to crack it: First of all, let's give operation # a name; let's call it Bloggs. (You can call all functions Bloggs. It will help you keep track of what you're doing.)

Finding Jim's answer is just a matter of careful plugging in. What you need to do is to find the value of the following very intimidating complex fraction:

$$\frac{1}{2} \# \frac{1}{3} = \frac{1}{\frac{1}{2} - \frac{1}{3}}$$

$$= \frac{1}{\frac{3}{6} - \frac{2}{6}}$$

$$= \frac{1}{\frac{1}{6}}$$

$$= 6$$

Jim's answer, therefore, is choice A.

There are usually about three function problems on every SAT. One of the three will be extremely difficult. If you're not trying to score in the 700s, you should probably skip it. On the others, work very, very carefully and don't make careless mistakes.

WORD PROBLEMS I

Most word problems can be solved quickly by working backward or plugging in. But there will be a few algebra word problems on your SAT that will be more complicated. You'll still be able to answer them, but you should save them for last.

In solving a word problem that can't be done by working backward or plugging in, you should simply translate the problem into an equation. As we said earlier, equations are a kind of shorthand. You will be able to set up equations easily if you train yourself to notice words that are longhand versions of arithmetic symbols. Here are some words and their equivalent symbols:

WORD	SYMBOL
is	=
of, times, product	×
what (or any unknown value)	any letter (x, k, b)
more, sum	+
less, difference	−
ratio, quotient	÷

Here are two examples:

Words: 14 is 5 more than x

Equation: $14 = x + 5$

Words: If $\frac{1}{8}$ of a number is 3, what is $\frac{1}{3}$ of the same number?

Equation: $\frac{1}{8} n = 3$, $k = \frac{1}{3} n$

WORD PROBLEM II

In solving word problems, you should be familiar with the following formulas:

1. distance = (rate)(time). (This is the most frequently tested formula on the SAT. It can appear in several forms, including time = $\frac{\text{distance}}{\text{rate}}$.)
2. total price = (number of items)(cost per item)
3. sale price = (original price) – (%discount)(original price)

Summary

1. Math-class algebra takes too much time on the SAT. Do it our way instead.

2. In working backward on an SAT algebra word problem, you put numeric choices into the problem until you find one that works.

3. Plugging in is the technique for problems whose answer choices contain letters. It has three steps:
   A. Pick numbers for the letters in the problem.
   B. Using your numbers, find an answer to the problem.
   C. Plug your numbers into the answer choices to see which choice equals the answer you found in step B.

4. When you plug in, use "good" numbers—ones that are simple to work with and make the problem easier to manipulate.

5. Plugging in works on problems containing inequalities, but you will have to be careful and follow some different rules. Plugging in *one* number is seldom enough; to find Jim's answer you may have to plug in several, including ones with special properties.

6. You should plug in whenever you don't know what a number is, but you can also plug in when you have numbers that are too big, too ugly, or too inconvenient to work with.

7. If a problem contains an expression that can be factored, you should factor it immediately. If it contains an expression that already has been factored, you should unfactor it.

8. ETS has two favorite quadratic expressions. Be sure you know them cold in both factored and unfactored form:

$$x^2 - y^2 = (x + y)(x - y)$$
$$x^2 + 2xy + y^2 = (x + y)^2$$

9. Don't "solve for x" or "solve for y" unless you absolutely have to. (Don't worry; your math teacher won't find out.) Instead, look for direct solutions to SAT problems. ETS never uses problems that require time-consuming computations or endless fiddling with big numbers. There's always a trick—if you can spot it.

10. In solving simultaneous equations, simply add or subtract the equations.

11. Learn to recognize SAT function problems. They're the ones with the funny symbols.

12. If you come across a word problem you can't beat by working backward or plugging in, simply translate the problem into an equation and solve it.

CHAPTER ELEVEN

Geometry

SAT Geometry Problems: Cracking the System

About a third of the math problems on your SAT will involve geometry. Fortunately, you won't need much specific knowledge of geometry to solve them. You won't have to prove any theorems and you won't need to know many terms. You'll have to use a few formulas, but they will be printed on the first page of each math section in your test booklet.

In this chapter we will teach you

1. the fundamental facts you *must* know to solve SAT geometry problems
2. how to find Jim's answers and avoid careless mistakes by guesstimating
3. how to find Jim's answers by plugging in
4. the advanced principles that will help you on harder problems

Basic Principles: Fundamentals of SAT Geometry

The SAT doesn't cover any really difficult geometry, but you will have to have a thorough knowledge of several fundamental rules. You will use these fundamentals in applying the techniques that we will teach you later in the chapter. You don't need to linger over these rules if you have already mastered them. But be sure you understand them *completely* before you move on.

For the sake of simplicity, we have divided SAT geometry into four basic topics:

1. degrees and angles
2. triangles
3. circles
4. rectangles and squares

DEGREES AND ANGLES

1. A circle contains 360 degrees. In ancient times, it was believed that the sun revolved around the earth and that it required 360 days to do so. Every day, it was thought, the sun moved $\frac{1}{360}$th of the total distance it had to travel around the earth.

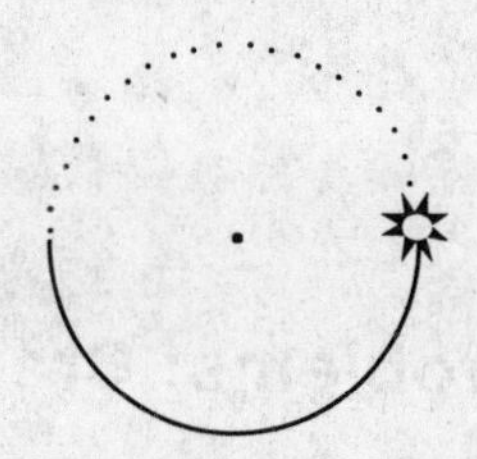

We know today that the earth revolves around the sun, not the other way around, and that it takes 365 days to do so. When the conventions of geometry were created, though, the older idea was incorporated. Every circle, therefore, is said to contain 360 degrees. Each degree is $\frac{1}{360}$th of the total distance around the outside of the circle. It doesn't matter whether the circle is large or small; it still has exactly 360 degrees.

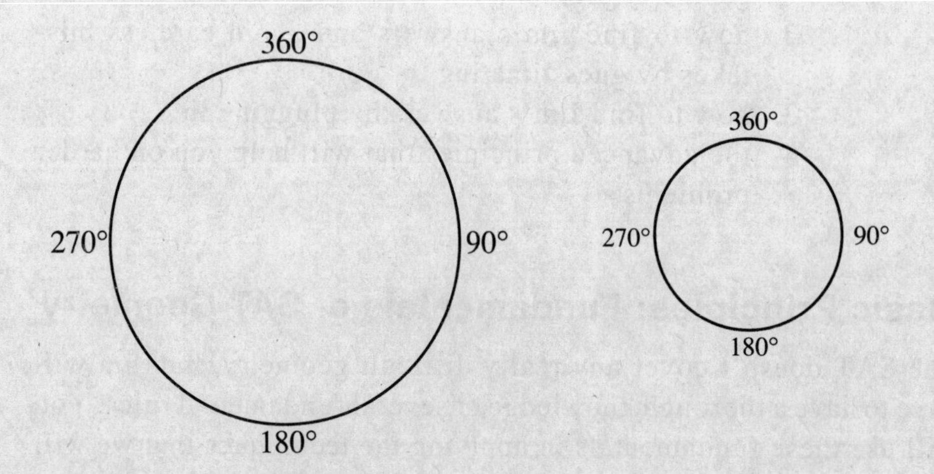

2. When you think about angles, remember circles. An angle is formed when two line segments extend from a common point. If you think of the point as the center of a circle, the *measure of the angle* is the number of degrees enclosed by the lines when they pass through the edge of the circle. Once again, the size of the circle doesn't matter; neither does the length of the lines.

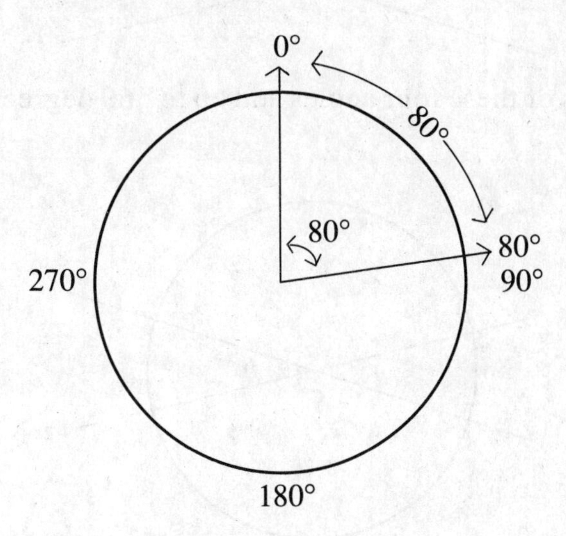

3. A line is a 180-degree angle. You probably don't think of a line as an angle, but it is one. Think of it as a *flat* angle. The following drawings should help:

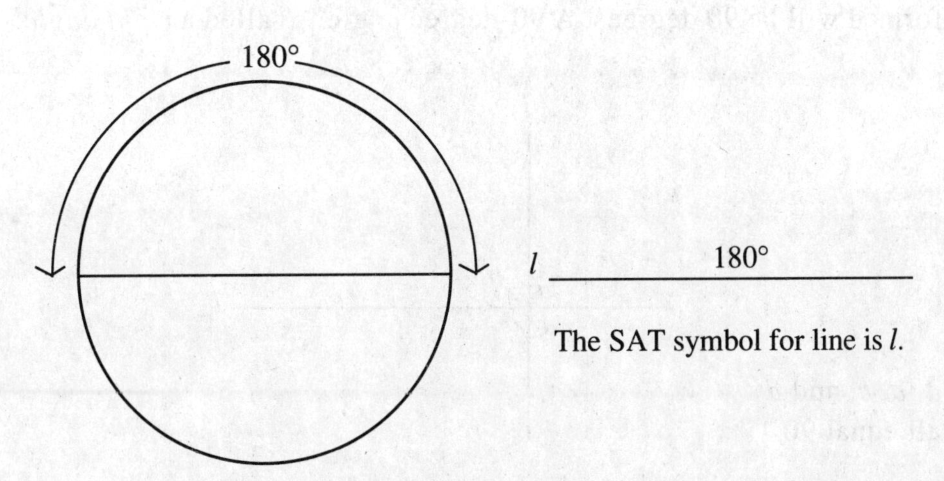

The SAT symbol for line is l.

4. When two lines intersect, four angles are formed. The following diagram should make this clear. The four angles are indicated by letters.

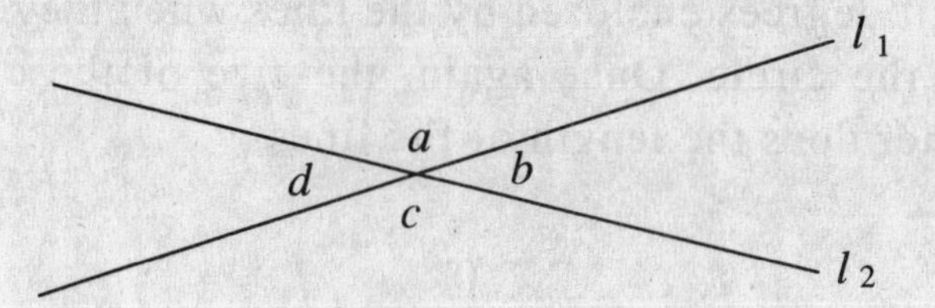

The measures of these four angles add up to 360 degrees. (Remember the circle.)

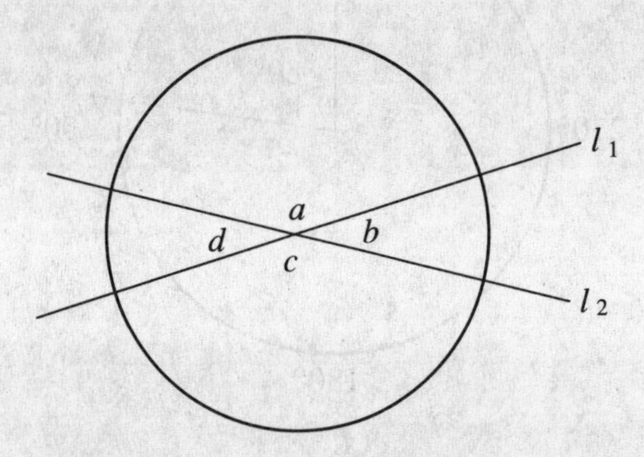

$a + b + c + d = 360$

If two lines are perpendicular to each other, each of the four angles formed will be 90 degrees. A 90-degree angle is called a *right angle*.

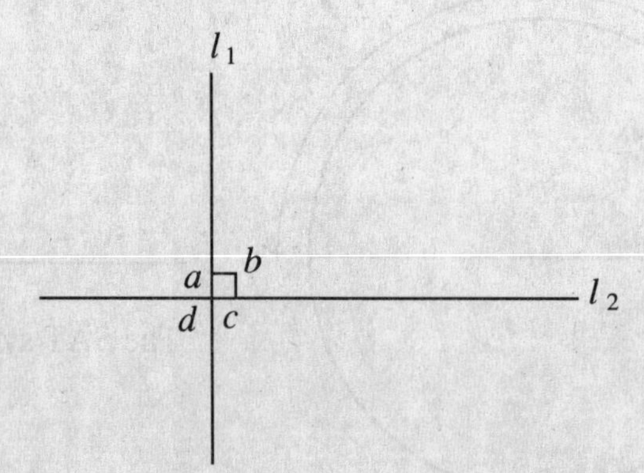

a, b, c, and d
all equal 90

The little box at the intersection of the two lines is the symbol for a right angle. If the lines are not perpendicular to each other, then none of the angles will be right angles, but angles opposite each other will have the same measures. Such angles are called *vertical angles*. They are like mirror images, or like the blades and handles of a pair of scissors. In the following diagram, angles a and c are equal; so are angles b and d. The total of all four angles is still 360 degrees.

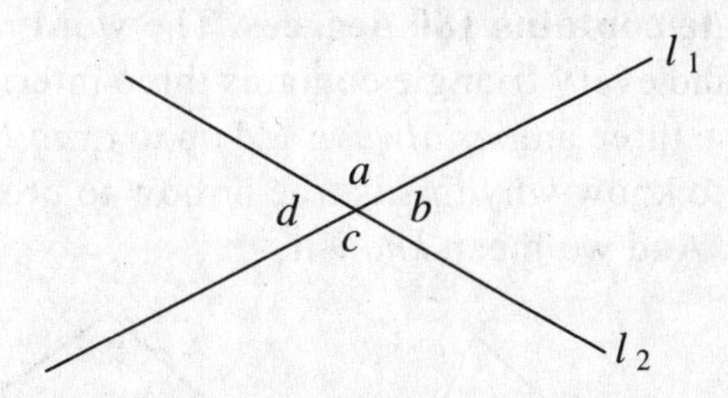

$a + b + c + d = 360$

It doesn't matter how many lines you intersect through a single point. The total measure of all the angles formed will still be 360 degrees.

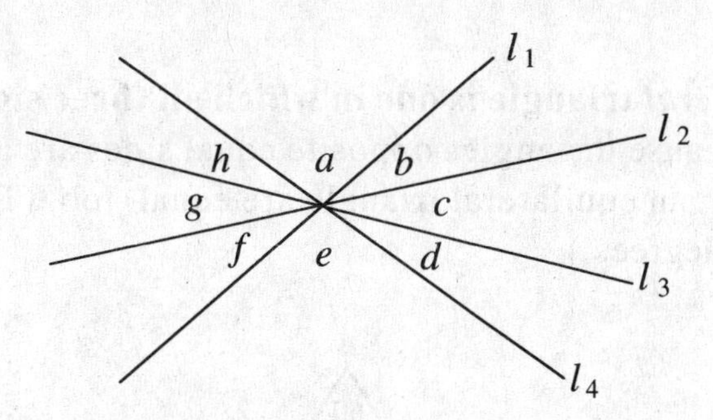

$a + b + c + d + e + f + g + h = 360$

5. **Fred's theorem: When two parallel lines are cut by a third line, angles that *look* equal *are* equal.** Fred is a teacher in one of our schools. Parallel lines are lines that never intersect, like the lines on notebook paper. In the following drawing, angle a has the same measure as angles c, e, and h; angle b has the same measure as angles d, f, and g.

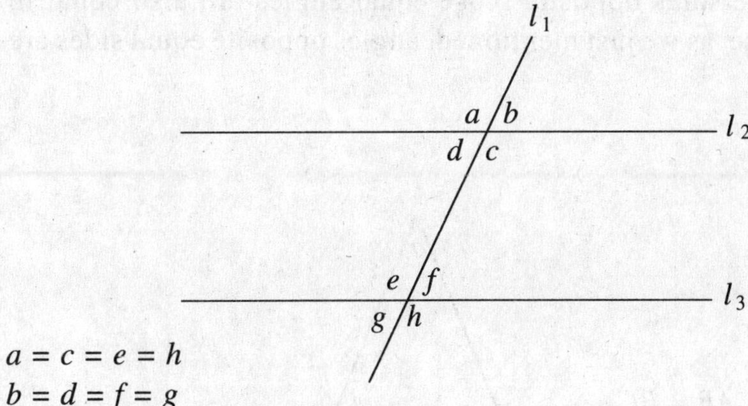

$a = c = e = h$
$b = d = f = g$

You should be able to see that angles a, b, c, and d add up to 360 degrees. So do angles e, f, g, and h.

TRIANGLES

1. Every triangle contains 180 degrees. The word *triangle* means "three angles," and every triangle contains three interior angles. The measures of these three angles *always* add up to *exactly* 180 degrees. You don't need to know why this is true or how to prove it. You just need to know it. And we mean *know* it.

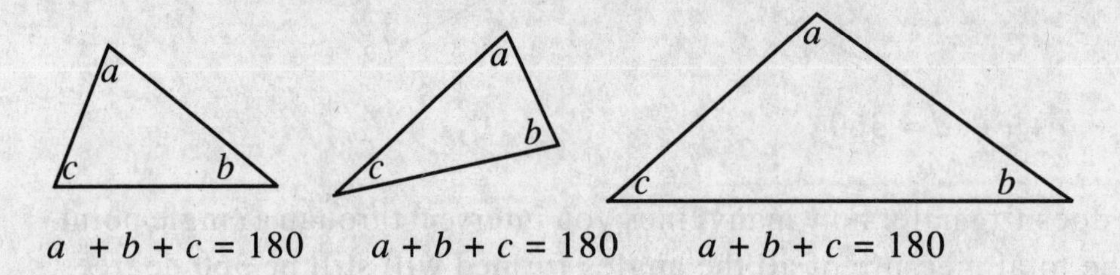

2. An *equilateral* triangle is one in which all three sides are equal in length. Because the angles opposite equal sides are also equal, all three angles in an equilateral triangle are equal, too. (Their measure is always 60 degrees.)

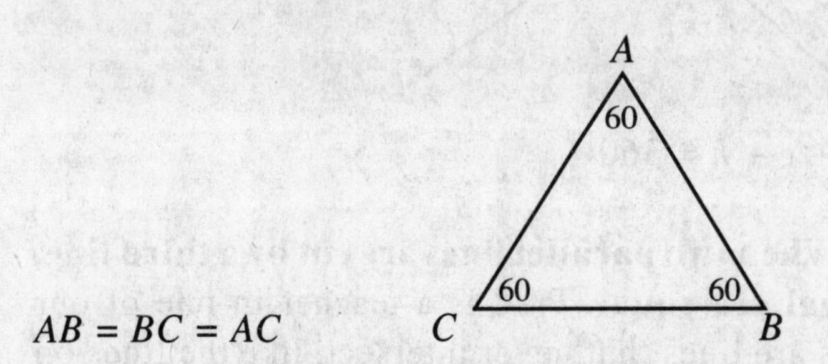

3. An *isosceles* triangle is one in which two of the sides are equal in length. The sides opposite those equal angles are also equal in length, because, as we just mentioned, angles opposite equal sides are also equal.

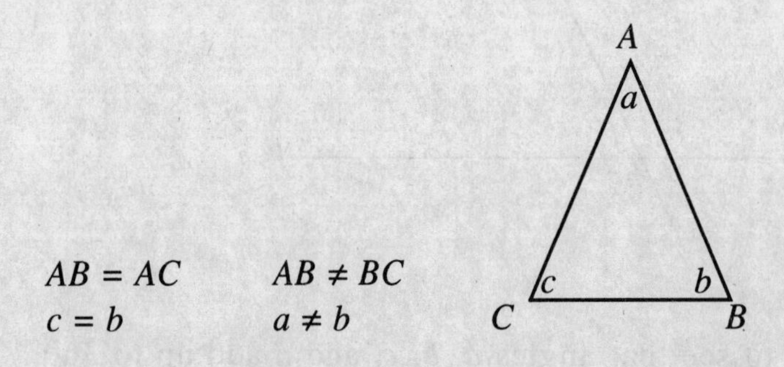

4. A *right triangle* is a triangle in which one of the angles is a right angle (90 degrees). The longest side of a right triangle is called the hypotenuse.

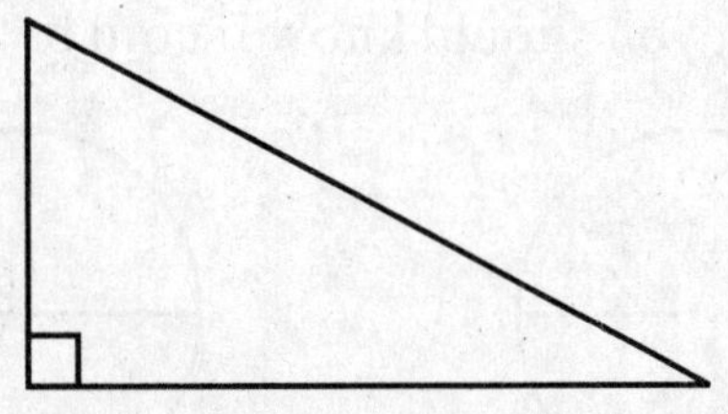

Some isosceles triangles are also right triangles.

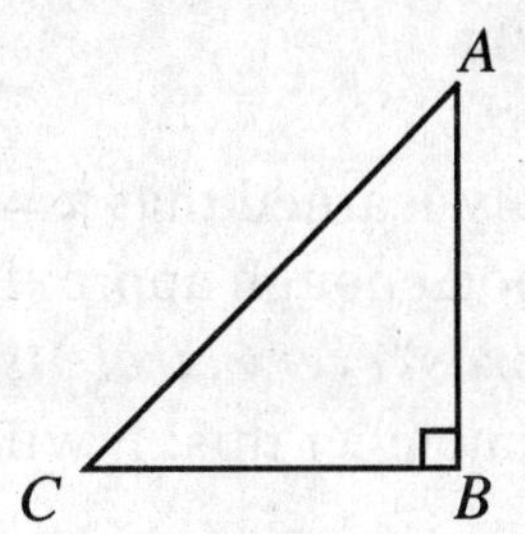

$AB = BC$

5. The perimeter of a triangle is the sum of the lengths of its sides.

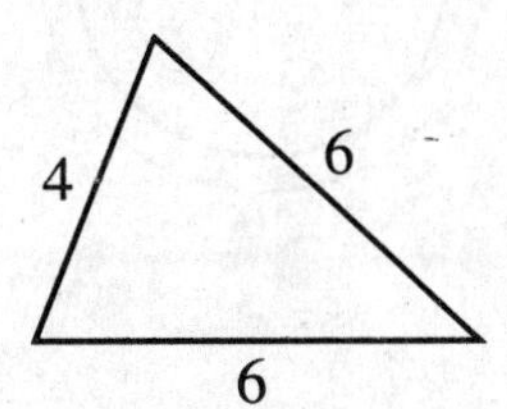

perimeter = 16

6. The area of a triangle is: $\frac{\textbf{altitude} \times \textbf{base}}{\textbf{2}}$

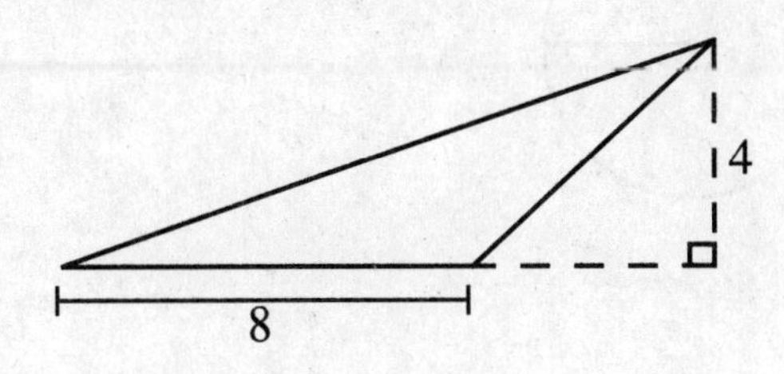

area = $\frac{4 \times 8}{2} = 16$

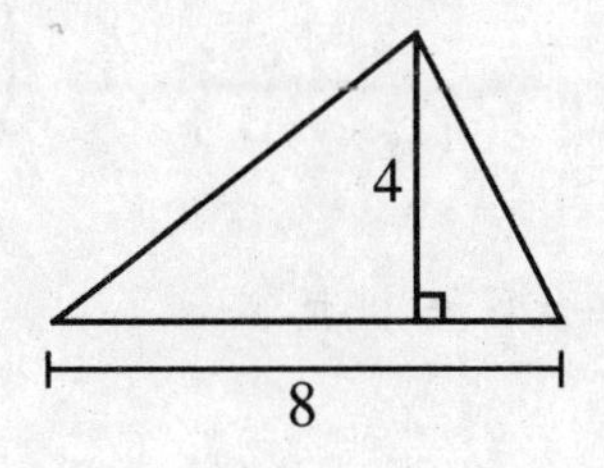

area = $\frac{4 \times 8}{2} = 16$

CIRCLES

1. The circumference of a circle is $2\pi r$ or πd, where r is radius of the circle and d is the diameter. You'll be given this information in your test booklet, but you should know it cold before you take the test.

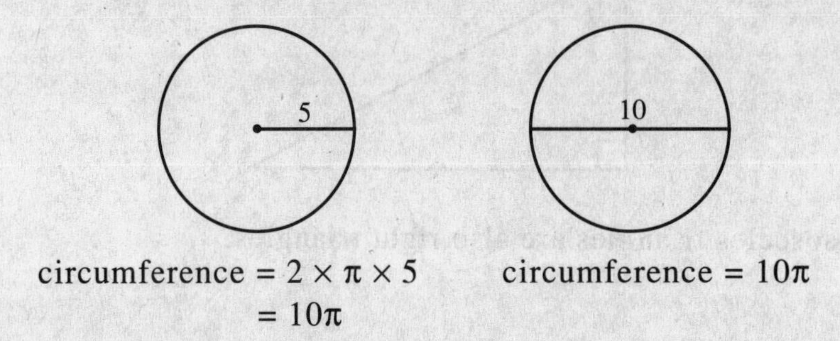

circumference = $2 \times \pi \times 5$
= 10π

circumference = 10π

In math class you probably learned that $\pi = 3.14$ (or even 3.14159). On the SAT, $\pi = 3$ is a good enough approximation, and much easier to work with. *In other words, every circle is about three times as far around as it is across.* Remember this: It will be helpful to you on the test.

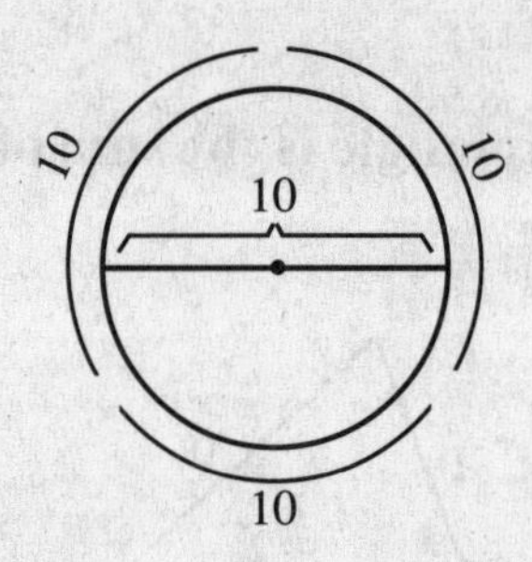

circumference = about 30

2. The area of a circle is πr^2, where r is the radius of the circle.

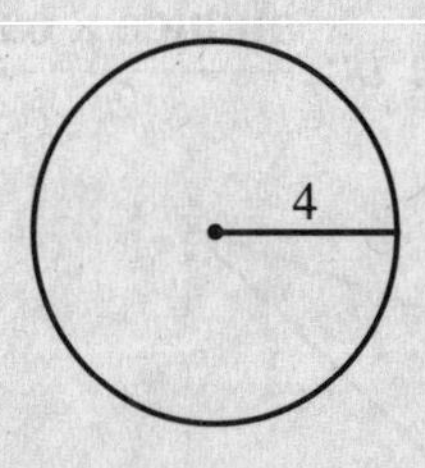

area = $\pi 4^2 = 16\pi$

RECTANGLES AND SQUARES

1. The perimeter of a rectangle is the sum of the lengths of its sides. Just add them up.

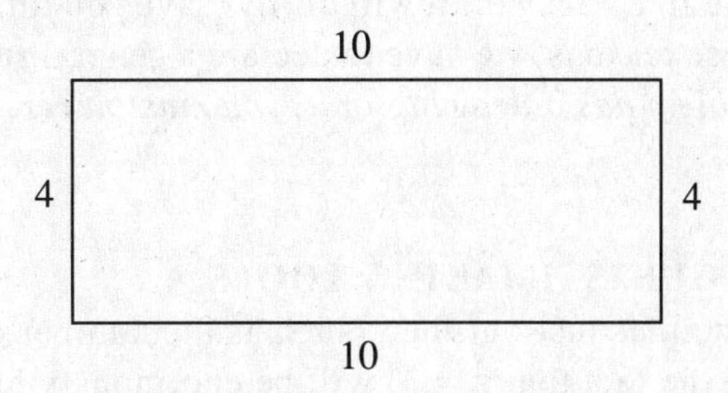

perimeter = 10 + 4 + 10 + 4 = 28

2. The area of a rectangle is length × width. The area of the preceding rectangle, therefore, is 10 × 4, or 40.

3. A square is a rectangle whose four sides are all equal in length. The perimeter of a square, therefore, is four times the length of any side. The area is the length of any side squared.

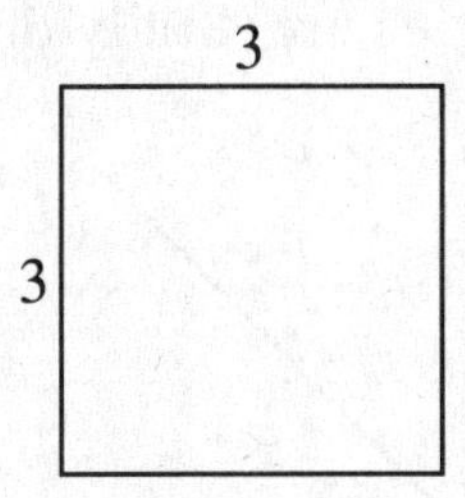

perimeter = 12
area = 9

Basic Principles: Guesstimating

In many SAT geometry problems, you will be presented with a drawing in which some information is given and asked to find some of the information that is missing. In most such problems, Jim expects you to apply some formula or perform some calculations, often an algebraic one. But you'll almost always be better off if you look at the drawing and make a rough estimate of Jim's answer (based on the given information) before you try to work it out. We call this "guesstimating." It will often enable you to find Jim's answer without working the problem out at all.

Guesstimating is extremely helpful on SAT geometry problems. At the very least, it will enable you to avoid careless mistakes. It will allow you to eliminate *immediately* answer choices that could not possibly be Jim's answer. It will *always* save you time and points.

For these reasons, we have to declare a general rule: *If an SAT geometry problem has a drawing in it, you must never, never, never leave it blank.*

THE BASIC GUESSTIMATING TOOLS

The basic principles just outlined (such as the number of degrees in a triangle and the fact that $\pi = 3$) will be enormously helpful to you in guesstimating on the SAT. You should also know the values of the following square roots. Be sure to memorize them before moving on.

Square Roots

$\sqrt{1} = 1$

$\sqrt{2} = 1.4$

$\sqrt{3} = 1.7$

$\sqrt{4} = 2$

You will also find it very helpful if you have a good sense of how large certain common angles are. Study the following examples.

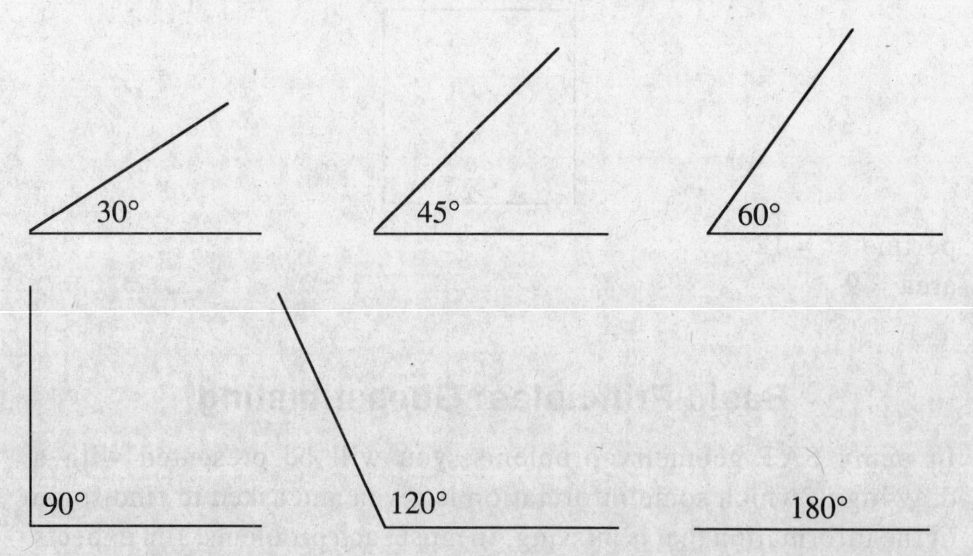

To get a little practice using the material you've memorized to guesstimate, do the following drill.

DRILL

Guesstimate the following values. You can check your answers on page 284.

1. $\sqrt{2} - 1 =$
2. $3\sqrt{\pi} =$
3. $2\sqrt{2} =$
4. $\sqrt{\frac{3}{4}}$
5. $\sqrt{18}$

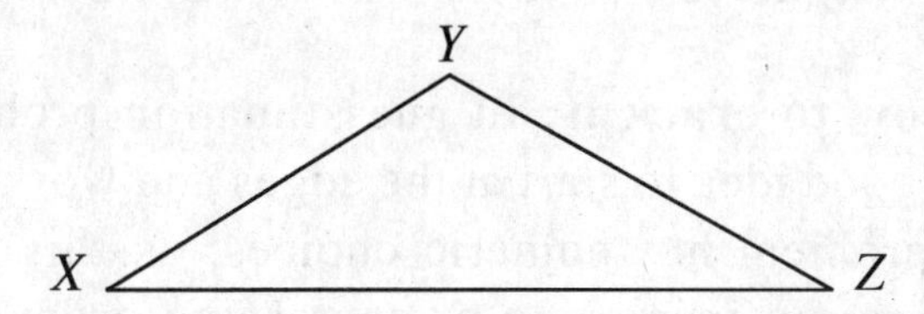

6. In the figure above, given $XY = 16$, estimate all angles and the lengths of other sides.

HOW TALL IS THE CEILING?

If your father stood next to a wall in your living room and asked you how tall the ceiling was, what would you do? Would you get out your trigonometry textbook and try to triangulate using the shadow cast by your father? Of course not. You'd look at your father and think something like this: "Dad's about 6 feet tall. The ceiling's a couple of feet higher than he is. It must be about 8 feet tall."

Your guesstimation wouldn't be exact, but it would be close. If your mother later claimed that the ceiling in the living room was 15 feet height, you'd be able to tell her with confidence that she was mistaken.

You'll be able to do the same thing on the SAT. *Every geometry figure on your test will be drawn exactly to scale unless there is a note* in that problem *telling you otherwise*. That means that you can trust the proportions in the drawing. If line segment *A* has a length of 2 and line segment *B* is exactly half as long, then the length of line segment *B* is 1. All such problems are ideal for guesstimating.

Look at the following example:

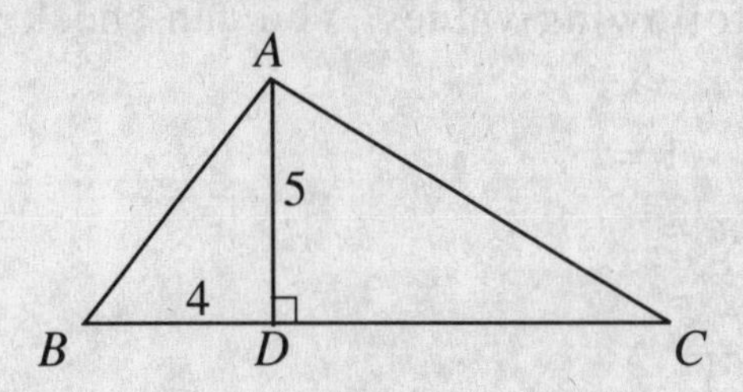

10. If the area of ΔABC in the figure above is 30, then the length of DC is

(A) 2 (B) 4 (C) 6 (D) 8 (E) 12

Here's how to crack it: In guesstimation problems like this, it's usually a good idea to start at the edges and work your way in. When an SAT problem has numeric choices, as this one does, they are always given in increasing or decreasing order of size. Choices at either extreme will be the easiest to dispute and hence the easiest to eliminate if they are wrong.

Look at the drawing. Line *DC* is obviously a good bit longer than line *BD*. Since $BD = 4$, we know for certain that *DC* has to be greater than 4. That means we can eliminate choices A and B. Just cross them out so you won't waste time thinking about them again. They couldn't possibly be correct.

Now look at *DC* again. Is it 3 times as long as *BD*? No way. That means choice E can be eliminated as well.

We've narrowed it down to choice C or D. Does *DC* look like it's twice as long as *BD*, or like it's one and a half times as long? That's all you have to decide.

(Jim's answer is D. Notice that you found it without having to use the area of the triangle, which was given in the problem.) Here's another example:

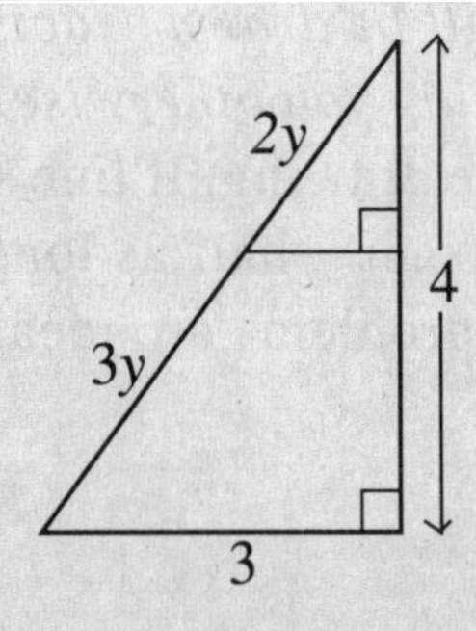

13. In the figure above, $y =$

(A) 1 (B) 2 (C) 3 (D) 4 (E) 5

Here's how to crack it: You can use any of a number of guesstimating approaches in solving this problem. Here's one of them:

The hypotenuse of the little triangle is $2y$. That means that y equals half the length of the hypotenuse. Is half the length of the small hypotenuse larger or smaller than 3 (the base of the triangle)? Smaller, obviously. Therefore, you can eliminate choices C, D, and E, all of which are *larger*.

You now know that y has to be either 1 or 2. You can probably see that it has to be 1. (Jim's answer, therefore, is *A*. Don't get careless on this problem and select choice E after figuring out that $5y$ has to equal 5.)

Here's one final example. It's a good bit harder than the others, but you still shouldn't have trouble with it.

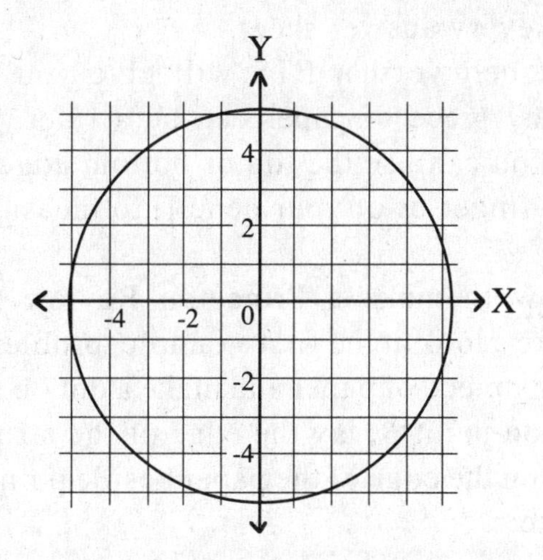

29. What is the circumference of the circle in the figure above?

(A) 5π (B) 10π (C) $\frac{25}{2}\pi$ (D) 20π (E) 25π

Here's how to crack it: Let's say you've forgotten the formula for circumference and don't have the time to look it up. What do you do? Just count "squares." If you count units along the rim of the circle, you get about 7 for a quarter of the way around the circle. That means that the entire circumference is approximately 28. Now look at the choices:

(A) 5π is about 15. Could this be Jim's answer? No. Eliminate.

(B) 10π is about 30. A good possibility.

(C) $\frac{25}{2}$ is 12.5. Therefore, $\frac{25}{2}\pi$ is about 37.5. Could this be Jim's answer? It doesn't seem likely; it's a good bit more than 28.

(D) 20π is about 60. That's way off. Eliminate.

(E) 25π is about 75. That's even further off. Eliminate.

(Jim's answer is choice B. This problem didn't turn out to be very hard after all, did it?)

WHEN YOU CAN'T EYEBALL, MEASURE

Sometimes you won't be able to tell just by looking whether one line is longer than another. In these cases you should actually *measure* what you need to know. How will you do this? By using the *ruler* that ETS provides on every answer sheet.

You don't believe that ETS will give you a ruler on your answer sheet? Any piece of paper can be a ruler, if you mark off distances on it. You can use the top or bottom edge of your answer sheet (or of your finger or of your pencil) to measure distances and solve problems.

Here's how to make a Princeton Review ruler with your answer sheet. Take a look at the first example, problem number 10, on page 206. Take any piece of paper and make a dot on the bottom edge. Now put the dot on point B, lay the edge of the strip along BD, and mark another dot on the edge of the paper beside point D. Here's what it should look like:

What's the length of the space between the dots? It's exactly 4, of course—the same as the length of BD in the diagram. You now have a ruler. You can use it to measure the length of DC, which is what the problem asks you for.

You can make your ruler as precise as you need to. By placing the ruler against side AD and noting the difference between its length and the length of BD, you'll be able to mark off your ruler in units of 1.

You can even use your Princeton Review ruler to measure the circumference of a circle or the length of a curved line. Just carefully turn the paper around the curved distance you want to measure, mark off the distance on your ruler with your pencil, and then compare the ruler with some known distance in the problem.

Here's how it works. Look at the last example, problem number 29, on the page 207. Take any piece of paper, turn it around the circle, mark off the distance, and measure it on the grid in the problem. You'll come up with a length of about 30, just as you did by eyeballing.

Important Note

You'll have to make a new ruler for each problem on which you need to measure something. ETS figures are drawn to scale (unless they're labeled otherwise), but they aren't all drawn to the *same* scale. A ruler that measures 4 on one diagram won't measure 4 on another. Also, don't forget to erase your markings after you've finished each problem, so that they don't throw off ETS's grading machines.

YOU CAN ALSO MEASURE ANGLES

ETS is also kind enough to give you a protractor. Where? On any of the three square corners of your answer sheet. The square corner of a sheet of paper is a perfect 90-degree angle, like this:

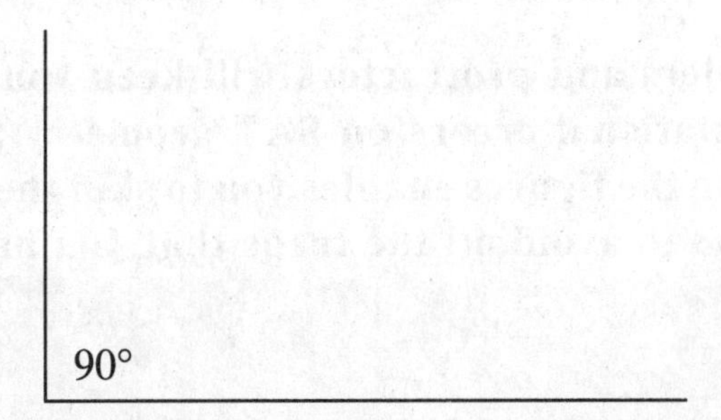

If you fold the paper on the diagonal, taking care not to leave a crease, you end up with a perfect 45-degree angle, like this:

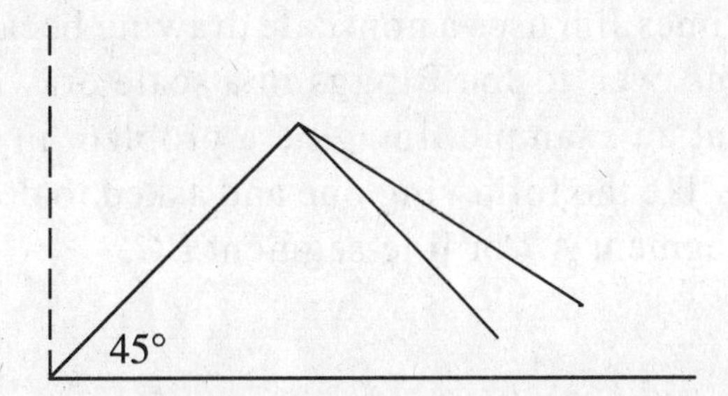

With a tool like this, you'll be able to measure almost any angle with a fair degree of accuracy. Actually, if you practice eyeballing angles, you may never need to consult the corner of your answer sheet. If you spend an hour or so teaching yourself to guesstimate the size of angles just by looking at them, you'll improve your SAT score. In fact, you should be able to answer at least one question on your SAT without doing anything except eyeballing or measuring. Here's an example:

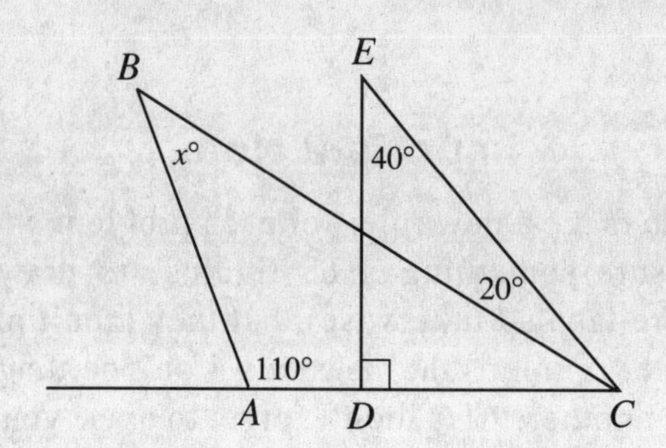

6. In the figure above, $x =$

(A) 15 (B) 20 (C) 30 (D) 40 (E) 50

Here's how to crack it: By using your page-corner protractor you should be able to see that x is a little bit less than 45. (You should also be able to tell this just by eyeballing.) Therefore, you can definitely eliminate answer choices A, B, and E. Your best choice is D. (It is also Jim's answer.)

Using rulers and protractors will keep you from making careless computational errors on SAT geometry problems. Because measuring the figures enables you to skip the arithmetic, it also enables you to avoid all the traps that Jim has laid for Joe Bloggs.

WHAT IF A DIAGRAM IS NOT DRAWN TO SCALE?

Don't worry if a diagram is *not* drawn to scale. In many cases you will simply be able to *redraw* the diagram in your test booklet and then measure. Sometimes Jim uses a nonscale drawing because his answer would be obvious even to Joe Bloggs in a scale drawing.

Let's look at an example. Imagine a problem in which you are given a drawing like the following one and asked to determine which is bigger, line segment *AB* or line segment *BC*.

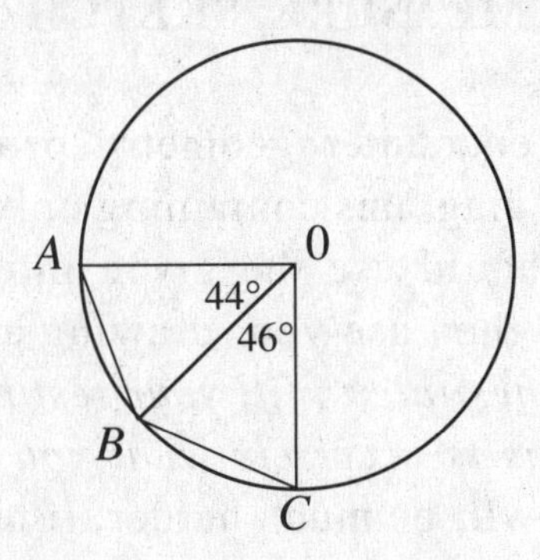

Note: Not drawn to scale

Here's how to crack it: This figure is not drawn to scale, so simply measuring the segments won't help. In addition, Jim has drawn the figure so that the segments seem to be the same length. What should you do? *Redraw the figure in your test booklet exaggerating the difference in the given information.* In this case, you are given the measures of two angles. One angle is a little larger than the other, but both seem to be about the same size in the drawing. All you have to do is redraw the figure exaggerating this difference. Since one angle is bigger than the other, you should make it *much* bigger. Your drawing should look something like this:

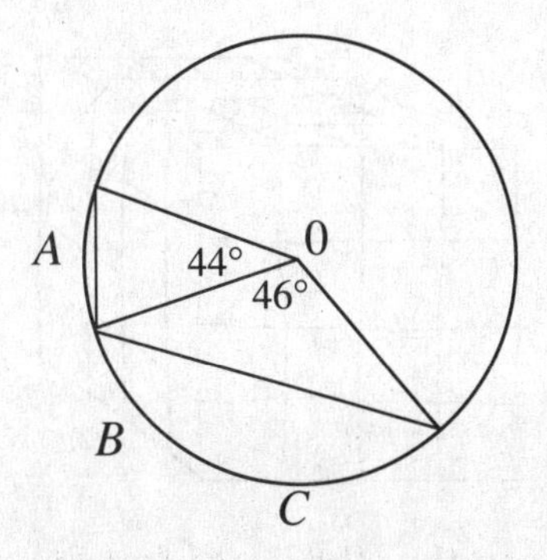

Now you shouldn't have any trouble seeing that line segment *BC* has to be bigger than line segment *AB*. Jim used a nonscale drawing because his answer would have been obvious if he had not.

Sometimes you will find it helpful to take a nonscale drawing and *redraw it to scale*. This can be somewhat time-consuming if the problem is complicated, but it may give you a shortcut to Jim's answer. Just use your ruler to redraw the figure based on the information given you.

WHEN YOU CAN'T MEASURE, SKETCH AND GUESSTIMATE

You will sometimes encounter geometry problems that have no diagrams, or that have diagrams containing only partial information. In these cases, you should use the given information to *sketch* a complete diagram and then use your drawing as a basis for guesstimating. *You must not hesitate to fill your test booklet with sketches and scratch work: This is precisely what you are supposed to do.* Finding Jim's answer will be much harder, if not impossible, if you don't take full advantage of the materials ETS gives you.

Here's an example:

10. All faces of a cube with a 4-meter edge are covered with striped paper. If the cube is then cut into cubes with 1-meter edges, how many of the 1-meter cubes have striped paper on exactly one face?

    (A) 24 (B) 36 (C) 48 (D) 60 (E) 72

Here's how to crack it: This problem doesn't have a diagram. It would be much easier to solve if it did. What should you do? Draw a diagram, of course! Just sketch the cube quickly in your test booklet and mark it off into 1-meter cubes as described. Your sketch should look like this:

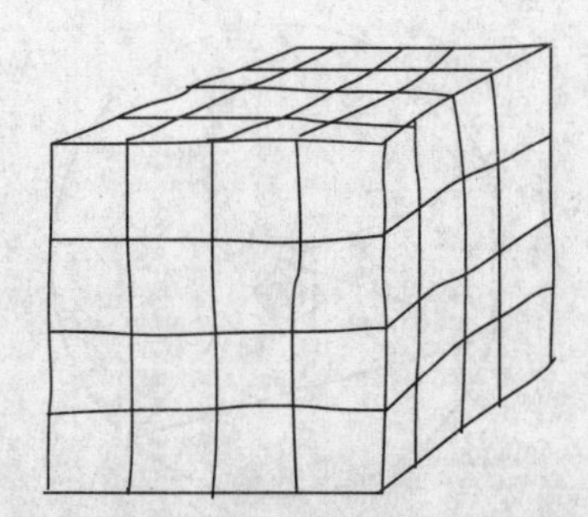

You should be able to see that there are four cubes on each side of the big cube that will have striped paper on only one face. Since a cube has six sides, this means that Jim's answer is choice A.

Basic Principles: Plugging In

As you learned in Chapter Ten, plugging in is one of the most helpful techniques for solving SAT algebra problems. It is also very useful on geometry problems. On some problems, you will be able to plug in guesstimated values for missing information and then use the results either to find Jim's answer directly or to eliminate answers that could not possibly be correct.

Here's an example:

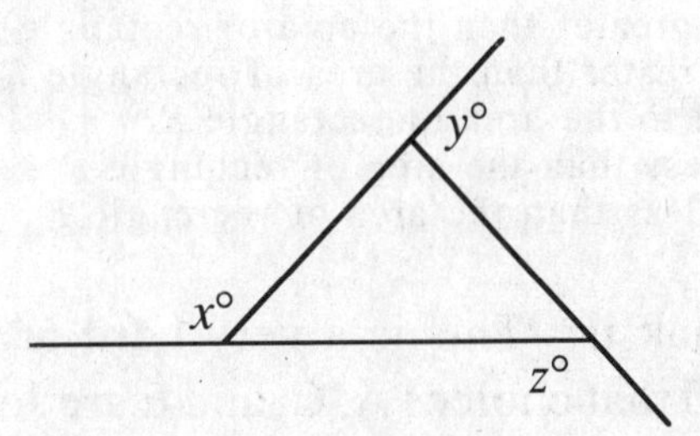

18. In the figure above, $x + y + z =$

(A) 90 (B) 180 (C) 270 (D) 360 (E) 450

Here's how to crack it: We don't know the measures of the interior angles of the triangle in the drawing, but we do know that the three interior angles of *any* triangle add up to 180, and 180 divided by 3 is 60. Now, simply plug in 60 for the value of each *interior* angle.

This doesn't give you Jim's answer directly; the problem does not ask you for the sum of the interior angles. But plugging in does enable you to find Jim's answer. Look at the redrawn figure:

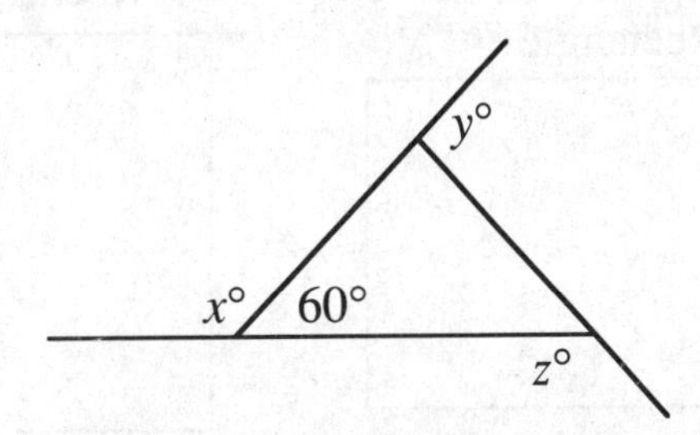

If the marked interior angle is 60, what must x be? Remember that every line is a 180-degree angle. That means that the measure of x must be $180 - 60$, or 120. You can now do the same thing for the other two angles. Using this method you find that x, y, and z each equal 120. That means that $x + y + z = 360$. Jim's answer, therefore, is choice D.

Alternate solution: It is possible to solve this problem by guesstimating. Angle x looks like it's about, oh, 135 degrees; angle y looks like about 100 degrees; angle z looks like about 120. (Don't spend a lot of time eyeballing; you don't have to be very precise.) What does that add up to? 355. Not bad!

Guesstimating like this won't always give you exactly Jim's answer, but it will usually enable you to eliminate at least three of the four incorrect choices. Other kinds of geometry problems also lend themselves to plugging in. Here's an example:

25. The length of rectangle S is 20 percent longer than the length of rectangle R, and the width of rectangle S is 20 percent shorter than the width of rectangle R. The area of rectangle S is

(A) 20% greater than the area of rectangle R
(B) 4% greater than the area of rectangle R
(C) equal to the area of rectangle R
(D) 4% less than the area of rectangle R
(E) 20% less than the area of rectangle R

Here's how to crack it: This is a very hard problem. You should recognize first of all that choices A, C, and E are Joe Bloggs attractors and should be eliminated. Even if you don't see this, though, you'll be able to find Jim's answer by sketching and plugging in.

In plugging in, always use numbers that are easy to work with. Twenty percent equals one-fifth; the easiest number to work with, therefore, is 5. Let's say that the length of rectangle R is 5; that means that the length of rectangle S, which is 20 percent longer, must be 6. You can use 5 again in figuring widths. If the width of rectangle R is 5, then the width of rectangle S, which is shorter, must be 4. You should come up with two sketches that look like this:

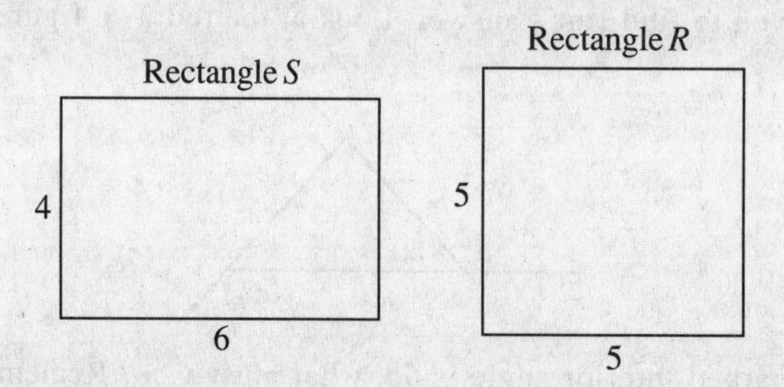

R turns out to be a square, but that's all right; squares are rectangles, too. The area of rectangle S is 24; the area of R is 25. The area of S, which is what the problem asks for, is thus a little bit less than the area of R. In fact, it is 4 percent less, although you don't need to figure it out exactly. Jim's answer is choice D.

Advanced Principles: Beyond the Fundamentals

THE PYTHAGOREAN THEOREM

The Pythagorean theorem states that in a right triangle (a triangle with one interior angle that is exactly 90 degrees), the square of the hypotenuse equals the sum of the squares of the other two sides. As we told you earlier, the hypotenuse is the *longest* side of a right triangle; it's the side that doesn't touch the right angle. The square of the hypotenuse is its length squared. Applying the Pythagorean formula to the following drawing, we find that $c^2 = a^2 + b^2$

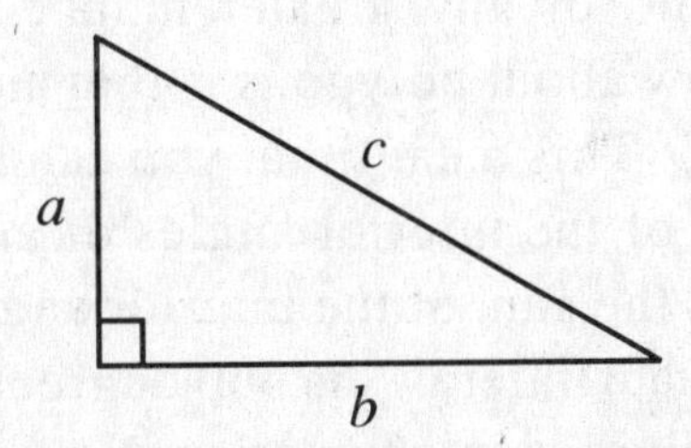

Jim makes fairly frequent use of math problems that require you to know the Pythagorean formula. Fortunately, he is extremely predictable in how he does so. If you memorize the formula and the proportions of a few common triangles, you will have a big advantage on these problems.

The most common Pythagorean triangle on the SAT has sides measuring 3, 4, and 5 or multiples of those numbers, as in the following two examples:

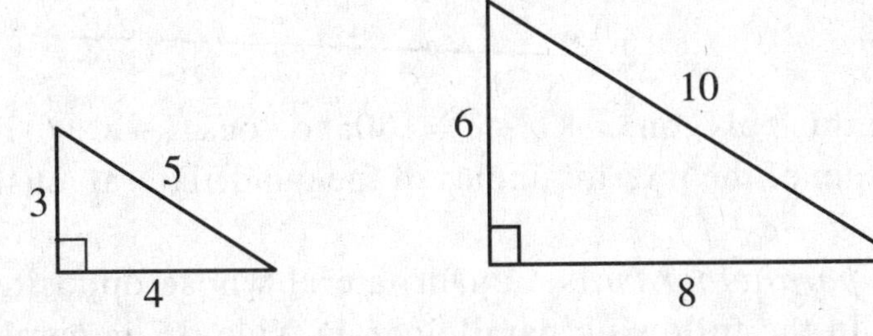

You should also be on the lookout for problems in which the application of the Pythagorean theorem is not obvious. For example, every rectangle contains two right triangles. That means that if you know the length and width of the rectangle, you also know the length of the diagonal, which is the hypotenuse of both triangles. Here's an example:

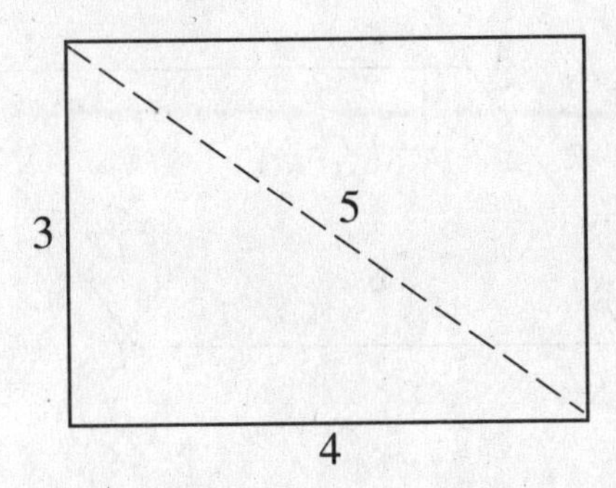

POLYGONS

Polygons are two-dimensional figures with three or more straight sides. Triangles and rectangles are both polygons. So are figures with five, six, seven, eight, or any greater number of sides. The most important fact to know about polygons is that any one of them can be *divided into triangles*. This means that you can always determine the sum of the measures of the interior angles of any polygon.

For examples, the sum of the interior angles of any four-sided polygon (called a "quadrilateral") is 360 degrees. Why? Because any quadrilateral can be divided into two triangles, and a triangle contains 180 degrees. Look at the following example:

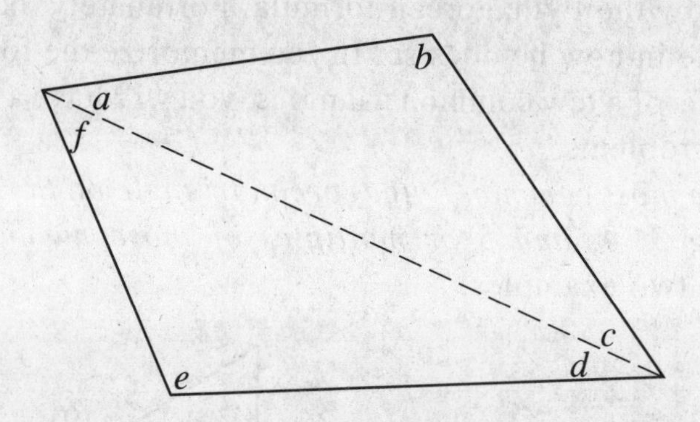

In this polygon, $a + b + c = 180$; so does $d + e + f$. That means that the sum of the interior angles of the quadrilateral must be 360 ($a + b + c + d + e + f$).

A *parallelogram* is a quadrilateral whose opposite sides are parallel. In the following parallelogram, side AB is parallel to side CD, and AD is parallel to BC. Because a parallelogram can also be thought of as a pair of parallel lines intersected by another pair of parallel lines, *Fred's theorem applies to it:* Interior angles that *look* equal *are* equal. In the drawing, therefore, the interior angle at point A is equal to the one at point C, and the one at point B is equal to the one at point D.

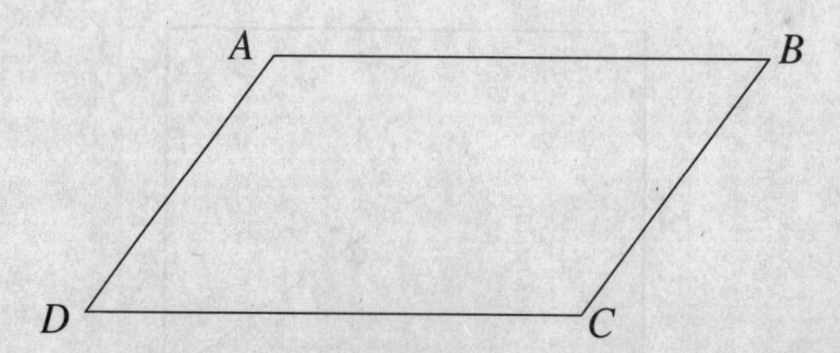

ANGLE/SIDE RELATIONSHIPS OF TRIANGLES

The *longest* side of any triangle is opposite the *largest* interior angle;

the *shortest* side is opposite the *smallest* angle. In the following triangle, side A is longer than side B, which is longer than side C, because angle a is larger than angle b, which is larger than angle c.

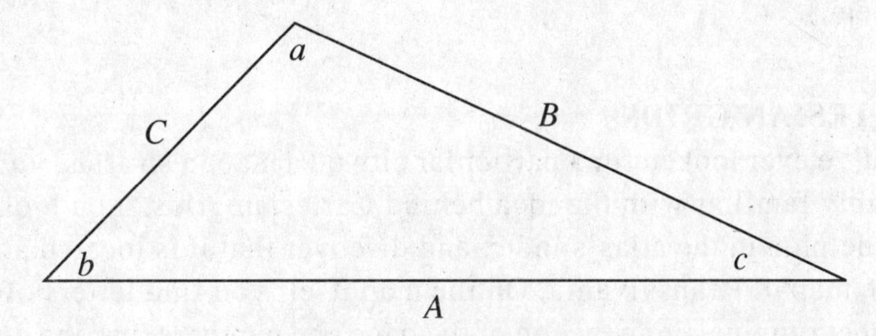

The same rule applies to isosceles and equilateral triangles. An isosceles triangle, remember, is one in which two of the sides are equal in length; therefore, the angles opposite those sides are also equal. In an equilateral triangle, all three sides are equal; so are all three angles.

VOLUME

You'll never have to know the formula for the *volume* of any geometric figure except a *rectangular solid* (a box or a cube) on the SAT. That formula is *length* × *width* × *height*. Since length, width and height are equal in a cube, the volume of a cube can be calculated simply by *cubing* (where do you think you get the name?) the length of any of the sides.

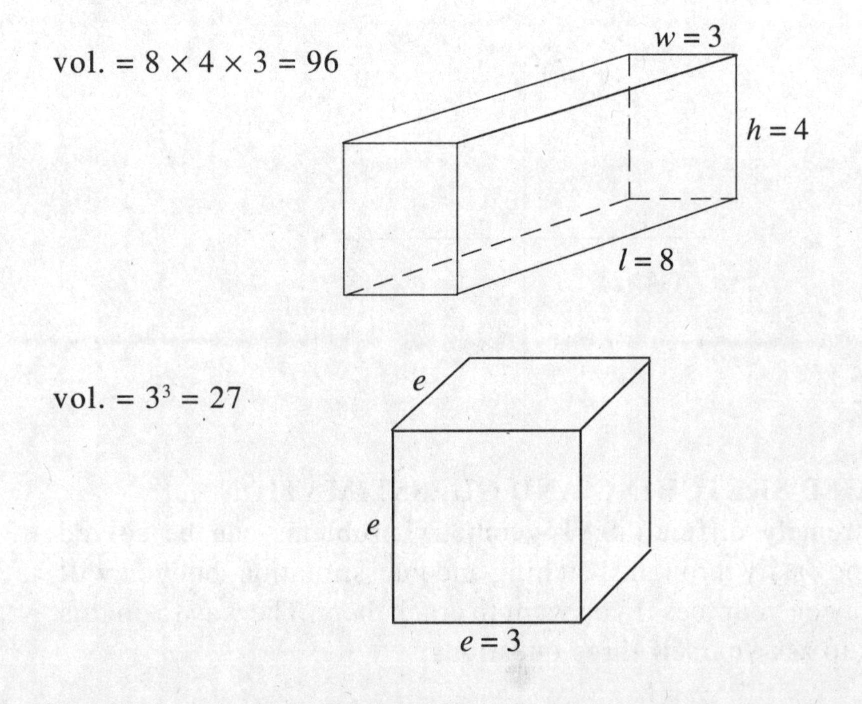

(In extremely rare cases, ETS will ask you a question that will require you to find the volume of a figure other than a rectangular solid. In any such case, the formula will be provided with the problem.)

CARTESIAN GRIDS

If you've ever looked for a particular city on a map in an atlas, you're probably familiar with the idea behind Cartesian grids. You look up Philadelphia in the atlas's index and discover that it is located at D5 on the map of Pennsylvania. On the map itself you find letters of the alphabet running along the top of the page and numbers running down one side. You move your finger straight down from the D at the top of the page until it is at the level of the 5 along the side, and there you are: in Philadelphia.

Cartesian grids work the same way. The standard grid is shaped like a cross. The horizontal line is called the *X-axis*; the vertical line is the *Y-axis*. The four areas formed by the intersection of the axes are called *quadrants*. The location of any quadrant can be described with a pair of numbers (x, y), just the way you would on a map. (0,0) are the coordinates of the intersection of the two axes (also called the "origin"). (1,2) are the coordinates of the point one space to the right and two spaces up. (–1,5) are the coordinates of the point one space to the left and five spaces up. (–4,–2) are the coordinates of the point four spaces to the left and two spaces down. All these points are located on the following diagram:

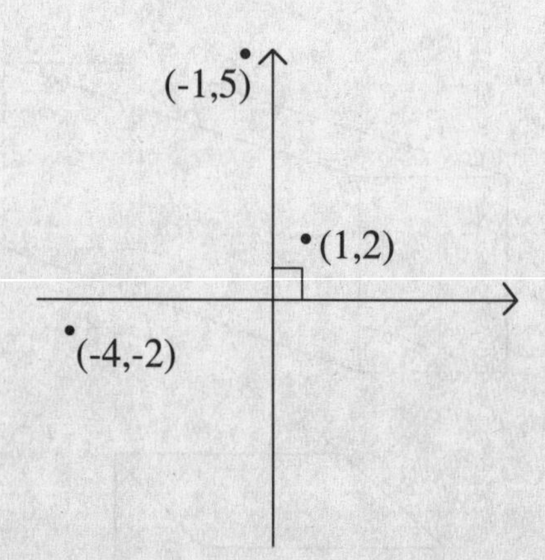

ADVANCED SKETCHING AND GUESSTIMATION

Some extremely difficult SAT geometry problems can be solved quickly and easily through sketching and guesstimation, but you will have to stay on your toes if you want to crack them. The way to do this is always to ask yourself three questions:

1. What information have I been given?
2. What information have I been asked to find?
3. What is the relation between them?

Here's an example. It was the second hardest problem on the SAT in which it appeared:

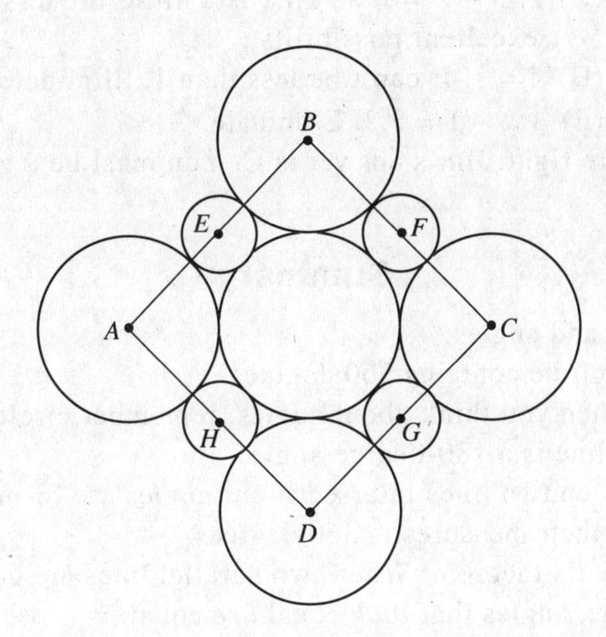

24. Four circles of radius 2 with centers A, B, C, and D are arranged symmetrically around another circle of radius 2, and four smaller equal circles with centers E, F, G, and H each touch three of the larger circles as shown in the figure above. What is the radius of one of the small circles?

(A) $\sqrt{2} - 2$ (B) $\sqrt{2} - 1$ (C) $2\sqrt{2} - 2$
(D) 1 (E) $3\sqrt{2} - 1$

Here's how to crack it: First answer the three questions:

1. I have been given the radius of a large circle.
2. I have been asked for the radius of a small circle.
3. Both are distances and both, therefore, can be measured.

What at first appeared to be an extremely difficult geometry problem now reveals itself to be a simple matter of measurement. Mark off the distance of one large-circle radius along the edge of your answer sheet. This equals 2. Now align your ruler on a small-circle radius. The small-circle radius is smaller, obviously. How much smaller? You can probably see that it is a little bit less than half as long. That means that the answer to the question is "a little bit less than 1."

Now turn to the answer choices and solve them one at a time:

(A) $\sqrt{2}$, as you know, equals 1.4, so $\sqrt{2} - 2 = -0.6$. A distance cannot be negative. Eliminate.

(B) $\sqrt{2} - 1 = 0.4$. This is less than 1, but a lot less. A possibility.

(C) $2\sqrt{2} - 2 = 0.8$. This is a little bit less than 1. An excellent possibility.

(D) $1 = 1$. It can't be less than 1. Eliminate.

(E) $3\sqrt{2} - 1 = 3.2$. Eliminate.

You're right. Jim's answer is C. You must be a genius!

Summary

1. Degrees and angles:
   A. A circle contains 360 degrees.
   B. When you think about angles, remember circles.
   C. A line is a 180-degree angle.
   D. When two lines intersect, four angles are formed; the sum of their measures is 360 degrees.
   E. Fred's theorem: When two parallel lines are cut by a third line, angles that *look* equal *are* equal.

2. Triangles:
   A. Every triangle contains 180 degrees.
   B. An equilateral triangle is one in which all three sides are equal in length, and all three angles are equal in measure (60 degrees).
   C. An isosceles triangle is one in which two of the sides are equal in length, and all three angles are equal in measure (60 degrees).
   D. A right triangle is one in which one of the angles is a right angle (90 degrees).
   E. The perimeter of a triangle is the sum of the lengths of its sides.
   F. The area of a triangle is: $\frac{\text{altitude} \times \text{base}}{2}$

3. Circles:
   A. The circumference of a circle is $2\pi r$ or πd, where r is the radius of the circle and d is the diameter.
   B. The area of a circle is πr^2, where r is the radius of the circle.

4. Rectangles and squares:
   A. The perimeter of a rectangle is the sum of the lengths of its sides.
   B. The area of a rectangle is length × width.
   C. A square is a rectangle whose four sides are all equal in length.

5. When you encounter a geometry problem on the SAT, *guesstimate* the answer before trying to work it out.

6. You must never skip an SAT problem that has a drawing with it.

7. You must know the following values:

$$\pi = 3$$
$$\sqrt{2} = 1.4$$
$$\sqrt{3} = 1.7$$

8. You must also be familiar with the size of certain common angles.

9. Most SAT geometry diagrams are drawn to scale. Use your eyes before you use your pencil.

10. When your eyes aren't enough, use the edges and corners of your answer sheet as rulers and protractors.

11. When a diagram is not drawn to scale, redraw it.

12. When no diagram is provided, make your own; when a provided diagram is incomplete, complete it.

13. When information is missing from a diagram, guesstimate and plug in.

14. The Pythagorean theorem states that in a right triangle, the square of the hypotenuse equals the sum of the squares of the other two sides.

15. Any polygon can be divided into triangles.

16. The *longest* side of any triangle is opposite the *largest* interior angle; the *shortest* side is opposite the *smallest* angle.

17. The volume of a rectangular solid is length × width × height. You will almost never have to calculate the volume of any other figure on the SAT.

18. You must know how to locate points on a Cartesian grid.

19. Some extremely difficult SAT geometry problems can be solved quickly and easily through sketching and guesstimation, but you will have to stay on your toes. The way to do this is always to ask yourself three questions:

    What information have I been given?
    What information have I been asked to find?
    What is the relationship between them?

CHAPTER TWELVE

Quantitative Comparisons

Quantitative Comparisons: Cracking the System

The scored 35-item math section on your SAT will contain a group of 20 quantitative comparison problems, or quant comps. For a number of years now the quant comps have always been problems 8-27 in this section. This section begins with a group of 7 ordinary math problems, followed by the 20 quant comps, followed by a concluding group of 8 less ordinary math problems.

The order of quant comps will progress from easy to difficult, as follows:

Items 8–14, easy
Items 15–22, medium
Items 23–27, difficult

What Is a Quantitative Comparison?

Here are the instructions for quant comps and three examples exactly as they will appear on your SAT:

Questions 8–27 each consist of two quantities, one in Column A and one in Column B. You are to compare the two quantities and on the answer sheet blacken space

A if the quantity in Column A is greater;
B if the quantity in Column B is greater;
C if the two quantities are equal;
D if the relationship cannot be determined from the information given,

Notes:

1. In certain questions, information concerning one or both of the quantities to be compared is centered above the two columns.
2. A symbol that appears in both columns represents the same thing in Column A as it does in Column B.
3. Letters such as x, n, and k stand for real numbers.
4. Since there are only four choices *NEVER MARK (E)*.

EXAMPLES	*Column A*	*Column B*	*Answers*
E1.	2×6	$2 + 6$	● Ⓑ Ⓒ Ⓓ
	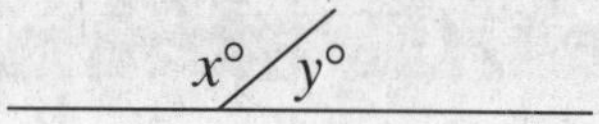		
E2.	$180 - x$	y	Ⓐ Ⓑ ● Ⓓ
E3.	$p - q$	$q - p$	Ⓐ Ⓑ Ⓒ ●

Jim's answer to the first example is A, because the quantity in Column A (12) is greater than the quantity in Column B (8). Jim's answer to the second example is C. You know from Chapter Eleven that $x + y = 180$; $180 - x$, therefore, must equal y, and the two quantities are the same. Jim's answer to the third example is D. Since you can't tell what p or q is, you can't determine whether one quantity is greater than the other.

Be sure that you know these instructions cold before you take the SAT. If you have to look them up each time you answer a question, you'll be wasting time and robbing yourself of points.

Important Note

Even though there are just four answer choices on quant comp problems, your SAT answer sheet will have five circles for each one. Be *very* careful that you darken the proper circle in answering these problems. The only possible choices are A, B, C, and D. If you mark circle E on a quant comp, your answer will count as omitted.

SAT answer sheets used to have just four circles for quant comp answers. ETS changed the format of the answer sheet in an effort to frustrate a coaching technique taught in Princeton Review schools.

To start out, let's look at a very simple quant comp example:

Column A	*Column B*
$2 + 2$	2×2

Your task, remember, is to determine the relationship between the quantity in Column A and the quantity in Column B. The quantity in Column A is 4; so is the quantity in Column B. Will this always be true? Yes, $2 + 2$ will always equal 4, and so will 2×2. Therefore, the correct answer is C, "the two quantities are equal."

Suppose we rewrite the problem as follows:

$3 + 2$	2×2

The quantity in Column A now equals 5, while the quantity in Column B still equals 4. Because $3 + 2$ will always equal 5, and 5 will always be greater than 4, the correct answer now is A, "the quantity in Column A is greater."

Let's rewrite the problem one more time:

$x + 2$	$2 - x$

What's the answer now? Suppose that x equals 5. In that case, the quantity in Column A would be greater than the quantity in Column B. But x can be *any* number; suppose it's 0. In that case, the two quantities would be equal. Now suppose that x equals -2. In that case the quantity in Column B would be greater than the quantity in Column A.

In other words, depending on which numbers we plug in for x, we can make choice A, B, *or* C seem to be the correct answer. That means that *none* of these answers is *always* correct. Jim's answer has to be D, "the relationship cannot be determined from the information given."

The Information Given

Many quant comps contain given information that you are supposed to use in solving the problem. This information is placed *between* the two columns. Here's an example:

	Column A	*Column B*
	During a 100-day period last year, it rained on exactly 40 days.	
9.	Percent of days when it did not rain	40%

Here's how to crack it: The statement centered between the columns is the given. You are supposed to use it in solving the problem.

You shouldn't have any trouble with this one. Since it rained on 40 percent of the days, 60 percent must have been dry. The quantity in Column A is thus greater than the quantity in Column B, and Jim's answer is A.

Quant Comps Are Quick but Tricky

Most students are able to answer quant comps very quickly. Answering 20 quant comps usually takes much less time than answering 20 regular math questions. Because of this, many students breathe a sigh of relief when they come to the quant comp section.

But this apparent ease is deceptive. Quant comps go quickly because certain answers tend to *seem* correct immediately. Because of this, Joe Bloggs loves quant comps. When he looks at a question, he doesn't have to think very long before an "obvious" answer choice jumps off the page.

This Is Bad New for Joe, but Good News for You

Since certain answer choices on quant comps have a strong tendency to *seem* correct to Joe Bloggs, he quickly finds himself in the same predicament he is in on the rest of the SAT:

1. On easy questions the answers that seem right to him really are right, so he earns points.
2. On medium questions his hunches are sometimes right and sometimes wrong, so he just about breaks even.

3. On difficult questions the answers that seem right to him are always wrong, so he loses points.

This is unlucky for Joe, but very lucky for you. Quant comps are the easiest math questions to crack because the Joe Bloggs attractors are easy to spot—*if you know what to look for and if you are careful.* You can use POE, the process of elimination, to eliminate obviously incorrect choices, improve your guessing odds, and zero in on Jim's answer.

Mathematical Content

In terms of mathematical content, most quant comps will seem familiar to you. You'll find arithmetic problems, algebra problems, and geometry problems. You will be able to solve most of these problems by using the techniques we have already taught you.

Solving Quant Comps: Basic Principles

Not all quant comps can be solved simply by using the techniques we have already taught you. Quant comps are a unique problem type, and there are a number of special rules and techniques that apply only to them.

Even on quant comps that can be solved simply by using techniques you already know, there are still some unique features that you need to be familiar with. For instance, some regular techniques must be modified slightly for quant comps. We'll start with some basic principles and then move on to some more advanced ones.

QUANT COMPUTATION

Many quant comps can be solved without any sort of computation. Look at the following example:

25. Area of a circle with diameter 12	Surface area of a sphere with diameter 12

Here's how to crack it: Do you remember the formula for the surface area of a sphere? No?

Good! You don't need it.

Just use your common sense to picture what you're being asked to compare: the area of a circle—say, a paper plate—and the surface area of a sphere—say, a beach ball with the same diameter as the plate. Which is bigger? It's obvious: the surface of the beach ball. (Imagine trying to cover the beach ball completely with the paper plate. It can't be done!) Jim's answer is B.

NUMBERS ONLY

If a quant comp problem contains nothing but numbers, choice D *cannot* be Jim's answer.

In a quant comp that has no variables, it will always be possible to obtain a definite solution. For example, the quantity 2 + 2 can only have one value: 4. The quantity $2 + x$, on the other hand, can have an infinite number of values, depending on what you plug in for x.

When you see a quant comp that contains only numbers, therefore, you can eliminate choice D right off the bat. This tilts the odds in your favor, of course, which means that even if you can't get any further, you should guess among the remaining choices.

Here's an example:

11. $10 - (8 - 6 - 4)$ $\qquad\qquad$ $10 - 8 - (6 - 4)$

Here's how to crack it: This problem contains nothing but numbers. Therefore, it *must* have a solution, and choice D can be eliminated.

(Jim's answer is A. Because you know you are always to perform *first* any operations enclosed in parentheses, you can see that the quantity in Column A equals 12, while the quantity in Column B equals 0.)

EQUATIONS

Think of the quantities in Column A and Column B as the two sides of an equation; all rules that apply to equations also apply to them.

You know that you can add the same number to both sides of an equation, or subtract the same number, or multiply both sides by the same number, or divide them by the same number. *You can also do all of this with quant comps.*

Here's an example:

8. $\frac{1}{4} + \frac{1}{2} + \frac{1}{13}$ $\qquad\qquad$ $\frac{1}{13} + \frac{1}{2} + \frac{1}{3}$

Here's how to crack it: Before doing anything else, you should notice that this quant comp contains nothing but numbers and that choice D, therefore, cannot possibly be Jim's answer.

Your next impulse may be to find a common denominator for all those fractions. Don't you dare! You can solve this problem in a second by eliminating common terms from both sides.

The quantities in Column A and Column B both include $\frac{1}{2}$ and $\frac{1}{13}$. That means you *subtract both fractions from both sides*. Doing so leaves you with the following:

$\frac{1}{4}$ $\qquad$ $\frac{1}{3}$

It should be obvious to you now that Jim's answer has to be B, because $\frac{1}{3}$ is bigger than $\frac{1}{4}$. (Don't make the common careless error of thinking that $\frac{1}{4}$ is bigger than $\frac{1}{3}$ because 4 is bigger than 3!)

SIMPLIFICATION

In the preceding section, we told you that you *can* simplify expressions by performing the same operations on both sides. Now we are going to tell you that you *must*. Very often on quant comps, you will be able to find Jim's answer by doing nothing more than simplifying the terms.

Here's an example

18. 20×6.24 $\qquad$ $\frac{624}{5}$

Here's how to crack it: First of all, you should realize that you can eliminate choice D immediately. This problem contains nothing but numbers; therefore, the relationship between the two quantities *can* be determined.

Now you can look at the problem. The first thing to do is get rid of that fraction in Column B. You can do that by multiplying *both* sides by 5, which yields the following:

100×6.24 $\qquad$ 624

Since 100×6.24 *equals* 624, you can see that the quantities are equal and that Jim's answer is C.

LENGTHY CALCULATIONS = WRONG ANSWERS

If you have to do a lengthy or laborious calculation to find your answer, then you've probably missed the trick. Quant comps are fast. Even on difficult problems, Jim's solution method is usually quick, assuming you can figure out what it is. As a result, *you should always think twice before beginning a time-consuming calculation.*

Here's an example:

12. $(8 \times 73) + (8 \times 13)$ $\qquad$ $8(73 + 13)$

Here's how to crack it: Before you start to multiply out all those numbers, you should stop and take another look at the problem. Jim would never ask a question in which all he wanted was to see whether you could multiply and add a handful of numbers without making a mistake. There *must* be a shorter solution. What is it?

In this case, the solution hinges on whether or not you realize that an 8 can be factored out of the quantity in Column A. Doing this yields the expression 8(73 + 13), which is identical to the quantity in Column B. In other words, the quantities are the same and Jim's answer is C.

Solving Quant Comps: Medium and Difficult Questions

ATTACKING HUNCHES

On medium and difficult quant comps, you should *attack* your hunches. Joe Bloggs's hunches begin to let him down after question 17. Jim's answers, which seemed right to him on the easy question, now begin to seem wrong. By the time Joe gets to question 23, his hunches are invariably leading him to incorrect choices.

What does this mean for you? It means that on medium and difficult questions, you should be extremely suspicious of choices that *seem* to be obvious or correct. In fact, you should attack these very choices. For example, when it is obvious that one column *could* be greater than the other, you should attack that column and try to find a case where the *other* column could be greater.

Here's an example:

$x > 0$

22. $x^2 + 1$ $\qquad$ $x^3 - 1$

Here's how to crack it: It is easy to think of a value for x that would make the quantity in Column B greater than the quantity in Column A. How about 4? You know that $4^3 - 1$ equals 63, and $4^2 + 1$ equals 17. Because 63 is greater than 17, the correct answer *could* be B.

But would Column B *always* have to be greater than Column A? This is what you have to find out. (Before you do, notice that you have already eliminated choices A and C as possibilities: C is out because if one quantity is even *sometimes* greater than the other, the two quantities cannot *always* be equal; A is out because if Column B is even *sometimes* greater than Column A, then Column A cannot *always* be greater than Column B.)

The easiest number greater than 0 to plug in is 1. Doing so produces a value of 2 for Column A and a value of 0 for Column B. In other words, when you plug in 1, the value in Column A is greater—just the opposite of what happened when you plugged in 4. Since you have now found a case in which Column A *could* be greater than Column B, you can also eliminate choice B as a possibility. The only choice left is D—Jim's answer.

PLUGGING IN

When you plug in on quant comps, remember the numbers with special properties: negatives, fractions, 0, and 1.

In ordinary algebra problems on the SAT, you don't have to be very careful about which numbers you plug in. Since you're only looking for numbers that make the equations work, you can just pick numbers that are easy to work with. This is what we taught you in Chapter Ten.

Quant comps, though, are a little different. On these questions you are looking for answers that *always* work. A single exception, therefore, is enough to make an answer choice wrong. The key to finding Jim's answer on hard questions is being certain that you've taken into account all possible exceptions. This is why Joe Bloggs has trouble on medium and difficult quant comps.

This is a hard fact for many students to keep in mind. In plugging in on quant comps, they are attracted naturally to the numbers we use most often: positive whole numbers. But there are many other numbers, and Jim loves to write quant comp problems that depend on the special qualities of these numbers. In fact, many difficult quant comps are difficult *only because* these numbers must be considered in finding a solution, and Joe Bloggs forgets to consider them.

Because this is true, you should always ask yourself the following question on quant comp plug-ins:

Would my answer be different if I plugged in a negative number, a fraction, 0, or 1?

To find out whether it would, you should plug in one of each until you have found a definite answer.

Here's an example:

$x^2 > y^2$

26. $x - y$ 0

Here's how to crack it: When Joe Bloggs solves this problem, he plugs in easy positive integers—say, 3 for x and 2 for y. Because 3 – 2 = 1, and 1 is greater than 0, he selects A as his answer. What happens? He loses points.

This is a number 26—a very hard question. If finding the answer were as easy as plugging in 3 and 2, Joe Bloggs would get this question right and it would be in the easy third. There must be something Joe has forgotten

Indeed there is. Joe has forgotten the special cases. If you want to find Jim's answer, you're going to have to remember.

First, try plugging in negative numbers instead of positive ones: –3 for x and –2 for y. $(-3)^2$ is 9; $(-2)^2$ is 4. Because 9 is greater than 4, you've fulfilled the requirement in the given.

Now look at Column A. What is $x - y$ now? It is –1. Is –1 greater than 0? No, it's less than 0.

Before plugging in negatives, you had already proved that Jim's answer couldn't be B or C. (Do you see why?) Now you've proved that it also can't be A. This means that it must be D. (It is.)

SKETCHING AND GUESSTIMATING

You must also be very careful about sketching and guesstimating on medium and difficult quant comp geometry problems.

Ordinary guesstimating can occasionally be misleading on these problems for the same reason that ordinary plugging in can be misleading on quant comp algebra. Because a single exception is enough to disqualify an answer choice, you must be certain that you have considered all the possibilities. Approximate answers are usually good enough on ordinary geometry problems, but they are very often *wrong* on geometry quant comps.

Here's an example:

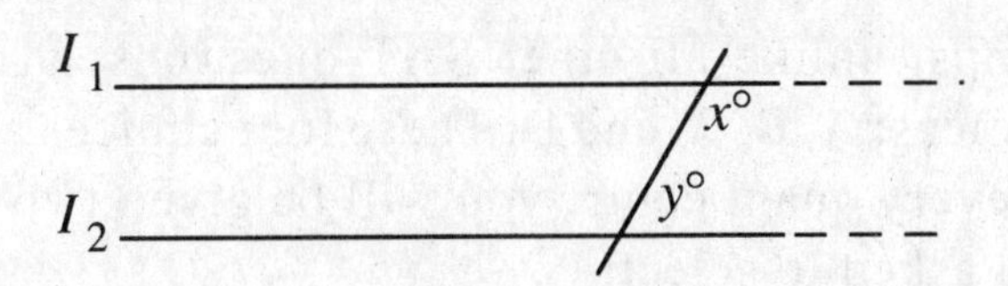

Lines l_1 and l_2 meet when extended to the right.

21. $x + y$ 180

Here's how to crack it: By simply eyeballing and guesstimating (or using your Princeton Review protractor) you would decide that $x + y$ equals *about* 180 degrees. Is Jim's answer therefore C?

No! You know from the given that the two lines are *not* parallel, even though they look it. So $x + y$ can only be a *little bit less* than 180. Jim's answer, therefore, must be B. (It is.)

On problems like this, it will help you to redraw the figure in exaggerated form. The given says that the two lines meet somewhere to the right. Redraw the figure so that they meet *immediately*, something like this:

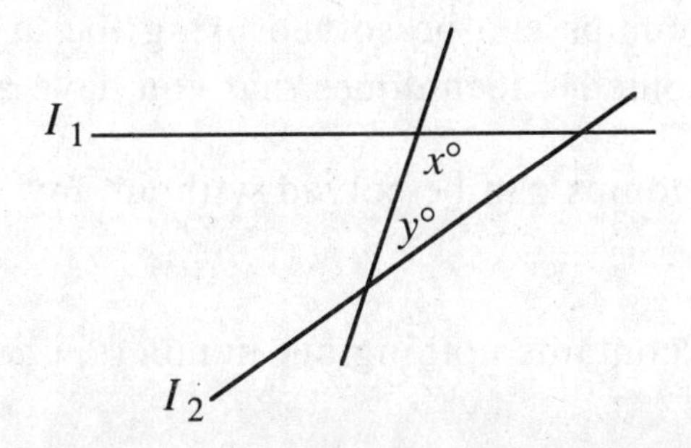

Now the difference between $x + y$ and 180 is very easy to see.

Always note the number on quant comps. On medium and difficult questions, you should be extremely suspicious of answer choices that seem correct immediately, or that you arrive at quickly and without much thought (unless you arrive at them by using our techniques!).

Summary

1. Quant comps, unlike all other SAT questions, offer only four answer choices: A, B, C, and D. These four choices are always the same. On every quant comp, you will be given two quantities or values and asked to select:

   Choice A if you think the first quantity is *always* greater than the second

   Choice B if you think the second quantity is *always* greater than the first

   Choice C if you think the two quantities are *always* equal

   Choice D if you think that it cannot be determined whether one quantity will *always* be greater than or equal to the other.

2. Many quant comps contain given information that you are supposed to use in solving the problem. This information is placed *between* the two columns.

3. Quant comps are ideal for POE, because the Joe Bloggs attractors are easy to spot—*if you know what to look for and if you are careful.*

4. Many quant comps can be solved using the arithmetical, algebraic, and geometric techniques that you have already learned.

5. Many quant comps can be solved without any sort of computation.

6. If a problem contains nothing but numbers, choice D *cannot* be Jim's answer.

7. Think of the quantities in Column A and Column B as the two sides of an equation; all rules that apply to equations also apply to them.

8. If a quant comp can be simplified, simplify it.

9. If you have to do a lengthy or laborious calculation to find your answer, then you've probably missed the trick.

10. On medium and difficult quant comps, *attack* your hunches.

11. When you plug in on quant comps, remember the numbers with special properties: negatives, fractions, 0, and 1.

12. You must also be very careful about sketching and guesstimating on medium and difficult quant comp geometry problems.

13. Always note the number on quant comps. On medium and difficult questions, you should be extremely suspicious of answer choices that *seem* correct immediately, or that you arrive at quickly and without much thought (unless you arrive at them by using our techniques!).

PART FOUR

HOW TO CRACK THE TEST OF STANDARD WRITTEN ENGLISH

You Lose

One of the five scored sections on your SAT will be the Test of Standard Written English (TSWE). This is a 30-minute, 50-question test that is a sort of miniature version of the English Composition Achievement Test (ECT). It is scored on a scale that runs from 20 to 60+; you can miss about four or five questions and still earn a score of 60+.

For most students, the TSWE is a no-win proposition. ETS says that it is "intended to be used to help the college you attend choose an English course appropriate for your ability." But in fact colleges don't use the test this way. There probably aren't three colleges in the country that use TSWE scores for this. Instead, virtually all colleges that consider the scores use them in making admissions decisions—a purpose for which the test was not designed. Some admissions officers will look at your TSWE score as a measure of your "writing ability." Others will use it as a standard for judging your application essay. (If you submit an excellent essay but earn a mediocre TSWE score, they'll assume that your mother wrote your essay.)

Many guidance counselors, taking ETS at its word when it says TSWE scores won't affect admissions decisions, advise their students not to get too worked up about it. This is very bad advice. Most college admissions officers don't know much about interpreting test scores of any kind, but they are really in the dark about TSWE scores. If your score is lower than the admissions officers (for whatever reason) expect it to be, you will be penalized.

The TSWE is a stupid, badly written test that will sap your energy and make it harder for you to do your best on the SAT. Unfortunately, though, you're stuck with it for the time being. (ETS and the College Board are going to get rid of it in 1994.) You don't really have any choice except to try to earn the highest score you can. We'll do our best to help you do that.

Organization and Order of Difficulty

If you've already taken ETS's ECT, then you know roughly what to expect on the TSWE. The TSWE contains two types of questions, both of which are also used on the ECT: *usage questions* and *sentence corrections*. These questions are arranged as follows:

25 usage questions (easy, medium, difficult)
15 sentence corrections (easy, medium, difficult)
10 usage question (medium, difficult)

Difficulty classifications for the TSWE are relative; a "difficult" question on the TSWE is roughly the equivalent of a medium question on the ECT. If you were good at taking the ECT, you shouldn't have any trouble with the TSWE, as long as you don't get careless.

WHAT the TSWE Tests

Generally speaking, the TSWE will test you on the following:

1. *Basic grammar*, including subject-verb agreement, noun-pronoun agreement, and correct verb tense
2. *Sentence structure*, including parallel structures, sentence fragments, and run-ons
3. *Word choice*, including diction (using the correct word) and idioms

You will *not* be tested on spelling, capitalization, grammatical terms, or specific grammatical rules. (If you don't know what a dependent clause is but do know how to write and recognize grammatical English, you'll do fine.) Punctuation marks will play only a very secondary role. *You don't need to run out and memorize a lot of grammatical rules.*

Format

Rather than try to describe the two types of questions on the TSWE, we'll simply reprint the direction and examples provided by ETS. As usual, you should know these instructions cold before you go to take the test.

USAGE QUESTIONS

Directions: The following sentences contain problems [that is, mistakes] in grammar, usage, diction (choice of words), and idiom.

Some sentences are correct.

No sentence contains more than one error.

You will find that the error, if there is one, is underlined and lettered. Assume that elements of the sentence that are not underlined are correct and cannot be changed. In choosing answers, follow the requirements of standard written English.

If there is an error, select the one underlined part that must be changed to make the sentence correct and blacken the corresponding space on your answer sheet.

If there is no error, blacken answer space Ⓔ.

EXAMPLE:

The region has a climate so severe that plants
A
growing there rarely had been more than twelve inches
B C
high. No error
D E

SAMPLE ANSWER:
Ⓐ Ⓑ ● Ⓓ Ⓔ

SENTENCE CORRECTIONS

Directions: In each of the following sentences, some part or all of the sentence is underlined. Below each sentence you will find five ways of phrasing the underlined part. Select the answer that produces the most effective sentence, one that is clear and exact, without awkwardness or ambiguity, and blacken the corresponding space on your answer sheet. In choosing answers, follow the requirements of standard written English. Choose the answer that best expresses the meaning of the original sentence.

Answer Ⓐ is always the same as the underlined part. Choose answer Ⓐ if you think the original sentence needs no revision.

EXAMPLE:

Laura Ingalls Wilder published her first book and she was sixty-five years old then.

(A) and she was sixty-five years old then
(B) when she was sixty-five years old
(C) at age sixty-five years old
(D) upon reaching sixty-five years
(E) at the time when she was sixty-five

SAMPLE ANSWER:
Ⓐ ● Ⓒ Ⓓ Ⓔ

Usage Questions: Basic Principles

"NO ERROR"

Choice E—"No error"—is correct almost exactly one-fifth of the time. In the first 25-question section, therefore, you should expect to find approximately 5 questions whose correct answer is E. Don't waste a lot of time searching for errors where none exist.

WHAT IS UNDERLINED

Remember that a part of the sentence that is *not* underlined may make something underlined incorrect. So don't simply focus on the words that are underlined.

PUNCTUATION

Punctuation errors show up once or twice in the sentence correction section but almost never in the usage questions. Don't spend a lot of time fretting about whether all the commas are in the right places.

PRONOUNS

Among the most common errors tested in usage problems are ones involving pronouns. Before you do anything else, make certain that all pronouns are correct. Here's an example:

3. When her (A) and her friends (B) went to the movie, they (C) had trouble finding (D) a place to park. No error (E)

Here's how to crack it: The correct answer is A. That *her* ought to be *she*. You can always test pronouns by simplifying the sentence and seeing if it still sounds right. To simplify this sentence, leave out "and her friends." This gives you the following: "When her went to the movie . . ." If that sounds correct to you, you are going to have trouble on the TSWE.

NUMBER

You should always determine whether the subject is a singular or plural. Then check the verb. If the subject is plural, the verb must be plural as well. Here's an example:

4. The members of the steering committee, though (A) relatively (B) inexperienced, is (C) doing a good (D) job with planning. No error (E)

Here's how to crack it: The correct answer is C. The subject of the sentence is *members*, not *committee*, which means that the *is* should be *are*.

TENSE

Similarly, you must make certain that every verb in the sentence is in the proper tense. Here's an example:

> 6. When John plays (A) tennis with his brother, he (B) showed off by using (C) his expensive (D) new racket. No error (E)

Here's how to crack it: The correct answer is A. Even though the clause "When John plays tennis with his brother" is perfectly grammatical by itself, it doesn't agree with the rest of the sentence. *Plays* should be *played* to agree with *showed off*.

ADVERBS

Keep an eye out for adjectives used in place of adverbs, and vice versa. Here's an example:

> 19. Rum and Coke, which (A) had been (B) a favorite of all his friends, was forgotten (C) with the rapid increasing (D) number of scotch drinkers. No error (E)

Here's how to crack it: The correct answer is D. *Rapid* should be *rapidly*.

AMBIGUITY

Ambiguity is lack of clarity. Most often ambiguous sentences contain pronouns that have no clear antecedents (*antecedents* are the nouns that pronouns represent). This isn't much of a problem in spoken English, because we can usually figure out what pronouns represent by paying attention to context or the speaker's tone of voice. Not so in written English.

When checking for this sort of mistake, play dumb. Don't guess what the writer meant or make up a context in which the sentence would be correct as written. Antecedents in TSWE sentences must be *clear*. Here's an example:

> 9. Football and baseball are both (A) popular sports, but it (B) has too much (E) violence for many people (C). No error (D)

Here's how to crack it: The correct answer is B. The subject of the sentence is plural (*football and baseball*), but the pronoun is singular (*it*). You can't tell from the sentence whether *it* represents football or baseball. A corrected version of this sentence would read something like this: "Football and baseball are both popular sports, but football has too much violence for many people."

DICTION, USAGE, AND IDIOM

Some TSWE sentences are easy enough to understand but contain slight errors in word choice or usage. You don't need a big vocabulary to answer these questions correctly, but you do need to read carefully. A sentence might contain a word that is *almost* right, but not quite. Here's an example:

13. When (A) the battle was over (B), the victorious soldiers rose (C) their (D) flag over the fort. No error (E)

Here's how to crack it: The correct answer is C; *rose* should be *raised*. Pay attention.

Sentence Corrections: Basic Principles

Many sentence correction problems contain errors of number, tense, and usage quite similar to those in usage questions. You should also keep in mind the following:

ANTICIPATE

In Chapter Seven, on sentence completions, we told you that you should try to *anticipate* the missing word or words as you read each sentence. You should do something very similar on TSWE sentence corrections. As you read each sentence, try to analyze what (if anything) is wrong before you even look at the choices. If you start plugging in the choices too early, you may find yourself with several possibilities that all sound sort of correct.

REMEMBER POE

If, when reading a sentence, you realize that something is definitely wrong with it, cross out choice A in your test booklet before considering the other choices. Choice A is always just a repeat of the underlined part of the sentence. Don't waste time by reading and rereading it as you consider the choices. As you look for your answer, you should also cross out choices that are obviously incorrect. If you use POE, the process of elimination, aggressively, you won't get confused.

CONCISENESS COUNTS

In weighing several possible answer choices, try the shortest one first. Good writing is usually more concise than bad writing. Shorter answers tend to be right more often than longer ones.

DANGLING MODIFIER

If a sentence starts with a verb ending in *-ing*, be very certain that the noun or pronoun following the comma is really the subject of that verb. Here's an example:

29. Working in the garden all afternoon, the sun burned him severely on the back of his neck.

(A) the sun burned him severely on the back of his neck
(B) a severe sunburn developed on the back of his neck
(C) he developed a severe sunburn on the back of his neck
(D) the back of his neck developed a severe sunburn
(E) the back of his neck was burned severely by the sun

Here's how to crack it: The sentence starts with *working*—a verb ending in *-ing*. The noun after the comma is *sun*. Is *sun* the subject of *working*? To put it another way, is it the sun that is working in the garden? No, of course not. The real subject of the verb *working* must be *he*. Thus, the correct answer to this question is C.

Whenever you see a sentence that begins like this, ask yourself: "What is the subject of the verb?" Then look after the comma and see if the noun or pronoun there is the one you were expecting. If not, you've found the error.

SENTENCE FRAGMENTS

Be on the lookout for incomplete sentences. If you read them too quickly, you may not notice that they are fragments. Here's an example:

29. When the committee met for the last time this year, the single most important piece of business still to be acted upon.

(A) still to be acted upon
(B) being still to be acted upon
(C) was acted upon
(D) they had not yet acted upon
(E) was still to be acted upon

Here's how to crack it: The correct answer is E. As originally written, the second clause of the sentence (the part after the comma) doesn't contain a verb. C, though grammatically correct, changes the meaning of the sentence.

RUN-ON SENTENCES

A run-on sentence consists of two complete sentences joined by a comma. Here's an example:

39. Of course they are a magnificent team, his good looks complement her innate ability to master anything.

(A) team, his good looks complement
(B) team; his good looks complement
(C) team: and his good looks complement
(D) team, consequently his good looks complement
(E) team; his good looks complementing

Here's how to crack it: The correct answer is B. In the original sentence, two complete sentences are incorrectly joined by a comma. Replacing the comma with a semicolon takes care of the problem.

CLUMSY WRITING

Sometimes the error in a sentence will simply be clumsy or redundant writing. Here's an example:

31. While working on math problems, Brenda quickly estimated and circled an approximate, if not exact, guess.

(A) an approximate, if not exact, guess
(B) an approximate guess
(C) an answer, if not exact
(D) an approximate, if not exactly an answer
(E) an answer

Here's how to crack it: The original sentence is doubly redundant. Since we are told that Brenda *estimated*, we don't need to be told that her answer was *approximate* (an estimate is approximate) or that it was *not exact* (which means the same thing as *approximate*). Choice B is more concise but still doubly redundant. The correct answer is E.

Here's another example:

34. During the boisterous party, Chris was swinging on the chandelier and shooting at light bulbs with a BB gun, and he thereby made the room dark.

(A) gun, and he thereby made the room dark
(B) gun, and therefore made the room dark
(C) gun and so the room was therefore dark
(D) gun, thereby making the room dark
(E) gun, and therefore this was making the room dark

Here's how to crack it: There's nothing really *grammatically* wrong with the original sentence. It's just awkward and wordy. The correct answer is D. Notice that it's the shortest of the choices.

PARALLELISM

Watch for parts of a sentence that are not parallel. Here's an example:

35. The ideal undergraduate curriculum teaches literature, science, and it also imparts an understanding of human civilization.

(A) and it also imparts an understanding of human civilization
(B) and imparts an understanding of human civilization
(C) imparting an understanding of human civilization
(D) and human civilization
(E) with an understanding of human civilization

Here's how to crack it: The original sentence lists three parts of an ideal curriculum, but these parts are not parallel: *Literature and science* are both simple nouns, while the underlined portion of the sentence is an entire independent clause. In any such list, all the elements must be of the same type—that is, they must be parallel. The correct answer is thus choice D.

PART FIVE

VOCABULARY

The Verbal SAT Is a Vocabulary Test

Despite ETS's talk about "scholastic aptitude" and "reasoning ability," the verbal SAT is primarily a vocabulary test. If you don't know the words on the test, you won't earn a good score. It's as simple as that.

The Princeton Review's techniques for beating the verbal SAT are intended to help you get the maximum possible mileage out of the words you do know. The bigger your vocabulary is, the more our techniques will help. But if your vocabulary is small, not even the Princeton Review will be able to do much about your score.

For this reason, it is extremely important that you get to work on your vocabulary immediately. Even if you have procrastinated until just a few days before the test, you can still improve your chances by studying this chapter in the time remaining.

Don't Memorize the Dictionary

Some students try to prepare for the SAT by sitting down with the dictionary and *reading* it. They start with the first word, *a,* and plow along—their eyelids growing heavy—until they get to, say, *agamogenesis* (a word that never has been, and never will be, tested on the SAT), and then they quit.

Some other students try to prepare for the SAT by learning only the very *hardest* words in the dictionary—words like *endogenous* and *endoblast*. Most of the popular SAT coaching books concentrate on words like this. The SAT is a test of how smart you are right? And smart people know a lot of big words right?

Forget it.

Only a tiny percentage of all the words in the English language are ever tested on the SAT. In fact, many of the same ones are tested over and over again. Virtually all of these are words you've heard before, even if you aren't sure what they mean.

There would never be a word as hard as *agamogenesis* on the SAT. Why? Because almost nobody has ever heard of it before. The SAT is a test for high-school juniors and seniors. If it tested *really* hard words, *every* kid in the country would get blown away.

What Kind of Words Does the SAT Test?

Generally speaking, the SAT tests the kind of words that an educated adult—your English teacher, for example—would know without having to look up. It tests the sort of words that you encounter in your daily reading, from a novel in English class to the daily newspaper.

We can even be a bit more specific than that. For nearly five years, we have used a computer to analyze the actual words tested on every SAT administered in the United States. Using the results of this analysis, we have compiled a vocabulary list that we call the Hit Parade. It contains the words tested most often on the SAT. These words tend to come up again and again. Your SAT vocabulary-building program should begin with them.

The Hit Parade

Well, here it is: the infamous, new and revised 1992 Princeton Review Hit Parade. Don't panic. Learning these words won't be as tedious as you think. You don't have to devour the whole list at once. Study a word in the car, in the shower, during television commercials, during dinner. Make a tape of the words and listen to it while you're jogging.

To beat the SAT you need more than a good vocabulary, but a good vocabulary is a great place to start. By learning the Hit Parade you'll be starting out in the right direction; learn this list, and you'll be learning words that you'll use long after the SAT is over.

These are the most commonly tested words on the SAT, *in order of their frequency on the exam,* weighted to reflect the frequency with which they turn up in Pam's answers. We've included short definitions to make it easier for you to learn. These definitions aren't always exactly like the ones you'll find in the dictionary; they're the definitions of the words *as they are tested on the SAT.*

Please keep in mind that these are not the *only* words you need to know for the SAT. They're just the words that have been tested most frequently in the past—words that SAT question writers tend to come back to over and over again. And remember, the words near the top of the list are more likely to turn up than the words near the bottom.

Some SATs are absolutely loaded with Hit Parade words; others don't contain as many. One of the most important things the Hit Parade will teach you is the *level* of the vocabulary on the test. Once you get a feel for this level, you'll be able to spot other possible SAT words in your reading. If you want to learn more, get a copy of our vocabulary builder, *Word Smart.* Good luck!

ostentatious showing off
contentious quarrelsome
reprove to scold; to find fault with
pessimism gloominess; a belief that the bad guys always win
cursory hasty; not thorough
profligate extremely wasteful; wildly extravagant
miser someone who hoards money
jocular joking
fracas uproar; brawl
caricature a satiric portrait or representation
corroborate to confirm
precarious dangerously unstable
expository explanatory
bolster to support; to prop up
daunt to intimidate; to discourage
apathy lack of emotion or interest
ambiguous having more than one meaning; vague
fervent passionate
vagrant a wandering homeless person; a tramp
undermine to weaken; to wear away the foundation of
oblivious unaware; unconscious
indifferent not caring one way or the other; lacking a preference; neutral
obscure unclear; clouded; partially hidden; hard to understand
objective without bias (*as opposed to subjective*)
revere to worship; to honor
discriminate to differentiate; to make a clear distinction; to see the difference
embellish to add details; to exaggerate
denounce to speak out against; to condemn
innovate to be creative; to introduce something new
stagnant not moving
candid honest; frank
impartial unbiased; neutral
discern to distinguish one thing from another
vulnerable capable of being harmed
hypocritical insincere
eccentric odd; unusual; quirky
disdain contempt; intense dislike
abstract theoretical; lacking substance (*the opposite of concrete*)
valid founded on fact or evidence
subtle not obvious; hard to spot
enigma mystery

inevitable unavoidable; bound to happen
inferred derived by reasoning; implied, as a conclusion
diverse varied
articulate speaking well
apprehensive fearful; worried
benevolent good; kind-hearted; generous
virulent very harmful (*like a virus*)
pious (piety) deeply religious
skeptical doubting
provincial narrow-minded; unsophisticated
resignation acceptance of a situation (*secondary meaning*)
illuminate to light up; make clear
resolution (resolve) determination (*also: the solution of a problem*)
servile overly submissive; cringing; like a servant
diligent hard-working
refute to disprove
anarchy lack of government; chaos
miser one who saves greedily
discord disagreement
inclined tending toward one direction
uniform constant; without variety
perceptive having keen understanding; discerning
superficial shallow; on the surface only
lucid (elucidate) clear; easy to understand
immune safe from harm; protected
aesthetic concerned with art or beauty (*not the same as ascetic*)
prodigal extravagant; wasteful
assess to estimate the value of; to measure
deter to prevent, especially by threatening
complacent smug; self-satisfied; overly confident
contempt disdain; hatred
eloquent speaking well; articulate
virtue moral excellence
vital essential; necessary
guile cunning; deceitfulness (*not the same as guilt*)
biased prejudiced; not neutral
censor to delete objectionable matter (*not the same as censure*)
monotonous without variety; tiresomely uniform
trivial unimportant; insignificant
profound (profundity) deep; insightful
enhance to improve; to augment
phenomenon an observable fact or occurrence

enduring lasting
advocate to speak in favor of; to support
solitude the state of being alone
tentative temporary; not final
contemporary living at the same time; modern
provocative (provoke) exciting; attracting attention
adversary an opponent; enemy
gravity (grave) seriousness (*secondary meaning*)
banal common; dull; ordinary
depravity moral corruption
temper to moderate; to soften (*secondary meaning*)
censure to blame; to criticize (*not the same as censor*)
extol to praise
indulgent pampering oneself; satisfying one's own desires
erratic irregular; without direction
insipid bland; boring; tasteless
euphony pleasant sound
antagonism opposition; hostility; resistance
arbitrary subject to individual judgment
austere severe; without frills
expedite (expedient) to make faster or easier
heresy an opinion violently opposed to established beliefs
compromise to settle by concession or surrender
condescend to talk down to
fallacious (fallacy) false; untrue
intangible abstract; not capable of being touched or felt
arrogant acting superior to others; snooty
compatible able to co-exist; harmonious
dubious doubtful
solicit to ask for; to seek
elusive (elude) tough to catch; hard to pin down
facilitate to make easier; to help
static stationary; not moving (*not the same as radio fuzz*)
ironic satiric; unexpected
irrational unreasonable; unpredictable
dogmatic stubbornly opinionated
flagrant shocking; outstandingly bad
frivolous not serious; trivial; silly
taciturn quiet; saying little
infamous notorious; scandalous
redundant repetitive; unnecessary; superfluous
authoritarian like a dictator

exhaustive thorough; complete
reticent quiet; uncommunicative; taciturn
fervor passion; zeal; great enthusiasm
scanty inadequate; minimal
dispassionate free from passion or spirit
pragmatic practical
didactic instructive
deference (defer) a show of respect
alleviate to lighten or relieve
vacillate to waiver between choices
endorse to approve of; to give support to
conspicuous easily seen; out in the open
negligence carelessness; neglect; indifference
ephemeral short-lived; fleeting; transitory
relegate to dismiss; to an inferior position
futile hopeless; worthless; useless
condone to forgive; to overlook
tranquility calmness
dissent disagreement
conciliate to soothe; to end a dispute; to reconcile
incessant unceasing; never ending
disparity inequality; different
disparage to speak badly of; to belittle
conventional ordinary; customary; normal; traditional
rigor harshness or severity
profuse flowing freely; generous; excessive
expedient useful for effecting a desired result
fastidious not easy to please; overly critical
prosaic uninspired; dull; banal
philanthropy a desire to help mankind
languid slow; tired; drooping; weak
astute perceptive; clever
authentic real; genuine
brevity briefness
relevant pertinent; important to know
incoherent impossible to understand; chaotic
mitigate to make milder; to make less severe
reprehensible shameful; bad
augment to add; to increase; to make bigger
engender to create; to produce
deride (derision) to ridicule; to make fun of
acclaim praise; applause; admiration

lethargic tired; languid; weak
fanatic one who is very devoted to a cause or an idea
novel new; unusual (*secondary meaning*)
solemn serious; grave
ambivalent undecided
indolence laziness
benign harmless
tedious boring; painstaking
amiable friendly
laud to praise
caustic burning; uncomplimentary
atrophy to waste away from lack of use
meander to wander randomly
instigate to start trouble
heed to obey
virtuoso an accomplished musician
predecessor the person who came before another
deplete to use up; to reduce
compliant submissive; obedient
inadvertent accidental; unintentional
acquiesce to agree finally; to go along with something
levity humor
belittle to put down; to disparage
extraneous irrelevant; extra; unnecessary
digress to stray from the subject
emulate to copy something admired; to imitate
appease to make peace with; to satisfy
sage (sagacious) a wise person
auspicious favorable; positive
universal existing or present everywhere
fickle unpredictable; capricious; whimsical
furtive secretive
remorse sadness; regret
repress to hold down
gullible overly trusting; willing to believe anything
respite a rest; a pause; a break
scrutinize to examine closely
coalesce to come together; to merge; to join
orthodox standard; commonly accepted; conventional (*not just in religion*)
innate inborn; inherited
preclude to prevent; to make impossible

efface to erase; to wipe out
marred damaged; bruised
ameliorate to make better; to improve
prodigious of enormous quantity or size
concise briefly and clearly stated
immutable unchanging; permanent
stoic indifferent to pleasure and pain; brave
innocuous harmless
credulous gullible; overly trusting
blasphemy heretical departure from accepted practice
lax careless; not diligent; relaxed
cryptic mysterious; puzzling; enigmatic
hinder to obstruct
esoteric understood only by a select few
pretentious pompous; self-important
incongruous not fitting in; out of place
unprecedented occurring for the first time; novel; never seen before
merger a joining; a uniting
pedestrian common; ordinary; banal (*secondary meaning*)
prudent careful; cautious
exemplary outstanding; setting a great example
sycophant a bootlicker; a brown noser
neutral unbiased; not taking sides; objective
rescind to repeal; to take back, formally
retract to take back (*e.g., a statement*)
fundamental essential; basic
rejuvenate to make young again
contrite apologetic; remorseful
exemplify to serve as an example of
nullify to negate; to make unimportant
vilify to speak of someone as a villain
hypothetical theoretical; for the sake of argument
nostalgic yearning for the good old days
assuage to soothe
saccharine overly sweet
stanza a section of a poem
jeopardy danger
supercilious haughty; arrogant
avarice greed
pivotal important; critical; crucial
blithe free-spirited; carefree
scrupulous careful; diligent; moral

volatile changeable; unstable; explosive
voluminous very large; spacious
peripheral on the edge; surrounding; unimportant
hedonistic pleasure-seeking; indulgent
amity friendship
benefactor a generous donor; someone who helps
apocryphal a doubtful origin; mythical
slander to defame; to speak maliciously of someone
animosity hatred
stringent strict; harsh; severe
hackneyed banal; over-used
amass to accumulate; to pile up
verbose wordy; overly talkative
trepidation fear
desecrate to profane a holy place
fortuitous accidental; happening by chance or luck
vehement urgent; passionate; forceful

How to Memorize New Words

Different people have different ways of memorizing new words. Some people find it easier to remember things if they write them down. Others find it helps to say them aloud. Many people say they can remember new things better if they review them right before they go to sleep. You should do what works best for you. Here are two methods that many Princeton Review students have found to be effective.

FLASH CARDS

You can make your own flash cards out of 3-by-5-inch index cards. Write the word on one side and the definition on the other. Then quiz yourself on the words, or practice with a friend. You can even carry a few cards around with you every day and work on them in spare moments—when you're riding the bus, for example.

One of the most important keys to memorizing new words is to start far enough in advance of the test so that you only have to learn a few each day. You'll be less likely to become confused if you tackle the Hit Parade one small chunk at a time—say, five words a day, starting with the first words on the list. You'll probably know a lot of the words already; there's no need to memorize those. Just be certain that you know each definition cold.

THE IMAGE APPROACH

The image approach involves letting each new word suggest a wild image to you, and then using that image to help you remember the word. For example, the word *enfranchise* means "to give the right to vote." (Women didn't become *enfranchised* in the United States until 1920, when the Nineteenth Amendment to the Constitution guaranteed them the right to vote in state and federal elections.) *Franchise* might suggest to you a McDonald's franchise—and you could remember the new word by imagining people lined up to vote in a McDonald's. The weirder the image the better. To give another example, the word *slake* means "to satisfy thirst." You might remember that by picturing yourself drinking an entire *lake* on a hot summer day.

Just Knowing They're There

You should also be sure that you can recognize the Hit Parade word whenever you see one, even if you can't remember what it means. Doing this is easier than you probably think. If you put any effort at all into memorizing the definitions, you'll remember the words themselves when you see them.

Why is this important? Because Hit Parade words make very good guesses when you're stumped on difficult verbal questions.

Other Words

As important as Hit Parade words are, they aren't the only words on the SAT. As you go about learning the Hit Parade, you should also try to incorporate other new words into your vocabulary. The Hit Parade will help you determine what *kinds* of words you should be learning—good solid words that are fairly difficult but not impossible.

One very good source of SAT words is the "Week in Review" section of the Sunday *New York Times*. If you live in an area where you can get the *Times* on Sunday, it's probably worth the effort to buy it and read it. (You'll learn something about the world as well.) Other well-written general publications are also good sources of SAT words.

What Do They Mean?

Before you can memorize the definition of a word you come across in your reading, you have to find out what it means. You'll need a dictionary for that. Pam uses two dictionaries in writing the SAT: the *American Heritage Dictionary* and the *Webster's New Collegiate Dictionary*. You should own a copy of one or the other. (You'll use it in college too—it will be a good investment.)

When you come across a new word, write it down, look it up, and remember it. You may want to start a special notebook for new words—you own SAT minidictionary. Keep in mind that most words have more than one definition. The dictionary will list these in order of their frequency, from the most common usage to the most obscure. ETS will sometimes trip you up by testing the third or fourth definition of a familiar-sounding word. For example, the word *pedestrian* turns up repeatedly on the SAT. When ETS uses it, though, it never uses it to mean a person on foot—the definition of pedestrian you're probably familiar with. It uses it to mean "common; ordinary; banal"—a secondary definition. Very often, when you see *easy* words on *hard* SAT questions, ETS is testing a second, third or fourth definition that you may not be familiar with.

Roots

Most of the words in the English language were borrowed from other languages at some point in our history. Many of the words you use every day contain bits and pieces of ancient Greek and Latin words that meant something similar. These bits and pieces are called "roots." The dictionary describes each word's roots by giving its *etymology*—a minihistory of where it came from. For example, the *American Heritage Dictionary* gives the following etymology for *apathy*, the sixteenth word on the Hit Parade: "Greek *apatheia*, for *apathés*, without feeling: *A*-(without) + *pathos*, feeling." Similar-sounding words, like *pathos*, *pathetic*, *sympathy*, and *empathy*, are all related and all have to do with feeling.

Many people say the best way to prepare for the SAT is simply to learn a lot of roots. Students who know a lot of roots, they say, will be able to "translate" any unfamiliar words they encounter on test. There is some truth in this; the more you know about etymology, the easier it will be to build your vocabulary. But roots can also mislead you. The hardest words on the SAT are often words that *seem* to contain a familiar root, but actually do not. For example, *audacity*, a hard word sometimes tested on the SAT, means "boldness or daring." It has nothing to do with *sound*, even though it *seems* to contain the root *aud-* from a Latin word meaning "to hear" (as in *audio*, *audiovisual*, or *auditorium*).

Still, learning about roots can be very helpful—if you do it properly. You should think of roots *not* as a code that will enable you to decipher unknown words on the SAT, but as a tool for learning new words and making associations between them. For example, *eloquent*, *colloquial*, *circumlocution*, and *eulogy* all contain the Latin root *loqu/loc*, which means to "speak." Knowing the root and recognizing it in these words will make it easier for you to memorize all of them. You should think of roots as a tool for helping you organize your thoughts as you build your vocabulary.

The worst thing you can do is try to memorize roots all by themselves, apart from words they appear in. In the first place, it can't be done. In the second place, it won't help.

The Root Parade

Just as the Hit Parade is a list of the most frequently tested words on the SAT in order of their frequency, the Root Parade is a list of the roots that show up most often in SAT vocabulary words. You may find it useful in helping you organize your vocabulary study. Don't try to memorize these roots. In approaching the Root Parade, you should focus on the *words*, using the roots simply as reminders to help you learn or remember the meanings. When you take the SAT, you may be able to prod your memory about the meaning of a particular word by thinking of the related words that you associate with it.

As was also true with the Hit Parade, the roots on the Root Parade are presented in order of their importance on the SAT. The roots at the top of the list appear more often than the roots at the bottom. Each root is followed by a number of real SAT words that contain it. (What should you do every time you don't know the meaning of a word on the Root Parade? Look it up!) Note that roots often have several different forms. Be on the lookout for all of them.

CAP/CIP/CEIPT/CEPT/CEIV/CEIT (TAKE)

capture
intercept
receptive
recipient
incipient
perceptive
percipient
anticipate
except
exceptional
exceptionable
susceptible
deception
conception
receive
conceit
accept
emancipate
precept

GEN (birth, race, kind)

generous
generate
degenerate
regenerate
genuine
congenial
ingenious
ingenuous
ingenue
homogeneous
heterogeneous
genealogy
indigenous
congenital
gender
engender
genre
progeny

DIC/DICT/DIT (tell, say, word)

predicament
condition
dictate
dictator
abdicate
predict
contradict
addict
malediction
benediction
extradite
verdict
indict
diction
dictum

SPEC/SPIC/SPIT (look, see)

perspective
aspect
spectator
spectacle
suspect
speculation
suspicious
auspicious
spectrum
specimen
introspection
respite
conspicuous
circumspect
perspicacious

SUPER/SUR (above)

surpass
superficial
summit
superlative
supernova
supercilious
superstition
superimpose
supersede
superfluous
sovereign

TENT/TENS/TEND/TENU (stretch, thin)

tension
extend
tendency
tendon
tent
contention
distend
tenuous
attenuate
portent

TEND (stretch, thin)

tentative
contend
tendentious

TRANS (across)

transfer
transaction
transparent
transgress
transport
transform
transition
transitory
transient
transmutation
transcendent
intransigent
traduce

DOC/DUC/DAC (teach, lead)

conduct
reduce
seduce
conducive
inductee
doctrine
document
docile
didactic
indoctrinate
traduce
induce

CO/CON/COM (with, together)

company
collaborate
conjugal
congeal
congenial
convivial
coalesce
contrition
commensurate
conclave
conciliate
comply
congruent

VERS/VERT (turn)

controversy
convert
revert
subvert
inversions
divert
diverse
aversion
extrovert
introvert
inadvertent
versatile
adversity

LOC/LOG/LOQU (word, speech)

eloquent
logic
apology
monologue
circumlocution
colloquial
eulogy
loquacious

LOC/LOG/LOQ (word, speech)

dialogue
prologue
epilogue
neologism
philology

SEN (feel, sense)

sensitive
sensation
sentiment
sensory
sensual
resent
consent
dissent
assent
consensus
sentry
sentinel

DE (away, down, off)

denounce
debility
defraud
decry
deplete
defame
delineate
deface
devoid
defile
desecrate
derogatory

NOM/NOUN/NOWN/NAM/NYM (name, order, rule)

name
anonymous
antonym
nominate
economy
astronomy
ignominy
renown
misnomer
nomenclature

CLA/CLO/CLU (shut, close)

closet
claustrophobia
enclose
disclose
include
conclude
exclusive
preclude
recluse
seclude
cloister

VO/VOC/VOK/VOW (call)

voice
vocal
provocative
advocate
equivocate
vocation
convoke
vociferous
irrevocable
evocative
revoke

MAL (bad)

malicious
malady
dismal
malfunction
malign
malcontent
malodorous
malefactor
malevolent
malediction
maladroit

FRA/FRAC/FRAG (break)

fracture
fraction
fragment
fragmentary
fragile
frail
refraction
refractory
infraction
infringe
fractious

OB (against)

objective
obsolete
oblique
obscure
obstruct
obstinate
obliterate
oblivious
obsequious
obfuscate

SUB (under)

- submissive
- subsidiary
- subjugation
- subliminal
- subdue
- subordinate
- sublime
- subtle
- subversion
- subterfuge

AB (from, away)

- abandon
- abhor
- abnormal
- abstract
- abdicate
- abstain
- absolve
- abstemious
- abstruse
- abrogate

GRESS/GRAD (step)

- progress
- regress
- retrogress
- retrograde
- gradual
- degrade
- downgrade
- aggressor
- digress
- transgress

SEC/SEQU (follow)

- second
- sequel
- sequence
- consequence
- inconsequential
- execute
- subsequent
- prosecute
- obsequious

PRO (much, for, a lot)

- prolific
- profuse
- propitious
- prodigious
- profligate
- prodigal
- protracted
- proclivity
- propensity
- prodigy

QUE/QUIS (ask, seek)

- inquire
- question
- request
- quest
- query
- querulous
- acquire
- acquisitive
- acquisition
- exquisite

SACR/SANCT/SECR (sacred)

sacred
sacrifice
sanctuary
sanctify
sanction
sacrosanct
consecrate
desecrate
execrable
sacrament

SCRIB/SCRIP (write)

scribble
describe
script
postscript
prescribe
proscribe
ascribe
inscribe
circumscribe

PATHY/PAS/PAT (feeling)

apathy
sympathy
empathy
antipathy
passionate
compassion
compatible
dispassionate
impassive

DIS/DIF (not)

dissonance
discrepancy
dispassionate
disparate

DIS/DIF (not)

disdain
dissuade
dismay
diffident
disparage

CIRCU (around)

circumference
circulation
circumstance
circumnavigate
circuitous
circumscribe
circumvent
circumlocutory

PART SIX

TAKING THE SAT

Tick, Tick, Tick . . .

The SAT is a week away. What should you do?

First of all, you should practice the techniques we have taught you on real SATs. If you don't own any real SATs, go buy a copy of *10 SATs* at your local bookstore. You should also take and score the diagnostic test at the back of this book. *The practice tests in most other SAT preparation books won't help you; they aren't enough like real SATs.* If you have more than a week, you can also order a copy of *5 SATs* directly from the College Board. Here's the address:

College Board Publications
Box 886
New York, NY 10101

You can also order by phone. The number is 800/323-7155. Visa and MasterCard are accepted. Copies of *5 SATs* are $7 each for the 1989 and 1991 editions.

You can also order the most recent edition of *10 SATs.* The price is $11.95.

A Good School Project

If your school's guidance office doesn't have a complete collection of released SATs, putting one together might make a good project for your student council. More than 50 real SATs have been made public since New York's Truth-in-Testing Law went into effect in 1980. Tracking all of them down will take some work, but studying real SATs is one of the best ways to improve SAT scores. The College Board has published collections of real tests called *4 SATs*, *5 SATs*, *6 SATs*, and *10 SATs*. Only recent editions of *5 SATs* and *10 SATs* are still available from the College Board. You might look for them in your own school library or in the libraries of other schools. In addition, other tests have been released through ETS's Question and Answer Service. Extra copies of these can sometimes be ordered from the College Board. Here are the address and phone number of the board's headquarters:

The College Board
45 Columbus Avenue
New York, NY 10023-6917
(212) 713-8000

Getting Psyched

The SAT is a big deal, but you don't want to let it scare you. Sometimes students get so nervous about doing well that they freeze up on the test and murder their scores. The best thing to do is to think of the SAT as a game. It's a game you can get good at, and beating the test can be fun. When you go into the test center, just think about all those poor slobs who don't know how to eyeball geometry diagrams.

The best way to keep from getting nervous is to build confidence in yourself and in your ability to remember and use our techniques. When you take practice tests, time yourself exactly as you will be timed on the real SAT. Develop a sense of how long 30 minutes is and how much time you can afford to spend on cracking difficult problems. If you know ahead of time what to expect, you won't be as nervous.

Of course, taking a real SAT is much more nerve-racking than taking a practice test. Prepare yourself ahead of time for the fact that 30 minutes will seem to go by a lot faster on a real SAT than it did on your practice tests.

It's all right to be nervous; the point of being prepared is to keep from panicking.

Should You Sleep for 36 Hours?

Some guidance counselors tell their students to get a lot of sleep the night before the SAT. This probably isn't a good idea. If you aren't used to sleeping 12 hours a night, doing so will just make you groggy for the test. The same goes for going out and drinking a lot of beer: People with hangovers are not good test-takers.

A much better idea is to get up early each morning for the entire week before the test and do your homework before school. This will get your brain accustomed to functioning at that hour of the morning. You want to be sharp at test time.

Before you go to sleep the night before the test, spend an hour or so reviewing the Hit Parade. This will make the list fresh in your mind in the morning. You might also practice estimating some angles and looking for direct solutions on real SAT math problems. You don't want top exhaust yourself, but it will help to brush up.

Furthermore

Here are a few pointers for test day and beyond:

1. You are supposed to take identification to your test center. ETS's definition of acceptable ID is "Any official document bearing the candidate's name and photograph, or name and description (driver's license, school ID, or current passport)."

   If you find yourself at the test center with *unacceptable* ID (one with name and signature only) you *should* be admitted anyway. According to the ETS rule book, you should be asked to fill out an identification verification form and then be allowed to take the test. If you really do turn out to be yourself, your scores will count.

   If you arrive without any identification at all, a literal-minded supervisor could turn you away. You can keep this from happening by quickly writing out a brief description of yourself and signing it. Your description probably won't count as "acceptable" ID, but it is ID and should allow you to take the test. You might also ask permission to call home and have someone drop off your driver's license while you're taking the test. That way you can have everything cleared up before you leave.

2. The only outside materials you are allowed to use on the test are No. 2 pencils (take four or five them, all sharp) and a wristwatch (an absolute necessity). Digital watches are best, but if it has a beeper, make sure you turn it off. If you have a calculator watch, be prepared to have it confiscated. Proctors should also confiscate other calculators, pocket dictionaries, word lists, portable computers, and the like. Proctors have occasionally also confiscated stopwatches and travel clocks. Technically, you should be permitted to use these, but you can never tell with some proctors. Take a watch and avoid the hassles.

3. Some proctors allow students to bring food into the test room; others don't. Take a soda and a candy bar with you and see what happens. If you don't flaunt them, they probably won't be confiscated. Save them until you're about halfway through the test. Remember that it takes about ten minutes for sugar to work its way to your tired brain. If the proctor yells at you, surrender them cheerfully and continue with the test.

4. You are going to be sitting in the same place for more that three hours, so make sure your desk isn't broken or unusually uncomfortable. If you are left-handed, ask for a left-handed desk. (The center may not have one, but it won't hurt to ask.) If the sun is in your eyes, ask to move. If the room is too dark, ask someone to turn on the lights. Don't hesitate to speak up. Some proctors just don't know what they're doing.

5. *Before* you start the test, make sure your booklet is complete. You can quickly turn through all the pages without reading them. Booklets sometimes contain printing errors that make some pages impossible to read. Last year more than ten thousand students had to retake the SAT because of a printing error in their booklets. This would not have happened had the students checked their booklets. Find out ahead of time and demand a new booklet if yours is defective. Also, check your answer sheet to make sure it isn't flawed.

6. You should get a five-minute break after the first hour of the test. Ask for it if your proctor doesn't give it to you. You should be allowed to go to the bathroom at this time. You should also be allowed to take a one-minute break at your desk at the end of the second hour. The breaks are a very good idea. They let you clear your head. Insist on them.

7. ETS allows you to cancel your SAT scores. Unfortunately, you can no longer cancel only your math, verbal, or TSWE score—it's all or nothing. You can cancel scores at the test center by asking your proctor for a "Cancellation Request Form." If you decide to cancel later on, you can do so by sending a telegram to ETS. You must do this before the Wednesday following the test.

   We recommend that you *not* cancel your scores unless you know you made so many errors, or left out so many questions, that your score will be unacceptably low. Don't cancel your scores because you have a bad feeling—students frequently have an exaggerated sense of how many mistakes they made, and it's possible you did much better than you realize.

8. Make sure you darken all your responses before the test is over. At the same time, erase any extraneous marks on the answer sheet. Seriously: A stray mark in the margin of your answer sheet can result in correct responses being marked wrong.

9. Don't assume that your test was scored correctly. Send away for ETS's Question and Answer Service. It costs money, but it's worth it. You'll get back copies of your answer sheet, a test booklet, and an answer key. Check your answers against the key and complain if you think you've been misscored. (Don't throw away the test booklet you receive from the Question and Answer Service. If you're planning to take the SAT again, save it for practice. If you're not, give it to your guidance counselor or school library.)

10. You deserve to take your SAT under good conditions. If you feel that your test was not administered properly (the high school band was practicing outside the window, your proctor hovered over your shoulder during the test) call us immediately at 1-800-333-0369 and we'll tell you what you can do about it.

PART SEVEN

ANSWER KEY TO DRILLS

Chapter 4

DRILL 1

(pages 43–45)

The worst mistake you can make on an analogy is to decide two words are unrelated when in fact they are related. Be careful.

4. To be incensed is to be very annoyed.
5. To babble is to speak foolishly.
6. A convict receives a sentence.
7. Unrelated.
8. Unrelated. Fuel is related to, say, an engine, but not to motion.
9. A sprint requires speed.
10. Unrelated. Lunatics are crazy, but they aren't necessarily violent.
11. Unrelated.
12. To strike is to refuse to work.
13. A building rests on a foundation. "A building has a foundation" isn't specific enough.
14. Muttering frustrates a listener. This is a weak relationship.
15. To sharpen a knife is to improve it. This is a good, solid relationship that is a little difficult to express in a sentence.
16. Victory is the successful outcome of a battle. This is a weak relationship.
17. Unrelated.
18. You play a cello with a bow.
19. A minute is a unit of time.
20. A snack is a tiny meal.
21. An audience attends a concert.
22. To eavesdrop is to listen secretly.
23. Fervor is a lot of emotion.
24. To emend is to correct or improve a text.
25. Pacifism is hatred of war.
26. A tirade is an angry speech. "A tirade is a kind of speech" isn't specific enough.
27. Unrelated.
28. A rebel is characterized by defiance.
29. A habitablc placc could have occupants.
30. To fade is to begin to disappear.
31. Forestry is the study (or care, or science) of trees.
32. To focus is to sharpen or improve an image. "You focus an image" isn't specific enough, since it doesn't reveal what focus means.
33. To defame is to ruin a reputation.
34. A bill is a request for payment. Payment satisfies a bill.
35. To abuse is to annoy greatly. "To abuse is to annoy" isn't good enough; the two words aren't synonyms.

36. To dwindle is to decrease in size.
37. To acquit is to find a defendant not guilty.
38. To be skeptical is to have doubt.
39. Unrelated.
40. An illicit act is without legality.
41. A casino is a place for gambling.
42. Unrelated.
43. A carol is a kind of song.
44. A boundary is the edge of a territory.
45. To guzzle is to drink quickly.
46. Unrelated.
47. A leap is a movement in dance. Not a strong relationship.
48. A pony is kept in a stable.
49. An ointment relieves something painful. Not a strong relationship.
50. A gallery displays the works of a painter.

DRILL 2
(*page 55*)

Here's the proper difficulty ranking of each group of words. A number 1 is easiest; a number 5 is hardest.

GROUP A
1. striped : lines
2. scribble : penmanship
3. urban : city
4. preamble : statute
5. banality : bore

GROUP B
1. trees : forest
2. mural : painting
3. finale : opera
4. taste : connoisseur
5. mendicant : beggar

GROUP C
1. word : sentence
2. mirror : reflection
3. reflex : involuntary
4. garrulous : speaker
5. arson : conflagration

GROUP D
1. fins : aquatic
2. novel : literature
3. loyal : devotion
4. threadbare : clothing
5. insurrectionist : docile

Group D was a tough call. Review these rearranged groups to get a feel for the progression of difficulty on the SAT.

Chapter 5

DRILL 1

(page 71)

Here are the six sentences in the reading passage that contain trigger words:

First Paragraph: "There is more than one kind of innovation at work in the region, of course, *but* I have chosen to focus on three related patterns of family behavior."

Third Paragraph: "They continue to migrate *but* on a reduced scale, often modifying their schedules of migration to allow children to finish the school year."

Fourth Paragraph: "The greatest amount of change from pattern I, *however,* is found in pattern III families, who no longer migrate at all."

"They not only work full time *but* may, in addition, return to school."

"*Although* these women are in the minority among residents of the region, they serve as role models for others, causing ripples of change to spread in their communities."

Fifth Paragraph: "*But* some of the women decided to stay at their jobs after the family's distress was over."

DRILL 2

(page 80)

Here are the same sentences and phrases again, with disputable words in italics:

(A) leads politicians to place *complete* reliance upon the results of opinion polls
(B) Baker's ideas had *no* influence on the outcome.
(C) Foreign languages should *never* be studied.
(D) *All* financial resources should be directed toward improving the work environment.
(E) the belief that nature is inscrutable and *cannot* be described

DRILL 3

(page 81)

Here are the same sentences and phrases again, with hard-to-dispute words in italics:

(A) New research *may* lead to improvements in manufacturing technology.
(B) *Not all* workers respond the same way to instruction.

(C) Improved weather was *but one of the many* factors that led to the record crop.
(D) *Most* scientists believe that continued progress is possible.
(E) Everyone *cannot* expect to be happy *all* the time.

Chapter 7

DRILL 1

(pages 113–114)

1.	financial monetary economic	
2.	hurt ravaged damaged	disappear end vanish
3.	boring unexciting lifeless	liveliness excitement style

DRILL 2

(pages 114–115)

1. Pam's answer is C. Choices A, B, E, and possibly D are all Joe Bloggs attractors, because they remind him of "critics," "book," "brilliant," and "author."

2. Pam's answer is B. Each of the other answer choices contains *one* word that makes sense in the sentence. Be careful!

3. Pam's answer is B. Many hard words here.

DRILL 3

(page 118)

GROUP A
1. interrupted
2. force..lacking
3. inevitable..mitigates

GROUP B
1. detect..overlook
2. postulate..explore
3. paradigm

GROUP C
1. vague..traditions
2. represent..diversity
3. certitudes..elusive

GROUP D
1. increased..inadequate
2. gullible..distant
3. parsimony..chary of

Chapter 9

DRILL 1

(page 143)

1. 109
2. 38
3. -3
4. 10
5. 15

DRILL 2

(page 144)

1. $(6 \times 57) + (6 \times 18)$
2. $51(52 + 53 + 54)$
3. $ab + ac - ad$
4. $x(y - z)$
5. $c(ab + xy)$

DRILL 3

(page 149)

1. 3
2. $\frac{31}{5}$
3. $-1\frac{4}{15}$ or $-\frac{19}{15}$
4. $\frac{1}{15}$
5. $\frac{6}{7}$
6. $\frac{2}{25}$
7. $\frac{4}{9}$

DRILL 4

(page 155)

1. 1.831
2. 14.58
3. 15
4. 0.005

DRILL 5

(page 159)

	Fraction	*Decimal*	*Percentage*
1.	$\frac{1}{2}$	0.5	50%
2.	$\frac{3}{1}$	3.0	300%
3.	$\frac{1}{200}$	0.005	0.5%
4.	$\frac{1}{3}$	0.3333	$33\frac{1}{3}\%$

Chapter 11

DRILL

(page 205)

1. 0.4
2. a little bit more than 5 or a little bit less than 6
3. 2.8
4. a little bit more than 0.85
5. A little bit more than 4
6. x = about 30°
   y = about 125°
   z = about 25°
   yz is about 16
   xz is about 30 (a little *less* than 32!)

   (None of these angle measurements is exact, but remember, you don't have to be exact when you guesstimate. Even a very rough guesstimation will enable you to eliminate one or two answer choices.)

PART EIGHT

DIAGNOSTIC TEST

The best way to learn our techniques for cracking the SAT is to practice them. The following diagnostic test will give you a chance to do that.

The diagnostic test was designed to be as much like a real SAT as possible. It contains two verbal sections, two math sections, a Test of Standard Written English, and an experimental section. Our questions test the same concepts that are tested on real SATs.

Since one of the sections in this test is experimental, none of the questions in it count toward your final score. The actual SAT will have an experimental section—verbal *or* math—that ETS now euphemistically terms an "equating section."

Some of the questions in the experimental section may have two answers or possibly no answers at all. Questions in this section may all be very easy or may all be incredibly tough. Furthermore, questions in this section may not be arranged in order of difficulty. If a section on your SAT seems bizarre, don't lose faith. Finish the section and start fresh on the next one. The weird section was probably experimental.

Sometimes it's easy to tell when a section is experimental; at other times it's not. If you *know* a section is experimental, relax on it, since it won't affect your score. If you can't tell which section is experimental, you'll have to treat them all like real sections.

When you take the diagnostic test, you should try to take it under conditions that are as much like real testing conditions as possible. Take it in a room where you won't be disturbed, and have someone else time you. (It's too easy if you time yourself.) You can give yourself a brief break halfway through, but don't stop for longer than five minutes or so. To put yourself in the proper frame of mind, you might take it on a Saturday morning.

After taking our test, you'll have a very good idea of what taking the real SAT will be like. In fact, we've found that students' scores on Princeton Review's diagnostic tests correspond very closely to the scores they earn on real SATs.

The answers to the questions and a scoring guide can be found on pages 319, 320, and 321. The answer sheet is at the back of the book.

If you have any questions about the diagnostic test, the SAT, ETS, or The Princeton Review, give us a call, toll-free, at 1-800-955-5585.

The following sample test was written by the authors and is not an actual SAT. The directions and format were used by permission of Educational Testing Service. This permission does not constitute review or endorsement by Educational Testing Service or the College Board of this publication as a whole or of any sample questions or testing information it may contain.

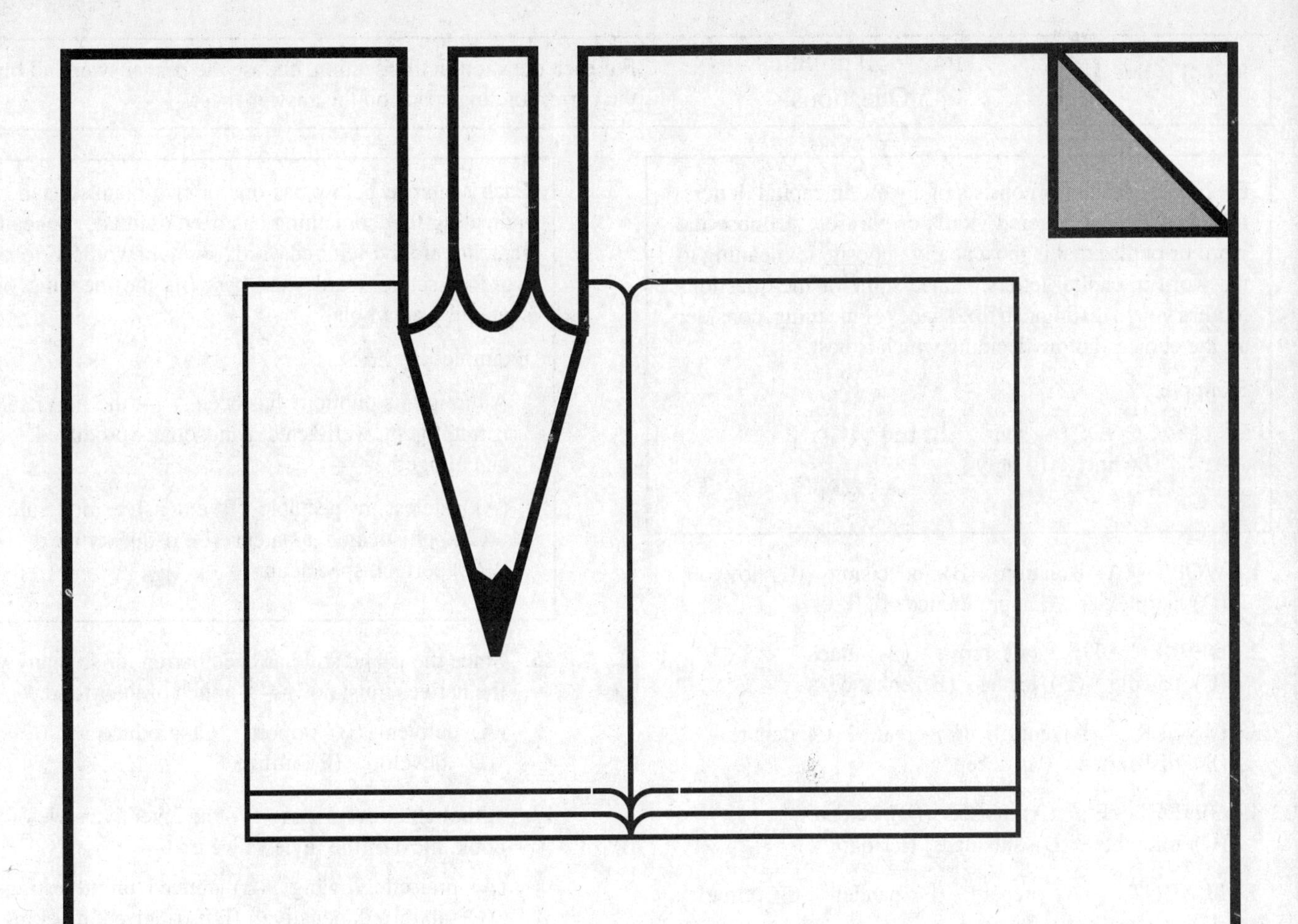

THE PRINCETON REVIEW DIAGNOSTIC

SCHOLASTIC APTITUDE TEST

SECTION 1 — Time—30 minutes, 45 Questions

For each question in this section, choose the best answer and blacken the corresponding space on the answer sheet.

Each question below consists of a word in capital letters, followed by five lettered words or phrases. Choose the word or phrase that is most nearly opposite in meaning to the word in capital letters. Since some of the questions require you to distinguish fine shades of meaning, consider all the choices before deciding which is best.

Example:

GOOD: (A) sour (B) bad (C) red (D) hot (E) ugly

(A) ● (C) (D) (E)

1. WOE : (A) isolation (B) indecision (C) joy (D) perplexity (E) preference

2. DEPRECIATE : (A) prove (B) attack (C) dawdle (D) locate (E) enhance

3. LINGER : (A) enroll (B) create (C) depart (D) dishearten (E) accept

4. OBJECTIVE : (A) biased (B) sincere (C) tolerable (D) subdued (E) dark

5. FLAUNT : (A) prepare (B) pander (C) remark (D) request (E) cover

6. FLAMBOYANCE : (A) preference (B) dullness (C) shame (D) vitality (E) formality

7. ARTICULATE : (A) definite (B) scholarly (C) bright (D) withdrawn (E) unclear

8. LUSH : (A) barren (B) insecure (C) harmful (D) extreme (E) astronomical

9. RECLUSIVE : (A) hopeful (B) supportive (C) unfaithful (D) sociable (E) aggressive

10. MEANDER : (A) travel directly (B) insinuate (C) dance gracefully (D) unblock (E) immerse

11. FLOUT : (A) make irrelevant (B) scatter (C) honor (D) overlook (E) remain innocent

12. EMPIRICAL : (A) farsighted (B) theoretical (C) completed (D) radical (E) farcical

13. SULLY : (A) punctuate (B) suffer (C) purify (D) acquiesce (E) facilitate

14. EVANESCENT : (A) permanent (B) silent (C) adroit (D) habitual (E) restless

15. PARSIMONIOUS : (A) impartial (B) relaxed (C) munificent (D) corpulent (E) courageous

Each sentence below has one or two blanks, each blank indicating that something has been omitted. Beneath the sentence are five lettered words or sets of words. Choose the word or set of words that best fits the meaning of the sentence as a whole.

Example:

Although its publicity has been ——, the film itself is intelligent, well-acted, handsomely produced, and altogether ——.

(A) tasteless..respectable (B) extensive..moderate (C) sophisticated..amateur (D) risqué..crude (E) perfect..spectacular

16. Since the island soil has been barren for so many years the natives must now —— much of their food.

(A) deliver (B) import (C) produce (D) develop (E) utilize

17. Although a few critics —— the inventive style of the book, most of the reviews were ——.

(A) praised..glowing (B) noticed..uninteresting (C) abhorred..negative (D) criticized..mocking (E) applauded..unfavorable

18. Since Jenkins neither —— nor defends either management or the striking workers, both sides admire his journalistic ——.

(A) criticizes..acumen (B) attacks..neutrality (C) confronts..aptitude (D) dismisses..flair (E) promotes.. integrity

19. Some anthropologists claim that a few apes have been taught a rudimentary sign language, but skeptics argue that the apes are only —— their trainers.

(A) imitating (B) condoning (C) instructing (D) acknowledging (E) belaboring

20. It is ironic that the —— insights of the great thinkers are repeated so often that they have become mere ——.

(A) original..clichés
(B) banal..beliefs
(C) dubious..habits
(D) philosophical..questions
(E) abstract..ideas

GO ON TO THE NEXT PAGE

Select the word of set of words that best completes each of the following sentences.

. The most frustrating periods of any diet are the inevitable ——, when weight loss —— if not stops.

(A) moods..accelerates (B) feasts..halts (C) holidays..contracts (D) plateaus..slows (E) meals..ceases

2. Since the author's unflattering references to her friends were so ——, she was surprised that her —— were recognized.

(A) laudatory..styles
(B) obvious..anecdotes
(C) oblique..allusions
(D) critical..eulogies
(E) apparent..motives

3. Mark was intent on maintaining his status as first in his class; because even the smallest mistakes infuriated him, he reviewed all his papers —— before submitting them to his teacher.

(A) explicitly (B) perfunctorily (C) honestly (D) mechanically (E) assiduously

4. The subtleties of this novel are evident not so much in the character —— as they are in its profoundly —— plot structure.

(A) assessment..eclectic
(B) development..trite
(C) portrayal..aesthetic
(D) delineation..intricate
(E) illustration..superficial

5. Since many disadvantaged individuals view their situations as —— as well as intolerable, their attitudes are best described as ——.

(A) squalid..obscure
(B) unpleasant..bellicose
(C) acute.. sanguine
(D) immutable..resigned
(E) political..perplexed

Each question below consists of a r... phrases, followed by five lettered pair... Select the lettered pair that best expres... similar to that expressed in the original pa...

Example:

YAWN : BOREDOM :: (A) dream : sleep
(B) anger : madness (C) smile : amusement
(D) face : expression (E) impatience : rebellion

26. SHIP : OCEAN :: (A) fish : gill (B) plane : air (C) child : bath (D) camel : water (E) car : passengers

27. WRESTLER : STRENGTH :: (A) goalie : skill (B) dancer : speed (C) marathoner : endurance (D) hiker : agility (E) fisherman : luck

28. BOTANY : PLANTS :: (A) agriculture : herbs (B) astronomy : stars (C) philosophy : books (D) anthropology : religion (E) forestry : evergreens

29. CENSUS : POPULATION :: (A) catalog : pictures (B) inventory : supplies (C) detonation : explosion (D) dictionary : words (E) election : tally

30. TAPESTRY : THREAD :: (A) pizza : pie (B) mosaic : tiles (C) ruler : divisions (D) computer : switch (E) car : engine

31. CONSTELLATION : STARS :: (A) earth : moon (B) center : circle (C) archipelago : islands (D) rain : water (E) maverick : herd

32. FODDER : HORSE :: (A) gas : automobile (B) wool : sheep (C) coop : poultry (D) mother : child (E) doe : deer

33. REFINE : OIL :: (A) winnow : wheat (B) harness : energy (C) mine : coal (D) mold : plastic (E) conserve : resource

34. PERSPICACIOUS : INSIGHT ::
(A) zealous : mobility
(B) audacious : hearing
(C) delicious : taste
(D) avaricious : generosity
(E) amiable : friendliness

35. VAGRANT : DOMICILE :: (A) pagan : morals (B) despot : leadership (C) arsonist : fire (D) exile : country (E) telephone : ear

GO ON TO THE NEXT PAGE

passage below is followed by questions based on its content. Answer all questions following a passage on the basis what is stated or implied in that passage.

t is easy to lose patience with science today. The stions are pressing: How dangerous is dioxin? What about w-level radiation? When will that monstrous earthquake strike California? And why can't we predict the weather better? But the evidence is often described as "inconclusive," forcing scientists to base their points of view almost as much on intuition as on science.

When historians and philosophers of science listen to this cacophony, some conclude that science may be incapable of solving all these problems any time soon. Many questions seem to defy the scientific method, an approach that works best when it examines straightforward relationships: If variable A is manipulated, what does this do to variable B? Such procedures can, of course, be very difficult in their own ways, but in experimental terms they are clean, elegant.

With the aid of Newton's laws of gravitational attraction, for instance, ground controllers can predict the path of a planetary probe with incredible accuracy. They do this by calculating, one at a time, the gravitational tugs from each of the passing planets until the probe speeds beyond the edge of the solar system. A much more difficult task is to calculate how two or three such tugs work at once. The unknowns can grow until riddles are impossibly knotty. Because of the turbulent and fickle whorls of the earth's atmosphere, for instance, scientists have struggled for centuries to predict the weather with precision.

This spectrum of explanatory power—from simple problems to those impossibly complex—has resulted in nicknames for fields of inquiry. "Hard" sciences, such as astronomy and chemistry, are said to yield precise answers, whereas "soft" ones, such as sociology and economics, admit a great degree of uncertainty.

36. The author's attitude toward those who have lost patie with science can best be described as
   (A) angry
   (B) patronizing
   (C) dismayed
   (D) confused
   (E) sympathetic

37. The author implies that when confronted with complex questions, scientists base their opinions
   (A) on theoretical foundations
   (B) more on intuition than on science
   (C) on science and intuition, in varying degrees
   (D) on observations and past experience
   (E) on experimental procedures

38. According to the passage, it can be inferred that the scientific method would work best in which of the following situations?
   (A) Predicting public reaction to a set of policy decisio
   (B) Identifying the factors which will predict a California earthquake
   (C) Predicting the amount of corn that an acre will yiel when a combination of different fertilizers is used
   (D) Determining the dangers of low-level radiation
   (E) Calculating how much a cubic centimeter of water will weigh when cooled under controlled conditior

39. The author suggests that accurately predicting the path a planetary probe is MORE difficult than
   (A) forecasting the weather
   (B) determining when an earthquake will occur
   (C) predicting economic behavior
   (D) explaining why people behave the way they do
   (E) determining the gravitational influence of one plane

40. According to the passage, hard science can be distinguished from soft science by which of the followir characteristics?
   (A) Producing more exact answers to its questions
   (B) Identifying important questions that need answers
   (C) Making significant contributions to human welfare
   (D) Creating debates about unresolved issues
   (E) Formulating theories to explain certain phenomena

GO ON TO THE NEXT PAGE

He walked through the streets of New York wearing a broad-brimmed hat, a dark business suit, a pale green satin shirt, a vest of white brocade, a huge black bow emerging from under his chin; and he carried a staff, not a cane, but an ebony staff surmounted by a bulb of solid gold. It was as if his huge body were resigned to the conventions of a prosaic civilization and its drab garments, but the oval of his stomach sallied forth, flying the colors of his inner soul.

These things were permitted to him, he thought to himself, because he was a genius. He was also president of the Architects' Guild of America. Ralston Holcombe did not subscribe to the views of his colleagues in the organization, for he was not a grubbing builder or a businessman. He was, he stated firmly, a man of ideals.

He denounced the deplorable state of American architecture. In any period of time, he declared, architects should build in the spirit of their own time and should not pick designs from the past. We could be true to history only by heeding her law, which demanded that we plant the roots of our art firmly in the reality of our own life. He decried the stupidity of erecting buildings that were Greek, Gothic, or Romanesque. Let us, he begged, abandon such unprincipled eclecticism. We are modern and must build in the style that belongs to our days. He had found that style—it was Renaissance.

He stated his reasons clearly. Inasmuch, he pointed out, as nothing of great historical importance had happened in the world since the Renaissance, we should consider ourselves still living in that period, and all the outward forms of our existence should remain faithful to the examples of the great masters of the sixteenth century.

He had no patience with the few who spoke of a modern architecture in terms quite different from his own; he ignored them; he stated that men who wanted to break with all of the past were lazy ignoramuses, and that one could not put originality above beauty. His voice trembled reverently on that last word.

He built like a composer improvising under the spur of a mystic guidance. He had sudden inspirations. He would add an enormous dome to the flat roof of a finished structure, or encrust a long vault with a gold-leaf mosaic. His clients turned pale, stuttered—and paid. His imperial personality carried him to victory in any encounter with a client's thrift; behind him stood the stern, unspoken, overwhelming assertion that he, above all others, was an Artist.

41. Which of the following titles would be the most appropriate for this passage?
(A) Ralston Holcombe, Architect for Our Times
(B) Ralston Holcombe, Spokesman for the Renaissance
(C) The Deplorable State of American Architecture
(D) A Portrait of Pomposity
(E) Inspiration in Modern Architecture

42. The author implies that Holcombe's torso
(A) is a reflection of his status as an architect
(B) provides a means of expressing his intelligence
(C) is an external symbol of his individuality
(D) overwhelms others despite his desire to conceal it
(E) represents his artistic importance

43. By "eclecticism" (line 23) the author means
(A) designing building without regard for principles
(B) creating buildings that employ styles of the past
(C) redefining previous periods of architecture
(D) ignoring historical precedents
(E) respecting the contributions of early artists

44. The author implies that the attitude of Holcombe's clients toward his "inspiration" is usually one of
(A) joy and anticipation
(B) shock and resignation
(C) discomfort and tolerance
(D) surprise and curiosity
(E) disgust and disillusionment

45. Which of the following best describes Holcombe's approach to the world of architecture?
(A) Defiant arrogance
(B) Sympathetic understanding
(C) Intrigued curiosity
(D) Respectful tolerance
(E) Enthusiastic inspiration

IF YOU FINISH BEFORE TIME IS CALLED, YOU MAY CHECK YOUR WORK ON THIS SECTION ONLY. DO NOT WORK ON ANY OTHER SECTION OF THE TEST.

STOP

SECTION 2 | Time—30 minutes 35 Questions | In this section solve each problem, using any available space on the pa for scratchwork. Then decide which is the best of the choices given a blacken the corresponding space on the answer sheet.

The following information is for your reference in solving some of the problems.

Circle of radius r: Area = πr^2; Circumference = $2\pi r$
The number of degrees of arc in a circle is 360.
The measure in degrees of a straight angle is 180.

Definitions of symbols:
= is equal to ≤ is less than or equal to
≠ is unequal to ≥ is greater than or equal to
< is less than || is parallel to
> is greater than ⊥ is perpendicular to

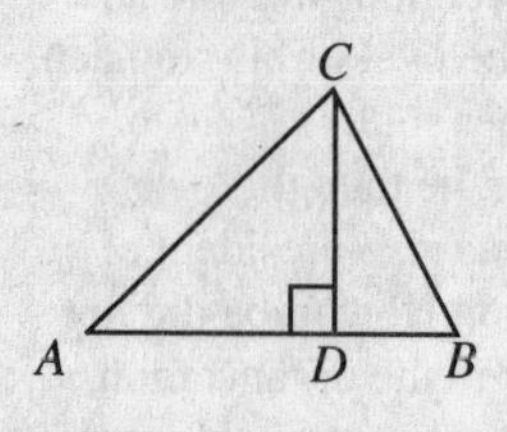

Triangle: The sum of the measures in degrees of the angles c a triangle is 180.
If $\angle CDA$ is a right angle, then

(1) area of $\Delta ABC = \frac{AB ¥ CD}{2}$

(2) $AC^2 = AD^2 + DC^2$

Note: Figures that accompany problems in this test are intended to provide information useful in solving the problems. They are dra as accurately as possible EXCEPT when it is stated in a specific problem that its figure is not drawn to scale. All figures lie in a pla unless otherwise indicated. All numbers used are real numbers.

1. $555,555 + (3 \times 10^5) =$

(A) 355,555
(B) 535,555
(C) 558,555
(D) 585,555
(E) 855,555

2. In which of the following patterns is the number of horizontal lines three times the number of vertical lines?

(A) 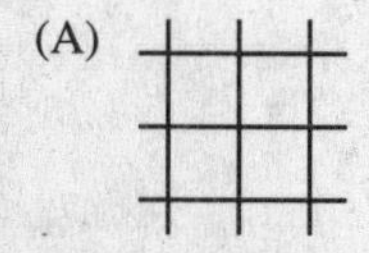 (B) (C)

(D) 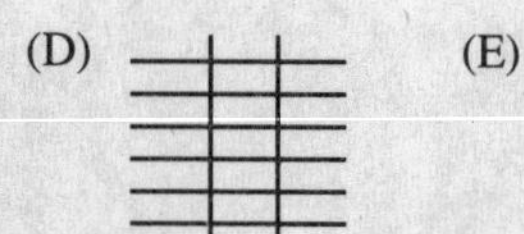 (E)

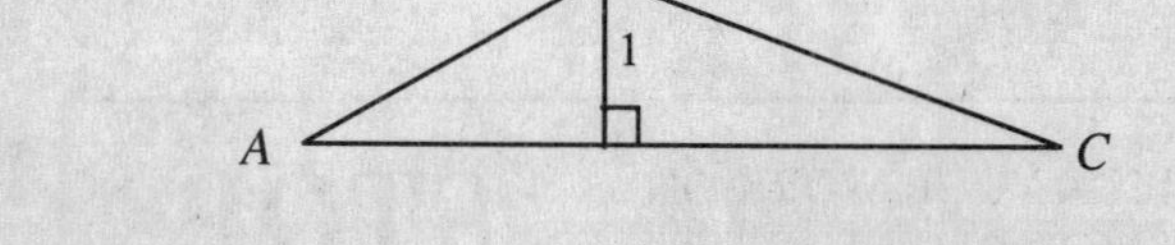

3. If $AC = 4$, what is the area of ΔABC above?

(A) $\frac{1}{2}$ (B) 2 (C) $\sqrt{7}$ (D) 4 (E) 8

4. If $x + y = z$ and $x = y$, then all of the following are true EXCEPT

(A) $2x + 2y = 2z$ (B) $x - y = 0$ (C) $x - z = y - z$

(D) $x = \frac{z}{2}$ (E) $z - y = 2x$

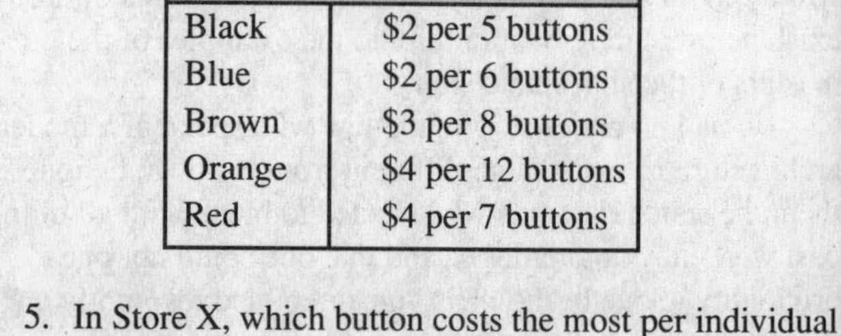

Price of Buttons in Store X	
Color	Price
Black	\$2 per 5 buttons
Blue	\$2 per 6 buttons
Brown	\$3 per 8 buttons
Orange	\$4 per 12 buttons
Red	\$4 per 7 buttons

5. In Store X, which button costs the most per individual unit?

(A) Black (B) Blue (C) Brown
(D) Orange (E) Red

6. Which of the following numbers can be written in the form $6K + 1$, where K is a positive integer?

(A) 70
(B) 71
(C) 72
(D) 73
(E) 74

7. What is the diameter of a circle with circumference 5?

(A) 25π (B) 10π (C) 5π (D) $\frac{5}{\pi}$ (E) $\frac{1}{5\pi}$

GO ON TO THE NEXT PAGE

2 2 2 2 2 2 2 2

)uestions 8-27 each consist of two quantities, one in :olumn A and one in Column B. You are to compare the wo quantities and on the answer sheet fill in oval

A if the quantity in Column A is greater;
B if the quantity in Column B is greater;
C if the two quantities are equal;
D if the relationship cannot be determined from the information given

N E RESPONSE WILL NOT BE SCORED.

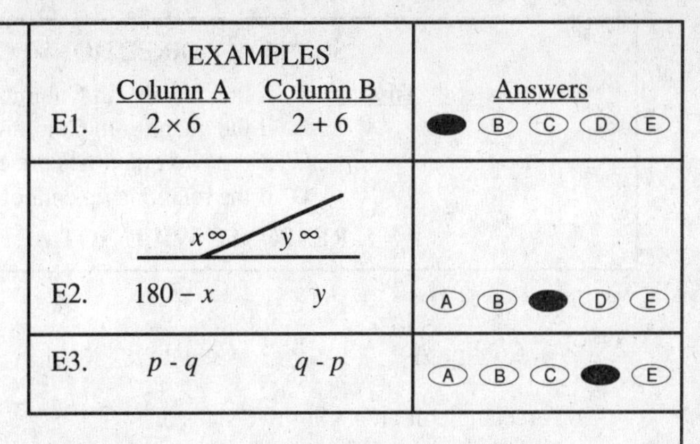

EXAMPLES

	Column A	Column B	Answers
E1.	2×6	$2 + 6$	● Ⓑ Ⓒ Ⓓ Ⓔ
E2.	$180 - x$	y	Ⓐ Ⓑ ● Ⓓ Ⓔ
E3.	$p - q$	$q - p$	Ⓐ Ⓑ Ⓒ ● Ⓔ

otes:

In certain questions, information concerning one or both of the quantities to be compared is centered above the two columns.

In a given question, a symbol that appears in both columns represents the same thing in Column A as it does in Column B.

Letters such as x, n, and k stand for real numbers.

Column A	Column B
$\frac{3}{7}$	$\frac{1}{2}$

$7a > 4b$

Column A	Column B
a	b

A cube has one red face, one white face, and the remaining faces are blue.

Column A	Column B
The number of faces that are blue	3

Michael had \$60, and lent one-third of it to Greg, who now has \$50.

Column A	Column B
Amount of money Greg originally had	Amount of money Michael now has

Column A	Column B
$\sqrt{3} + \sqrt{4}$	$\sqrt{5}$

	Column A	Column B
13.	$x + y$	90
14.	xy	$x\sqrt{y}$

The novelty clock above has hands which move at the correct speed, but counter-clockwise. The clock tells the correct time every 6 hours (at 6:00 and 12:00).

	Column A	Column B
15.	3 hrs. 15 minutes	Number of hours that have passed since 12:00

$9^n - 8^n = 1^n$

	Column A	Column B
16.	1	n

GO ON TO THE NEXT PAGE

SUMMARY DIRECTIONS FOR COMPARISON QUESTIONS

Answer: A if the quantity in Column A is greater;
B if the quantity in Column B is greater;
C if the two quantities are equal;
D if the relationship cannot be determined from the information given.

AN E RESPONSE WILL NOT BE SCORED.

	Column A	Column B

A rectangle of area 4 has two sides of length r and s, where r and s are integers.

17. r | s

List I
1
2
3
4
5

List II
2
3
4
5
6

18. The product of four different numbers from List 1 | The product of four different numbers from List 2

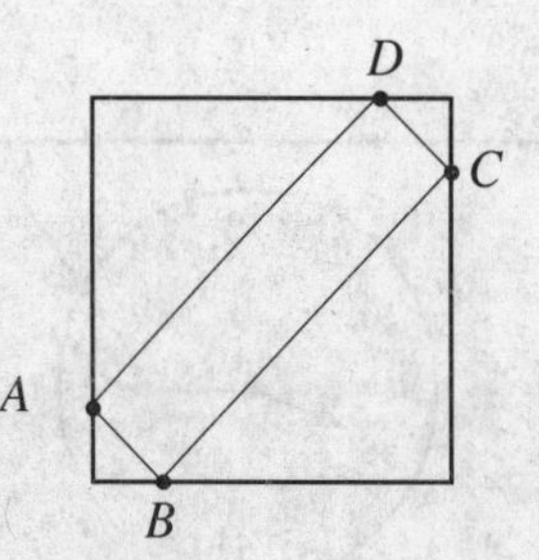

The area of the square is 25. Points A, B, C, and D are on the square.

19. 20 | Perimeter of the rectangle $ABCD$

$x = 3x + 1$

20. $-x$ | x

	Column A	Column B

x, y, and z are positive.
$x + y + z = 10$ and $x = y$

21. x | 5

22. The least even integer greater than –2 | 0

Cable lines cost $40 per 100 meters.

23. The cost in dollars of m meters of cable line. | $0.4m$

24. The number of distinct prime factors of 60 | The number of distinct prime factors of 30

25. x^2 | $(x + 1)^2$

$\frac{(a+b)}{c} = 0$

$(a + c) - b = a$

26. a | $-c$

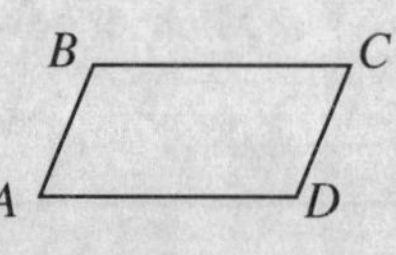

27. Area of parallelogram $ABCD$ if $AD = 1$, $CD = w$, and $\angle ADC \neq 90$ | Area of rectangle $EFGH$ if $EH = 1$ and $GH = w$

GO ON TO THE NEXT PAGE

Solve each of the remaining problems in this section using any available space for scratchwork. Then decide which is the best of the choices given and blacken the corresponding space on the answer sheet.

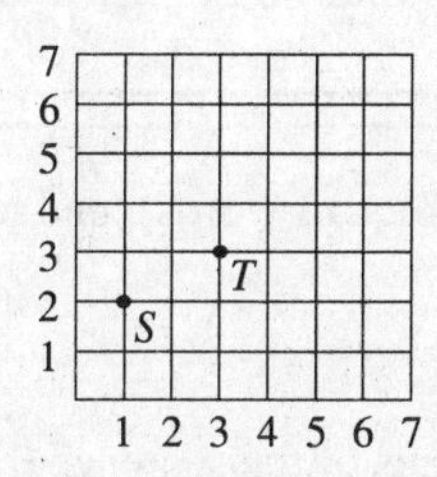

Which of the following points will lie on the line drawn through points S and T?

(A) (1, 1) (B) (3, 1) (C) (6, 4)
(D) (4, 4) (E) (5, 4)

The difference between $7\frac{1}{4}$ hours and $6\frac{3}{5}$ hours is how many minutes?

(A) 30 (B) 36 (C) 39 (D) 45 (E) 51

For all integers n not equal to 1, $\langle n \rangle = \dfrac{n+1}{n-1}$.

Which of the following has the greatest value?

(A) $\langle 0 \rangle$ (B) $\langle 2 \rangle$ (C) $\langle 3 \rangle$ (D) $\langle 4 \rangle$ (E) $\langle 5 \rangle$

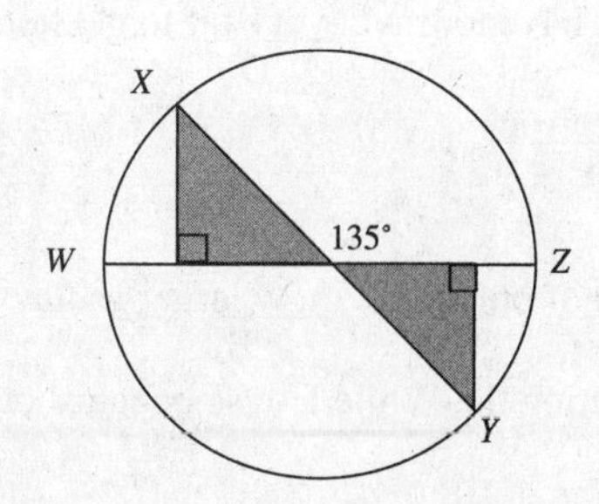

If segment WZ and segment XY are diameters with lengths of 12, what is the area of the shaded triangles?

(A) 36 (B) 33 (C) 30 (D) 18 (E) 12

32. If $w \neq 0$ and $w = 2x = 3y$, what is the value of $w + x$ in terms of y?

(A) $\frac{1}{5}y$ (B) y (C) $\frac{9}{2}y$ (D) $3y$ (E) $6y$

33. If $y = (x + 2)^2 + 1$, what is the minimum value of y?

(A) −2
(B) −1
(C) 0
(D) 1
(E) 5

34. Amy owes Berna \$2, Berna owes Cindy \$10, and Cindy in turn owes Amy money. How much does Cindy owe Amy if all three debts could be settled by having Berna pay \$1 to Amy and \$7 to Cindy?

(A) \$2
(B) \$3
(C) \$4
(D) \$5
(E) \$6

35. On a map, 1 centimeter represents 6 kilometers. A square on the map with a perimeter of 16 centimeters represents a region with what area?

(A) 64 km²
(B) 96 km²
(C) 256 km²
(D) 576 km²
(E) 8,216 km²

IF YOU FINISH BEFORE TIME IS CALLED, YOU MAY CHECK YOUR WORK ON THIS SECTION ONLY. DO NOT WORK ON ANY OTHER SECTION OF THE TEST.

STOP

SECTION 3

Time—30 minutes
50 Questions

The questions in this section measure skills that are important to writi well. In particular, they test your ability to recognize and use langua that is clear, effective, and correct according to the requirements standard written English, the kind of English found in most colle textbooks.

Directions: The following sentences contain problems in grammar, usage, diction (choice of words), and idiom.

Some sentences are correct.
No sentence contains more than one error.

You will find that the error, if there is one, is underlined and lettered. Assume that elements of the sentence that are not underlined are correct and cannot be changed. In choosing answers, follow the requirements of standard written English.

If there is an error, select one underlined part that must be changed to make the sentence correct and blacken the corresponding space on your answer sheet.

If there is no error, blacken answer space E.

EXAMPLE:

The region has a climate so severe that plants
A
growing there rarely had been more than twelve
B C
inches high. No error
D E

SAMPLE ANSWER

1. When Ms. Ruiz arrived at the holiday sale, she realized
A
that she had left her wallet at home and needs to go back
B C D
to get it. No error
E

2. If America were invaded by foreign forces, all able-
A B
bodied men would, without hardly a doubt, enlist at the
C D
nearest armed services recruitment center. No error
E

3. The pilot's carelessness, as well as her equipment's
A
malfunctioning, was responsible for the near-disaster at
B C D
Kennedy Airport. No error
E

4. Instead of concentrating on doing their homework as they
A B C
should, many teenagers watch television, talk on the
phone, and they listen to the radio. No error
D E

5. The twins wanted to be a member of the team, but the
A B
captain had already made her selections.
C D
No error
E

6. It's a good thing that the folks in the cast live close by;
A B
they won't have to travel very far to get home after the
C D
show. No error
E

7. The crowd of onlookers grew larger as the veterans whi
A B C
were picketing the White House began shouting. No er
D E

8. Of the nominees for the Nobel Prize in Literature this
A B
year, few are as qualified as the English novelist Antho
C D
Powell. No error
E

GO ON TO THE NEXT PAGE

The confrontation between domestic businesses and
A
foreign competitors has reached a dead-end that will take
B C
an Act of Congress to resolve. No error
D E

Psychologists have long debated the connection between
A B
violence on television plus actual crime. No error
C D E

The continual improvements in athletic training methods
A
has made performances that would have been considered
B C
impossible a generation ago everyday occurrences.
D
No error
E

A good teacher should not only convey information and
A B C
should also instill his students with a love for learning.
D
No error
E

Most of the contestants feel that the rules that pertains to
A B C
the race are far too strict. No error
D E

The building developer had hoped to keep the location
A
of the housing project a secret to prevent neighborhood
B C
resident groups from interfering. No error
D E

Unless scientists discover new ways to increase food
A
production, the earth will not be able to satisfy the food
B
needs for all its inhabitants. No error
C D E

16. Since the Senator has never broke any of his
A B
campaign promises, his third re-election appears
C
to be a virtual certainty. No error
D E

17. Not until each one of us take responsibility for world
A B C
peace will we ever move towards it. No error
D E

18. A number of scientists have begun speculating whether
A B
life actually began as crystals of clay rather than organic
C D
molecules. No error
E

19. Although Maria has a better voice than him, Larry
A B
insists on leading his class during the national anthem.
C D
No error
E

20. Revered as one of the world's most versatile geniuses,
A
Leonardo da Vinci excelled in every endeavor he at-
B
tempted and serving as a prototype for the Renaissance
C D
Man. No error
E

21. To have read that book in three days, Edwin would have
A
to sacrifice many of the enjoyable details of plot and
B C D
character development. No error
E

22. After checking her closets and drawers thoroughly, Katina
A B
walked through her old apartment one last time before
C
moving out. No error
D E

GO ON TO THE NEXT PAGE

23. After being hampered with (A) red tape and innumerable regulations for decades, (B) many businesses welcome (C) the trend towards fewer legal restrictions on (D) small companies. No error (E)

24. Florence is an exceedingly (A) beautiful city largely (B) because they (C) have successfully blended the modern (D) with the ancient. No error (E)

25. With the growing popularity (A) of word processors, the handwriting of many people (B) has become (C) barely intelligent. (D) No error (E)

GO ON TO THE NEXT PAGE

<u>Directions</u>: In each of the following sentences, some part or all of the sentence is underlined. Below each sentence you will find five ways of phrasing the underlined part. Select the answer that produces the most effective sentence, one that is clear and exact, without awkwardness or ambiguity, and blacken the corresponding space on your answer sheet. In choosing answers, follow the requirements of standard written English. Choose the answer that best expresses the meaning of the original sentence.

Answer (A) is always the same as the underlined part. Choose answer (A) if you think the original sentence needs no revision.

EXAMPLE:

Laura Ingalls Wilder published her first book <u>and she was sixty-five years old then</u>.

(A) and she was sixty-five years old then
(B) when she was sixty-five years old
(C) at age sixty-five years old
(D) upon reaching sixty-five years
(E) at the time when she was sixty-five

SAMPLE ANSWER

26. Positions in the police and fire departments once were traditionally filled by men, but <u>becoming increasingly popular among women.</u>

(A) becoming increasingly popular among women.
(B) have become increasingly popular among women.
(C) have among women increased in popularity.
(D) become increasingly popular among women.
(E) women have increasingly found them to be popular.

27. <u>Unless they become more responsible</u> about investing money, many college students will soon rebel against their administrations.

(A) Unless they become more responsible
(B) Unless becoming more responsible
(C) Unless colleges become more responsible
(D) Unless it becomes more responsible
(E) Unless more responsibility is shown

28. Today's computers <u>are becoming not only more varied and powerful but also less expensive.</u>

(A) are becoming not only more varied and powerful but also less expensive.
(B) not only are becoming more varied and powerful, they cost less.
(C) become not only more varied and powerful, they become less expensive.
(D) becoming more varied and powerful but also less expensive.
(E) become more varied and powerful, not only, but also less expensive.

29. Many parents and children argue often about responsibility; this would be avoided if <u>they had more trust in them.</u>

(A) they had more trust in them.
(B) their trust in them was more.
(C) their trust were more.
(D) the parents had more trust in them.
(E) the parents had more trust from their children.

30. Unprepared for such a strong rebuttal, <u>the lawyer's attempt at winning the case failed.</u>

(A) the lawyer's attempt at winning the case failed.
(B) the lawyer's attempt failed to win the case.
(C) the lawyer failed to win the case.
(D) the lawyer failed in his attempt to win the case.
(E) the lawyer attempted to win her case, but failed.

31. Goethe's poetry is <u>different from any others</u> in that it lyrically expresses profound thoughts.

(A) different from any others
(B) different from that of any other poet
(C) different from any other poet
(D) different than anyone else's
(E) different than anyone else

GO ON TO THE NEXT PAGE

32. It is true that plastic surgery can improve a person's outward appearance <u>but your personality will not change unless you make it.</u>

(A) but your personality will not change unless you make it.
(B) but your personality will not be changed unless you make it.
(C) but a personality will not change unless you make it.
(D) but a personality will not change without an effort.
(E) but a personality will not change unless you make an effort.

33. <u>After getting off the chairlift, Neil adjusted his boot buckles, polished his goggles, and skied down the slope.</u>

(A) After getting off the chairlift, Neil adjusted his boot buckles, polished his goggles, and skied down the slope.
(B) He got off the chairlift, Neil adjusted his boot buckles, polished his goggles, and skied down the slope.
(C) After getting off the chairlift, Neil adjusted his boot buckles and polished his goggles and then he skied down the slope.
(D) Neil, after getting off the chairlift, adjusted his boot buckles, polished his goggles, and was skiing down the slope.
(E) Getting off the chairlift, Neil adjusted his boot buckles, polished his goggles, and skied down the slope.

34. <u>The average person should eat more vegetables if they want to develop strong bodies and maintain their health.</u>

(A) The average person should eat more vegetables if they want to develop strong bodies and maintain their health.
(B) The average person should eat more vegetables to develop strong bodies and maintain their health.
(C) The average person should eat more vegetables if he wants to develop a strong body and maintain his health.
(D) The average person, wishing to develop a strong body and maintain his health, should eat more vegetables.
(E) The average person should eat more vegetables in order to develop strong bodies and maintain their health.

35. <u>When reading</u> the reviews of his recently published romantic novel, Father O'Malley threw his manuscript into a blazing fireplace.

(A) When reading
(B) Having read
(C) When he had read
(D) When he reads
(E) Reading

36. In today's newspaper <u>they said</u> the President was disliked by members of both parties.

(A) they said
(B) they said that
(C) an analyst was saying
(D) an analyst was quoted as saying
(E) it said an analyst quoted that

37. <u>When they first implicated him in it, Nixon denied any wrongdoing in the Watergate Scandal, but soon the evidence against him was overwhelming.</u>

(A) When they first implicated him in it, Nixon denied any wrongdoing in the Watergate Scandal, but soon the evidence against him was overwhelming.
(B) When Nixon was first implicated in the Watergate Scandal, he denied any wrongdoing and the evidence against him was soon overwhelming.
(C) When first implicated in the Watergate Scandal, the evidence against Nixon was soon overwhelming but he denied any wrongdoing.
(D) When he was first implicated in the Watergate Scandal, Nixon denied any wrongdoing, but soon he was overwhelmed by the evidence against him.
(E) Nixon first denied any wrongdoing in it, but soon the overwhelming evidence implicated him in the Watergate Scandal.

38. Michael Jackson <u>always has and probably will always be</u> one of the most exciting pop singers in the world.

(A) always has and probably will always be
(B) always has been and probably always will be
(C) always has been and probably will be
(D) has been and probably will be always
(E) always has and probably always will be

39. To survive an airplane hijacking, <u>it demands remaining calm</u> and well-behaved.

(A) it demands remaining calm
(B) it demands calmness
(C) one is demanded to remain calm
(D) one should remain calm
(E) demands one to remain calm

40. Vacationing in foreign countries provides one not only with relaxing experiences but also <u>cultures different from theirs are better understood.</u>

(A) cultures different from theirs are better understood.
(B) a better understanding of cultures different from theirs.
(C) with a better understanding of different cultures.
(D) cultures different from theirs are better understood.
(E) cultures, although different, are better understood.

GO ON TO THE NEXT PAGE

Even though the bill for an amendment appeared feasibly
A B
to the sponsoring congressman, it was voted down
C D
unanimously. No error
E

Since Edwin conscientiously practices diving every day
A
for hours after school, he is continually rising the
B C
difficulty of his dives. No error
D E

If everybody kept his car in good condition, he would find
A
that its value would diminish little over the years, if not
B C D
actually appreciate. No error
E

Dieting and exercise is not the answer to all weight
A B
problems, but they should do the trick for most waistlines.
C D
No error
E

My art history professor prefers Michelangelo's sculpture
A
to viewing his painting, although Michelangelo himself
B C
was more proud of the latter. No error
D E

46. Randy bought a new pair of pants because his last pair
A B
was just delivered to the laundry the morning of gradua-
C D
tion exercises. No error
E

47. Between the three old friends present there had been
A B C
many memorable experiences throughout the years.
D
No error
E

48. If the engineer had had competent assistants to help him
A B
finish the project, he would not have completed it so late.
C D
No error
E

49. Less college students are choosing liberal arts majors
A B
because the cost of a college education is prohibitive.
C D
No error
E

50. The purpose of Mark Twain's writings were not merely to
A
entertain but also to educate, although that doesn't
B
prevent one from enjoying his yarns. No error
C D E

IF YOU FINISH BEFORE TIME IS CALLED, YOU MAY CHECK YOUR WORK ON THIS SECTION ONLY. DO NOT MARK WORK ON ANY OTHER SECTION IN THE TEST. **STOP**

SECTION 4

Time—30 minutes
40 Questions

For each question in this section, choose the best answer and blac[k] the corresponding space on the answer sheet.

Each question below consists of a word in capital letters, followed by five lettered words or phrases. Choose the word or phrase that is most nearly opposite in meaning to the word in capital letters. Since some of the questions require you to distinguish fine shades of meaning, consider all the choices before deciding which is best.

Example:

GOOD: (A) sour (B) bad (C) red (D) hot (E) ugly

(A) ● (C) (D) (E)

1. DEPLORE: (A) indulge (B) approve (C) separate (D) entertain (E) weaken

2. CONCEAL: (A) deny (B) air (C) stiffen (D) insert (E) advance

3. INDEFATIGABLE: (A) durable (B) temperate (C) anonymous (D) independent (E) listless

4. FETID: (A) lengthy (B) sordid (C) stubborn (D) fragrant (E) unheralded

5. INCHOATE: (A) imaginative (B) essential (C) ancient (D) controlled (E) appreciative

6. ADULTERATE: (A) aspire (B) cleanse (C) agree (D) surpass (E) impede

7. ASTUTE: (A) dull (B) boring (C) moderate (D) favorable (E) legal

8. ABANDON: (A) significant progress (B) self-restraint (C) confident carriage (D) complete adjustment (E) outright humiliation

9. ESTRANGE: (A) befriend (B) conclude (C) whisper (D) alter (E) analyze

10. CONCATENATION: (A) inflammation (B) monotony (C) unraveling (D) opposition (E) dispassion.

11. FEROCIOUS: (A) meek (B) fragile (C) injurious (D) youthful (E) quick

12. INVEIGLE: (A) malinger (B) bombard (C) dissuade (D) expire (E) falter

13. OBLOQUY: (A) dearth (B) steadiness (C) blessing (D) envy (E) beauty

14. CONTEND: (A) beg (B) sojourn (C) disperse (D) acquiesce (E) dispel

15. ATROPHY: (A) whisper (B) flourish (C) criticize (D) reject (E) overthrow

Each sentence below has one or two blanks, each bla[nk] indicating that something has been omitted. Beneath t[he] sentence are five lettered words or sets of words. Choo[se] the word or set of words that best fits the meaning of t[he] sentence as a whole.

Example:

Although its publicity has been ——, the film itself is intelligent, well-acted, handsomely produced, and altogether ——.

(A) tasteless..respectable (B) extensive..moderate (C) sophisticated..amateur (D) risqué..crude (E) perfect..spectacular

● (B) (C) (D) (E)

16. Over a century ago Malthus predicted that human population growth would exceed increased food production, thus causing worldwide famine; his conclusion may have been premature, but we cannot yet say whether it was completely ——.

(A) histronic (B) scientific (C) unheeded (D) exaggerated (E) erroneous

17. The Constitution hopes to keep —— the concepts of liberty and democracy which this country upholds.

(A) public (B) mysterious (C) credulous (D) sacred (E) prudent

18. Shaken by two decades of virtual anarchy, the majority of people were ready to buy —— at any price.

(A) order (B) emancipation (C) hope (D) liberty (E) enfranchisement

19. As a person who combines care with ——, Marisa completed her duties with —— as well as zeal.

(A) levity..resignation (B) geniality..ardor (C) vitality..willingness (D) empathy..rigor (E) enthusiasm..meticulousness

20. Although bound to impose the law, a judge is free to use his discretion to —— the anachronistic barbarity of some criminal penalties.

(A) mitigate (B) understand (C) condone (D) provoke (E) enforce

GO ON TO THE NEXT PAGE

eplace each blank with the word(s) that best completes
e sentence.

Her shrewd campaign managers were responsible for the fact that her political slogans were actually forgotten clichés revived and —— with new meaning.

(A) fathomed (B) instilled (C) foreclosed
(D) instigated (E) foreshadowed

It was to proclaim their utter —— for popular conceptions of art that the Dadaists launched into a series of outrageous practical jokes.

(A) contempt (B) amusement (C) dread
(D) respect (E) hunger

Henry viewed Mélissa to be ——; she seemed to be against any position regardless of its merits.

(A) heretical (B) disobedient (C) contrary
(D) inattentive (E) harried

Our plans for the weekend are —— upon whether we will be able to use a second car for the long trip.

(A) reliable (B) reflected (C) contingent
(D) practicable (E) observant

It is not enough simply to want to do good in this troubled world; even —— must be practical if it is to be of any value.

(A) benevolence (B) power (C) speculation
(D) wealth (E) utility

Each question below consists of a related pair of words or phrases, followed by five lettered pairs of words or phrases. Select the lettered pair that best expresses a relationship similar to that expressed in the original pair.

Example:

YAWN : BOREDOM :: (A) dream : sleep
(B) anger : madness (C) smile : amusement
(D) face : expression (E) impatience : rebellion

26. POND : FISH :: (A) cage : zookeeper
(B) pasture : cow (C) mousetrap : mouse
(D) plain : wheat (E) gulf : water

27. ETERNAL : END ::
(A) indecent : exposure
(B) ephemeral : meaning
(C) intrinsic : sight
(D) indiscriminate : aim
(E) amicable : companionship

28. TRUNK : TREE :: (A) valley : mountain
(B) cavern : cave (C) petal : flower
(D) torso : body (E) animal : fence

29. URGE : COERCE :: (A) acknowledge : confirm
(B) take : usurp (C) summon : rally
(D) pressure : cook (E) create : destroy

30. MERITORIOUS : PRAISE ::
(A) captious : criticism
(B) kind : admiration
(C) questionable : response
(D) reprehensible : censure
(E) incredible : ecstasy

GO ON TO THE NEXT PAGE

Each passage below is followed by questions based on its content. Answer all questions following a passage on the basis of what is stated or implied in that passage.

To many people, the predictions of weather forecasters seem hardly more trustworthy than those of opinion pollsters. That view is unfair. Thanks largely to two technologies—the computer and the weather satellite—forecasting skill has improved dramatically over the past 25 years, and further gains can be expected.

Although dramatic, progress has been patchy. The prediction of large weather features such as big storms, jet streams, and high- and low-pressure systems over two to ten days (so-called "medium-range forecasts") truly is becoming a science. According to one common measure, the accuracy of medium-range forecasting has nearly doubled since computers were introduced: today's four-day forecasts are considered as reliable as the two-day projections of fifteen years ago. Locally, however, to work out what will happen in the next few hours remains much more error-prone, while long-term weather prediction is only just getting off the ground.

The problems in weather forecasting are partly conceptual, partly practical. Consider first the purely conceptual problems. Modern weather forecasting is based on a simple assumption: the atmosphere is a physical system and so it should obey physical laws that can be expressed in mathematical equations. Much of the physics of weather systems is known, but not all. The precise way in which rain clouds form and release their showers is still not fully understood. Nor are the details of interactions between the oceans and the atmosphere.

A second conceptual difficulty is mathematical. Computers are terrifically good at doing simple arithmetic very fast. Up to a point, they can even handle calculus. The trouble is that arithmetic and calculus work well only if the system they are being used to describe is linear. Broadly speaking, a system is linear if the sum of the causes acting on it gives the sum of their effects: for example, if a certain quantity of heat melts a certain mass of ice, then twice that quantity of heat will melt twice as much ice.

Weather is not a linear system: one cannot add up the various influences at work and obtain their total impact. There are countless feedback mechanisms. For example, an initial change in temperature may lead to changes in humidity, cloud formation, wind, and so on, which in themselves will in turn trigger a further change in temperature. The mathematical models used in weather forecasting can make some allowances for each feedback mechanisms, but only in an approximate and clumsy manner.

These conceptual problems are irksome, and a great deal of research is going into solving them. It would be misleading, however, to overemphasize them. So far, for all the gaps, meteorologists' understanding of weather systems and how to model them has run ahead of meteorologists' ability to apply their understanding. The main stumbling blocks are more mundane. They concern the provision of acurate, up-to-date data and the ability to manipulate them quickly.

31. The passage primarily concerns the
    (A) difference between medium-range and long-term weather forecasting
    (B) limitations of modern forecasting equipment
    (C) causes of weather systems
    (D) problems associated with long-term weather forecasting
    (E) application of mathematical models to scientific phenomena

32. According to the author, long-term weather forecastin[g is] difficult for all of the following reasons EXCEPT
    (A) weather systems are not linear
    (B) contemporary weather satellites are completely inadequate
    (C) the precise interaction between the oceans and th[e] atmosphere is unknown
    (D) computers are not yet adequate to handle the complex mathematics of weather forecasting
    (E) the physics of weather systems are uncertain

33. It can be inferred that in the paragraph immediately following this passage, the author will probably go on [to] discuss
    (A) the effect of conceptual models on weather syster[ms]
    (B) the development of previous forecasting models before the development of high-speed computers
    (C) the practical barriers that have kept weather forec[ast]ing from greater accuracy
    (D) the creation of statistical models by meteorologis[ts]
    (E) why meteorologists fail to take into account the effects of astronomical occurrences

GO ON TO THE NEXT PAGE

4. Which of the following inferences can be made about weather forecasting?

(A) Long-range weather prediction will reach its limit soon.
(B) Weather forecasting will become more reliable.
(C) Computers will eventually be able to make weather forecasting completely accurate.
(D) Weather satellites will become less prominent.
(E) Weather forecasting will have to adapt to a changing atmosphere.

5. Which of the following best describes the content of the passage?

(A) Technology's Struggle with the Elements
(B) Climate: A Conceptual Analysis
(C) Progress in Weather Forecasting: Slow but Sure
(D) A Collaboration of Science and Nature
(E) A Practical Approach to Weather Forecasting

6. The author's discussion suggests that

(A) conceptual and practical approaches to weather forecasting are in conflict and therefore prevent reliable forecasts
(B) attempts to control our climate are too conceptual
(C) four-day projections are still not adequate for modern needs
(D) certain fundamental assumptions now used in weather forecasting have yet to be completely validated
(E) the accuracy of his views depends on the future development of computers and weather satellites

7. The author provides information to answer which of the following questions?

(A) What triggers an initial change in temperature?
(B) Which purely conceptual difficulties of weather forecasting are still in dispute among meteorologists?
(C) Is there any hope for effective climate control?
(D) What exactly do meteorologists know about the physics of weather systems?
(E) What are the obstacles to effective weather forecasting?

38. It can be inferred from the passage that a weather forecaster could most accurately predict which of the following?

(A) total local snowfall in Chicago during January
(B) the direction of the movement of a high-pressure system
(C) the average temperature of a day exactly one year later
(D) how a given change in humidity will affect wind direction
(E) the sum of the causes of a linear weather system

39. According to the passage, computers are still less than accurate in forecasting the weather because they

(A) fail to describe weather in a linear way
(B) are not equipped with sufficient feedback mechanisms
(C) can effectively apply calculus and arithmetic only when describing simple systems
(D) are based on a mathematics which is consistently applicable only to big storms and jet streams
(E) analyze the data in objective ways only

40. The primary purpose of the author is to

(A) demonstrate a method
(B) analyze evidence
(C) debate a point
(D) raise an issue
(E) describe a problem

IF YOU FINISH BEFORE TIME IS CALLED, YOU MAY CHECK YOUR WORK ON THIS SECTION ONLY. DO NOT MARK WORK ON ANY OTHER SECTION IN THE TEST. **STOP**

SECTION 5

Time—30 minutes
25 Questions

In this section solve each problem, using any available space on the pa for scratchwork. Then decide which is the best of the choices given a blacken the corresponding space on the answer sheet.

The following information is for your reference in solving some of the problems.

Circle of radius r: Area $= \pi r^2$; Circumference $= 2\pi r$
The number of degrees of arc in a circle is 360.
The measure in degrees of a straight angle is 180.

Definitions of symbols:

= is equal to	≤ is less than or equal to
≠ is unequal to	≥ is greater than or equal to
< is less than	‖ is parallel to
> is greater than	⊥ is perpendicular to

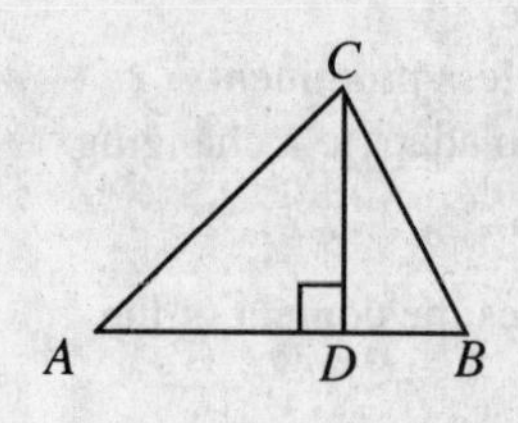

Triangle: The sum of the measures in degrees of the angles c a triangle is 180.
If $\angle CDA$ is a right angle, then

(1) area of $\Delta ABC = \frac{AB ¥ CD}{2}$

(2) $AC^2 = AD^2 + DC^2$

Note: Figures that accompany problems in this test are intended to provide information useful in solving the problems. They are draw as accurately as possible EXCEPT when it is stated in a specific problem that its figure is not drawn to scale. All figures lie in a pla unless otherwise indicated. All numbers used are real numbers.

1. If $9b = 81$, then $3 \times 3b =$

(A) 9
(B) 27
(C) 81
(D) 243
(E) 729

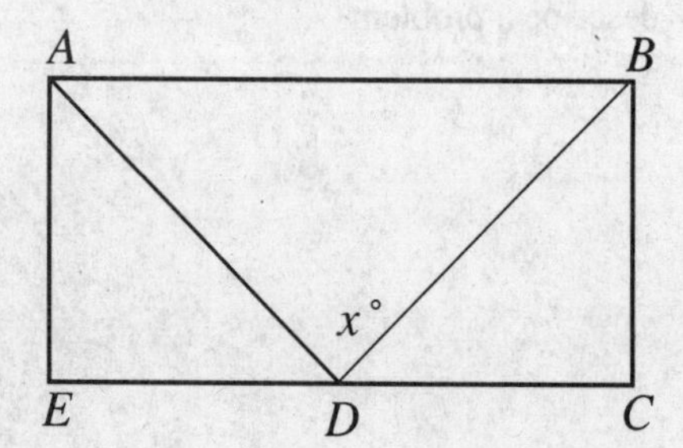

2. In the figure above, if $AE = ED = DC = CB$, then $x =$

(A) 60 (B) 75 (C) 90 (D) 120 (E) 135

3. $\frac{0.5 + 0.5 + 0.5 + 0.5}{4} =$

(A) 0.05 (B) 0.25 (C) 0.5 (D) 1 (E) 2.0

4. For any set of numbers S, $M(S)$ is defined as the maximum number of occurrences of any number in the set. For example, if $S = \{1, 2, 2, 2\}$ then $M(S) = 3$. If $S = \{2, 3, 3, 4, 5, 5, 6\}$ then $M(S) =$

(A) 0
(B) 2
(C) 4
(D) 6
(E) 8

A B C D

Note: Figure not drawn to scale

5. If $AB > CD$, which of the following must be true?

I. $AB > BC$
II. $AC > BD$
III. $AC > CD$

(A) I only (B) II only (C) III only
(D) II and III only (E) I, II, and III

GO ON TO THE NEXT PAGE

If 3 more than x is 2 more than y, what is x in terms of y?

(A) $y - 5$
(B) $y - 1$
(C) $y + 1$
(D) $y + 5$
(E) $y + 6$

If 8 and 12 each divide K without a remainder, what is the value of K?

(A) 16 (B) 24 (C) 48 (D) 96
(E) It cannot be determined from the information given.

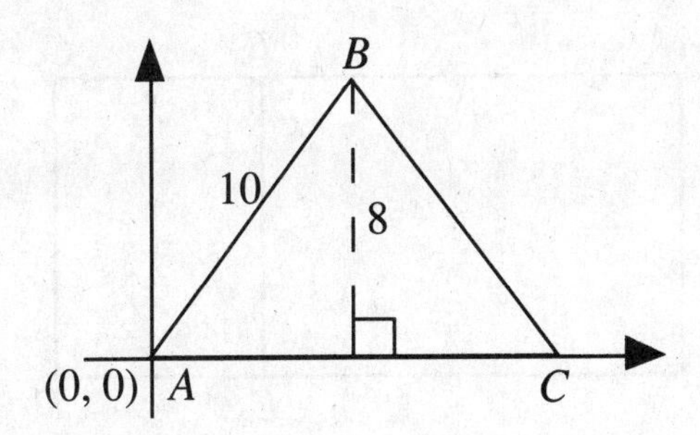

Side AB of the triangle ABC above must contain which of the following points?

(A) (3, 2) (B) (3, 5) (C) (4, 6)
(D) (4, 10) (E) (6, 8)

. If January 30th occurs on a Monday, on what day did January 1st occur?

(A) Sunday
(B) Monday
(C) Tuesday
(D) Friday
(E) Saturday

). Ricky bought grapes at a price of $1.19 per pound. Of the following, which is closest to the number of pounds Ricky bought if he paid $36 for the grapes?

(A) 31 (B) 30 (C) 29 (D) 28 (E) 18

11. Which of the following is closest to 4?

(A) 3.4
(B) 3.94
(C) 4.004
(D) 4.04
(E) 4.404

12. To the nearest thousand, what is the number of hours in a decade?

(A) 8,000
(B) 87,000
(C) 88,000
(D) 89,000
(E) 90,000

13. The Daily Newspaper has a particular format it likes to follow. There are six articles on the pages with even numbers, and seven articles on the pages with odd numbers. How many articles are there in today's paper if the paper has fifty-one pages beginning with page number one?

(A) 325 (B) 331 (C) 332 (D) 338 (E) 339

14. The product of (1 + 2), (2 + 3), and (3 + 4) is equal to half the sum of 20 and

(A) 10
(B) 85
(C) 105
(D) 190
(E) 1210

GO ON TO THE NEXT PAGE

15. Which of the following must be true?

I. The sum of two consecutive integers is odd.
II. The sum of three consecutive integers is even.
III. The sum of three consecutive integers is a multiple of 3.

(A) I only (B) II only (C) I and II only
(D) I and III only (E) I, II, and III

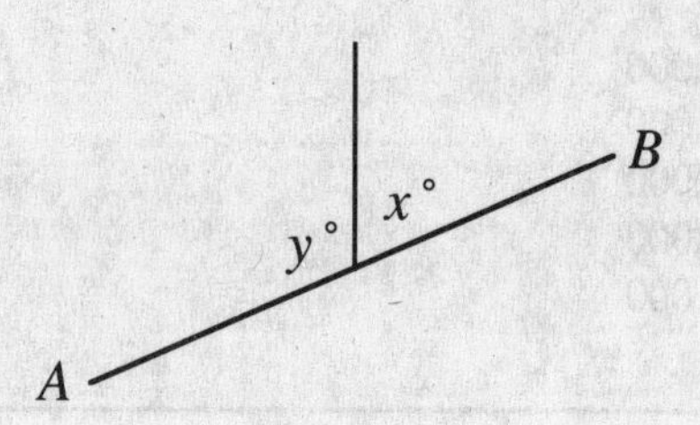

Note: Figure not drawn to scale.

16. In the figure above, if AB is a line segment and $3x = y$, what is the value of y?

(A) 45 (B) 60 (C) 90 (D) 120 (E) 135

17. What are all values of x such that $x^2 - 3x - 4$ is negative?

(A) $x < -1$ or $x > 4$
(B) $x < -4$ or $x > 4$
(C) $1 < x < 4$
(D) $-4 < x < 1$
(E) $-1 < x < 4$

18. At a certain school, 30 students study French, 40 stud[ents study] Spanish, 5 study both, and 10 study neither. How man[y] students are at this school?

(A) 70 (B) 75 (C) 80 (D) 85 (E) 90

19. If c is positive, what percent of $3c$ is 9?

(A) $\frac{c}{100}$ % (B) $\frac{c}{3}$ % (C) $\frac{9}{c}$ %

(D) 3% (E) $\frac{300}{c}$ %

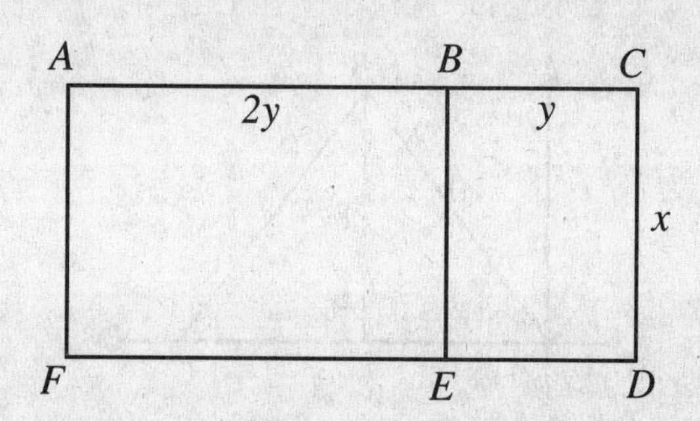

20. In the figure above, the area of rectangle $ACDF$ is how many times as great as the area of rectangle $BCDE$?

(A) 18 (B) 6 (C) 3 (D) 2
(E) It cannot be determined from the information give[n]

GO ON TO THE NEXT PAGE

The total number of integers between 1 and 200 inclusive that equal the cube of an integer is

(A) one (B) two (C) three
(D) four (E) five

If the price of dress A is three times the average price of 10 other dresses, what fraction of the total price of the 11 dresses is the price of dress A?

(A) $\frac{2}{13}$ (B) $\frac{3}{13}$ (C) $\frac{3}{11}$ (D) $\frac{3}{10}$ (E) $\frac{3}{4}$

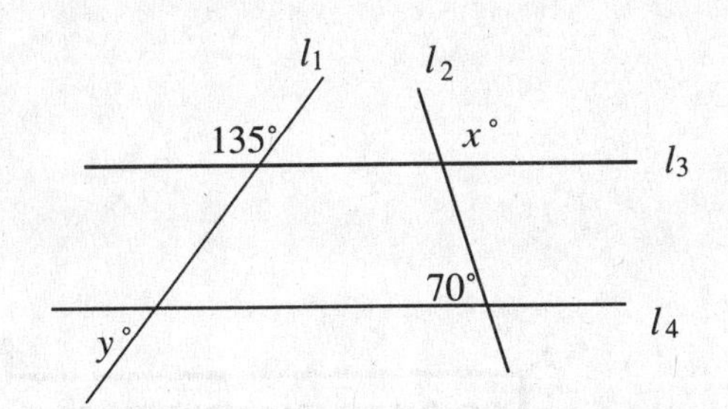

Note: Figure not drawn to scale.

If four lines intersect as shown in the figure above, $x + y =$

(A) 65 (B) 110 (C) 155 (D) 205
(E) It cannot be determined from the information given.

24. If $\frac{1}{x} + \frac{1}{y} = 6$ and $xy = 8$, what is the average (arithmetic mean) of x and y ?

(A) –7 (B) 12 (C) 14 (D) 24 (E) 48

25. If $4 < a < 7 < b < 9$, then which of the following best defines $\frac{a}{b}$?

(A) $\frac{4}{9} < \frac{a}{b} < 1$

(B) $\frac{4}{9} < \frac{a}{b} < \frac{7}{9}$

(C) $\frac{4}{7} < \frac{a}{b} < \frac{7}{9}$

(D) $\frac{4}{7} < \frac{a}{b} < 1$

(E) $\frac{4}{7} < \frac{a}{b} < \frac{9}{7}$

IF YOU FINISH BEFORE TIME IS CALLED, YOU MAY CHECK YOUR WORK ON THIS SECTION ONLY. DO NOT WORK ON ANY OTHER SECTION OF THE TEST. **STOP**

SECTION 6 | Time—30 minutes
40 Questions

For each question in this section, choose the best answer and blacken the corresponding space on the answer sheet.

Each question below consists of a word in capital letters, followed by five lettered words or phrases. Choose the word or phrase that is most nearly opposite in meaning to the word in capital letters. Since some of the questions require you to distinguish fine shades of meaning, consider all the choices before deciding which is best.

Example:

GOOD: (A) sour (B) bad (C) red (D) hot (E) ugly

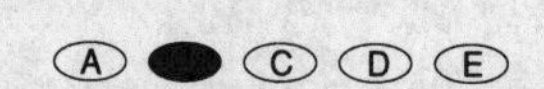

1. NEGLECT : (A) innocence (B) attention (C) expression (D) irrelevance (E) distraction

2. HUMID : (A) fresh (B) mild (C) cool (D) dry (E) feeble

3. DEFY : (A) submit (B) request (C) compete (D) cleverly deceive (E) allow disagreement

4. DEBASE : (A) uplift (B) assume (C) obey (D) decry (E) reject

5. RESERVE : (A) opposition (B) support (C) notice (D) injury (E) recklessness

6. GARISH : (A) adaptable (B) somber (C) explicable (D) generous (E) indifferent

7. IMPOSING : (A) uproarious (B) narrow (C) insignificant (D) random (E) secretive

8. PREDISPOSITION : (A) retention (B) delay (C) aversion (D) dissension (E) prescription

9. LATENT : (A) upright (B) straight (C) obvious (D) faithful (E) borne

10. VACILLATE : (A) hold fast (B) learn well (C) inflict (D) upset (E) peruse

GO ON TO THE NEXT PAGE

ach sentence below has one or two blanks, each blank dicating that something has been omitted. Beneath the ntence are five lettered words or sets of words. Choose e word or set of words that best fits the meaning of the ntence as a whole.

xample:

Although its publicity has been ----, the film itself is intelligent, well-acted, handsomely produced, and altogether ----.

(A) tasteless..respectable (B) extensive..moderate (C) sophisticated..amateur (D) risqué..crude (E) perfect..spectacular

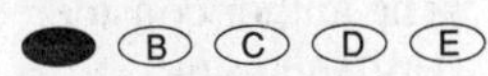

If it is true that morality cannot exist without religion, then does not the erosion of religion herald the —— of morality?

(A) regulation (B) basis (C) belief (D) collapse (E) value

Certain animal behaviors, such as mating rituals, seem to be ——, and therefore —— external factors such as climate changes, food supply, or the presence of other animals of the same species.

(A) learned..immune to
(B) innate..unaffected by
(C) intricate..belong to
(D) specific..confused with
(E) memorized..controlled by

. The former general led his civilian life as he had his military life, with simplicity and —— dignity.

(A) benevolent (B) informal (C) austere (D) aggressive (E) succinct

. Dr. Schwartz's lecture on art, while detailed and scholarly, focused —— on the pre-modern; some students may have appreciated his erudition, but those with more —— interests may have been disappointed.

(A) literally..medieval
(B) completely..pedantic
(C) expansively..technical
(D) voluminously..creative
(E) exclusively..comprehensive

5. Only when one actually visits the ancient ruins of marvelous bygone civilizations does one truly appreciate the sad —— of human greatness.

(A) perspicacity (B) magnitude (C) artistry (D) transience (E) quiescence

Each question below consists of a related pair of words or phrases, followed by five lettered pairs of words or phrases. Select the lettered pair that best expresses a relationship similar to that expressed in the original pair.

Example:

YAWN : BOREDOM :: (A) dream : sleep (B) anger : madness (C) smile : amusement (D) face : expression (E) impatience : rebellion

16. CAKE : DESSERT :: (A) coach : football (B) lawyer : jury (C) poet : writing (D) actor : troupe (E) pediatrician : doctor

17. BREEZE : HURRICANE :: (A) water : pebble (B) gulf : coast (C) eye : cyclone (D) sun : cloud (E) hill : mountain

18. IMMORTAL : DEATH :: (A) anonymous : fame (B) hopeless : situation (C) vital : life (D) indisputable : agreement (E) daily : year

19. DUEL : FIGHT :: (A) debate : argument (B) contest : referee (C) recess : intermission (D) match : tournament (E) act : play

20. LUBRICANT : FRICTION :: (A) motor : electricity (B) speed : drag (C) insulation : heat (D) adhesive : connection (E) muffler : noise

21. PARODY : IMITATION :: (A) stanza : verse (B) limerick : poem (C) novel : book (D) portrait : painting (E) riddle : puzzle

22. COMET : TAIL :: (A) traffic : lane (B) missile : trajectory (C) vessel : wake (D) engine : fuel (E) wave : crest

23. NEOLOGISM : LANGUAGE ::
(A) rhetoric : oratory
(B) syllogism : grammar
(C) innovation : technology
(D) iconography : art
(E) epistemology : philosophy

24. ADDENDUM : BOOK :: (A) signature : letter (B) vote : constitution (C) codicil : will (D) heading : folder (E) stipulation : contract

25. PENCHANT : INCLINED ::
(A) loathing : contemptuous
(B) abhorrence : delighted
(C) burgeoning : barren
(D) loss : incessant
(E) decision : predictable

GO ON TO THE NEXT PAGE

Each passage below is followed by questions based on its content. Answer all questions following a passage on the basis of what is stated or implied in that passage.

I was brought up to believe that sports would be the salvation of the black race in this country. As I grew to manhood, I was told repeatedly that sports represented the one area of American life in which a black man could proceed according to his own merit. For proof, I had only to look at the careers of exceptional individuals like Jesse Owens, Joe Louis, Jackie Robinson, and Willie Mays, with special attention to Paul Robeson at Rutgers and Jerome Holland at Cornell. I accepted the evidence, and when Holland was awarded the position of United States ambassador to Sweden, what had been up to that time merely a theory became for me an established fact. I often assured my friends that "for the black man, sports are the highroad to upward escalation, the proven way he will escape from the ghetto."

There was, of course, that distinctly awkward afternoon when a renowned sociologist rebuked me in an extremely serious manner: "All that you are saying is that if a young black possesses superhuman capabilities, if he can run like Jesse Owens, or play football like Jerome Holland, he can win for himself the normal decencies that the ordinary white man in this country takes for granted. We will have no social justice in this country until the day when an ordinary black, with no more than a ninth-grade education behind him and no outstanding skills, has full equality here on every level."

For a disturbing moment, I felt that I had caught a glimpse of what this radical scholar was proposing, but in my innocence I still dismissed both him and his argument. After all, the man was a known trouble-maker and might even have been a Communist. I reminded myself that the facts of the situation were irrefutable: blacks in the United States were finding a place for themselves in sports, and this would be their ultimate salvation. It was only years later that I discovered the truth of his words.

26. The author's attitude toward Jesse Owens, Joe Louis, Jackie Robinson was one of

(A) skeptical distaste
(B) hopeful admiration
(C) respectful disagreement
(D) sharp envy
(E) mild ambivalence

27. The author considered the accomplishments of Jerome Holland to be

(A) a sign that blacks were discriminated against
(B) evidence that blacks could accomplish a great dea through sports
(C) troubling in that Holland had to demonstrate superhum capabilities
(D) unbelievable and unlikely to be repeated
(E) proof that his sociologist friend was right

28. When he writes that the sociologist "might even have been a Communist," the author is being

(A) radical
(B) ironic
(C) laudatory
(D) political
(E) vague

GO ON TO THE NEXT PAGE

Charles Dickens, like untold millions of children all over e world throughout the ages, was enchanted by fairy tales. acknowledged the deep formative impact that the ondrous figures and events of fairy tales had on his ildhood and on his creative genius. Dickens understood that e imagery of fairy tales helps children better than anything se in their most difficult, yet most important and satisfying k: achieving a more mature consciousness to tame the aotic pressure of their unconscious.

Fairy tales, unlike any other form of literature, direct ildren to discover their identity and calling. These stories nt that a good, rewarding life is within one's reach despite versity. They promise that if one dares to engage in this arsome and taxing search, benevolent powers will come to e's aid, and that one will succeed. But fairy tales also warn at those who are too timid or narrow-minded to risk emselves must settle for humdrum existence.

In the past, those who loved fairy tales were often bjected to the scorn of pedants. But today many of our ildren are far more grievously bereaved; they are deprived the chance to know fairy stories at all. Most children now eet fairy tales, if they encounter them at all, only in prettified ersions that subdue their meaning and rob them of all deeper gnificance. One can see such versions in films and on levision, where fairy tales are turned into empty-minded tertainment.

Throughout history, the intellectual life of children largely epended on mythical and religious stories, and on fairy tales. his traditional literature fed children's imagination and imulated their fantasies. At the same time, these stories were major agent of the child's socialization. Children could learn ocial ideals from the material of myths, while fairy tales rovided patterns of behavior modeled on these ideals. These ere the images of the unconquered heroes. Achilles and dysseus, and of Hercules, whose life history showed that it is ot beneath the dignity of the strongest man to clean the lthiest stable.

9. The author cites Charles Dickens in order to
   (A) call attention to a person who began by writing fairy tales
   (B) demonstrate how fairy tale themes became incorporated into his work
   (C) support the author's scorn for those who adapt fairy tales for film and television
   (D) prove the formative influence of fairy tales on writers
   (E) provide an example of one who understands the importance of fairy tales to children

30. The author identifies all of the following as benefits children derive from fairy tales EXCEPT
    (A) expressing complex issues in language children can understand
    (B) serving as introductions to complex but rewarding lives
    (C) teaching children the wisdom of facing risks to achieve more fulfilling lives
    (D) helping children make sense of their inner conflicts
    (E) improving a child's imagination through models of vivid imagery

31. According to the passage, today's children seldom experience fairy tales in the original because these literary forms are
    (A) subject to the scorn of child development specialists
    (B) no longer available
    (C) not understandable to children
    (D) diluted to be entertaining
    (E) not relevant to the concerns of contemporary childhood

32. Which of the following best expresses the main idea of the passage?
    (A) Many of today's children lack the important socializing influences of myths and fairy tales.
    (B) Fairy tales provide models for human feelings and are therefore essential to good creative writing.
    (C) Families who expose children to the original fairy tales go against the advice of child development specialists.
    (D) The best way to tame a child's unconscious being is to allow him to experience fairy tales.
    (E) The diminishing importance of the role of fairy tales in child development explains today's problems.

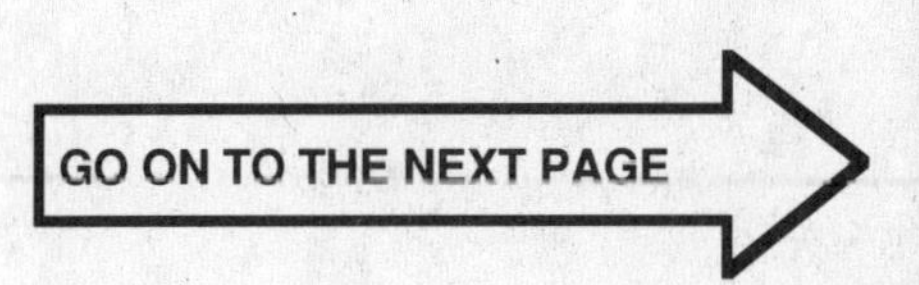

Schooling of fish is one of the most familiar forms of animal social behavior, but until recently it was little understood, possibly because of the impossibility of observing
Line minute changes in the position and the velocity of fish in a
(5) school under natural conditions. The fact that over the eons a great many species of fish have developed the ability to congregate in schools suggests that the behavior offers a considerable evolutionary survival advantage over those species that do not form schools. How the school is formed
(10) and maintained, however, is only beginning to be understood.

One of the most persistent misconceptions about fish schools is that they have a regular geometric form. Our work shows that the structure is a loose and probabilistic one, and that it results from each fish's applying a few simple rules.
(15) The first rule is that for each species there is a characteristic minimum approach distance within which neighbors do not come. The distance is usually about three-tenths of a body length. The minimum approach distance is not the distance that is generally maintained within the fish in a school,
(20) however. In each species there is a typical preferred distance to the nearest neighbor, which is usually about one body length. The spatial relations among the fish in a school change constantly as the fish adjust their speed and direction. For this reason the distance to the nearest neighbor is not uniform,
(25) even for a single fish. The preferred distance is a statistical abstraction, found by averaging the actual distances over a long period.

Fish of a particular species also tend to keep their nearest neighbor at a particular angle with respect to their body axis.
(30) Like the preferred distance, the preferred angle is a statistical quantity. At any given moment only a few fish may have their nearest neighbors at a preferred angle, but over the long period the preferred angle dominates. One useful measure of the degree of a school is the average ratio between the distance to
(35) the nearest neighbor and the distance to the second nearest neighbor. The closer the ratio to 1, the more uniform the structure. In a cubic lattice the ratio is exactly 1. The ratio varies considerably among species. For herring it is about 1.1, for pollack 1.3, and for cod 1.5. A ratio of 1.6 would be observed if the fish in the school took positions at random.

33. The author's observation that schooling is an evolut ary development suggests that
(A) schooling of fish is a specific learned behavior
(B) fish that do not swim in schools will become ex
(C) fish that swim in schools spend all their time in formation
(D) some species of fish that swim in schools did n always do so
(E) the habitat of a species of fish determines wheth form schools

34. By "probabilistic" (line 13) the author means that
(A) his conclusions are uncertain
(B) the structure of a school forms somewhat accord to chance
(C) there are statistical methods for determining hov school will form
(D) even species that usually swim in schools occasi ally break formation
(E) there are geometric rules for predicting a school' structure

35. It can be inferred that the author is now able to study schooling in fish because
(A) the author employed a new method for observin and measuring small changes in school formatio
(B) the author proved that evolution is responsible fc the longer periods of time
(C) new technology allows underwater study for lon periods of time
(D) new developments in statistical theory allow him predict the formation of schools of fish
(E) the author has successfully described the structur schools of several different species of fish

36. All of the following are behavioral rules used by fish swimming in the school EXCEPT the
(A) characteristic minimum approach distance
(B) typically preferred distance to the nearest neighb
(C) depth at which the school swims
(D) speed and direction of movement of the school
(E) preferred angle of body orientation

GO ON TO THE NEXT PAGE

The Supreme Court's recent decision allowing regional
erstate banks has razed one hedge in America's banking
ze, although many others still remain. Although the ruling
es not apply to very large money-center banks, it is a move
a liberalizing direction that could at last push Congress into
ming a sensible legal and regulatory system that allows
nks to plan their future beyond the next court case.

The restrictive laws the courts are interpreting are mainly
egacy of the bank failures of the 1930s. The current high
e of bank failures—higher than at any time since the great
pression—has made legislators afraid to remove the
trictions. While their legislative timidity is understandable,
s also mistaken. One reason so many American banks are
tting into trouble is precisely that the old restrictions make it
rd for them to build a domestic base large and strong
ough to support their activities in today's
ecommunicating, round-the-clock, around-the-world
ancial markets.

In trying to escape from this straitjacket, banks are taking
ormous, and what should be unnecessary, risks. For
ample, would a large bank be buying small, failed savings
nks at inflated prices if federal laws and states regulations
rmitted that bank to expand instead through the acquisition
financially healthy banks in the region? Of course not.

The solution is clear: American banks will be sounder
hen they are not geographically limited. The House of
epresentatives' banking committee has shown part of the
ay forward by recommending common-sensical, though
nited, legislation for a five-year transition to nationwide
nking. This would give regional banks time to group
gether to form counterweights to the big money-center
nks. Without this breathing space the big money-center
nks might soon sprawl across the country to become
igopolies. But any such legislation should be regarded as
ly a way station on the road towards a complete overhaul of
merican's creaking banking legislation.

7. The author's attitude towards the current banking laws is best described as one of
   (A) concerned dissatisfaction
   (B) tolerant disapproval
   (C) uncaring indifference
   (D) mild endorsement
   (E) great admiration

38. Which of the following best describes why the restrictive banking laws of the 1930s are still on the books?
   (A) The bank failures of the 1930s were caused by restrictive courts.
   (B) Banking has not changed in the past fifty years.
   (C) The Supreme Court rulings have adequately updated the existing laws.
   (D) The banking system is too restrictive, but no alternatives have been suggested.
   (E) Legislators apparently believe that banking problems similar to those of the depression still exist today.

39. The author argues that the change to a nationwide banking system should be
   (A) gradual, so that regional banks have a chance to compete with larger banks
   (B) postponed, until the consequences can be evaluated
   (C) immediate, because we cannot afford any more bank failures
   (D) reconsidered, in light of recent Supreme Court decisions
   (E) accelerated, to overcome legislative fear

40. Which of the following best expresses the main idea of the passage?
   (A) The current banking laws must be interpreted by the Supreme Court to be useful to today's banks.
   (B) Although there are currently many bank failures, the nature of banking has not really changed that much.
   (C) Money-center banks currently have too much power as compared with the regional banks.
   (D) Because current laws are not responsive to contemporary banking needs, banks have been forced to take needless and dangerous risks.
   (E) As a result of the many Supreme Court rulings liberalizing today's banking regulations, bank failures continue to occur.

IF YOU FINISH BEFORE TIME IS CALLED, YOU MAY CHECK YOUR WORK ON THIS SECTION ONLY. DO NOT MARK WORK ON ANY OTHER SECTION IN THE TEST. **STOP**

Your name (print) ______________________________
Last First Middle

Date ______________________

IMPORTANT: The following codes should be copied onto your answer sheet exactly as shown.

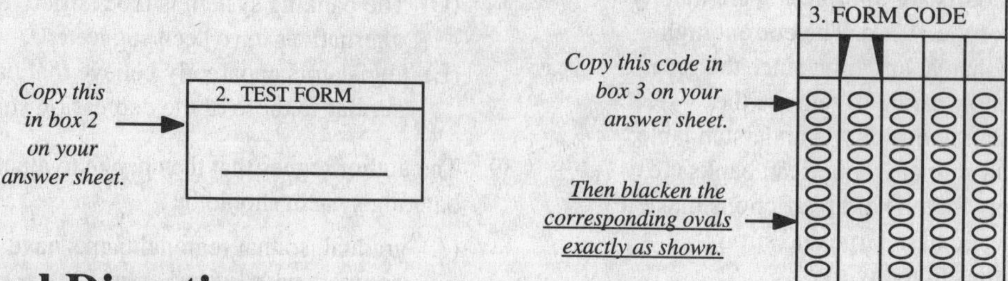

General Directions

This is a two-hour objective test designed to familiarize you with all aspects of the Scholastic Aptitude Test.

This test contains four sections, and you will be given 30 minutes to work on each section. The supervisor will tell you when to begin and end each section. During the time allowed for each section, you may work only on that particular section. If you finish your work before time is called, you may check your work on that section, but you are **not to work on any other section.**

You will find specific directions for each type of question found in the test. **Be sure you understand the directions before attempting to answer any of the questions.**

YOU ARE TO INDICATE ALL YOUR ANSWERS ON THE SEPARATE ANSWER SHEET:

1. The test booklet may be used for scratchwork. However, no credit will be given for anything written in the test booklet.
2. Once you have decided on an answer to a question, darken the corresponding space on the answer sheet. Give only one answer to each question.
3. As there are 50 numbered answer spaces for each section, be sure to use only those spaces that correspond to the test questions.
4. **Be sure that each answer mark is dark and completely fills the answer space.** Do not make any stray marks on your answer sheet.
5. If you wish to change an answer, erase your first mark completely--an incomplete erasure may be considered an intended response--and blacken your new answer choice.

Your score on this test is based on the number of questions you answer correctly minus a fraction of the number of questions you answer incorrectly. Therefore, it is improbable that random or haphazard guessing will alter your score significantly. However, if you are able to eliminate one or more of the answer choices as wrong, it is generally to your advantage to guess at one of the remaining choices. Remember, however, not to spend too much time on any one question.

If you have any questions, ask them of your supervisor now. Once the exam is in progress, the supervisor will not accept further questions.

DO NOT OPEN THIS TEST BOOKLET UNTIL YOU ARE TOLD TO DO SO.

DIAGNOSTIC TEST ANSWERS

Section 1		Section 2		Section 3		Section 4		Section 5		Section 6	
1. C	26. B	1. E	26. C	1. D	26. B	1. B	26. B	1. C		1. B	26. B
2. E	27. C	2. D	27. B	2. D	27. C	2. B	27. D	2. C		2. D	27. B
3. C	28. B	3. B	28. E	3. E	28. A	3. E	28. D	3. C		3. A	28. B
4. A	29. B	4. E	29. C	4. D	29. D	4. D	29. B	4. B		4. A	29. E
5. E	30. B	5. E	30. B	5. A	30. C	5. C	30. D	5. D		5. E	30. A
6. B	31. C	6. D	31. D	6. E	31. B	6. B	31. D	6. B		6. B	31. D
7. E	32. A	7. D	32. C	7. C	32. D	7. A	32. B	7. E		7. C	32. A
8. A	33. A	8. B	33. D	8. E	33. A	8. B	33. C	8. E		8. C	33. D
9. D	34. E	9. D	34. B	9. E	34. C	9. A	34. B	9. A		9. C	34. B
10. A	35. D	10. A	35. D	10. D	35. B	10. C	35. C	10. B		10. A	35. A
11. C	36. E	11. B		11. B	36. D	11. A	36. D	11. C		11. D	36. C
12. B	37. C	12. A		12. C	37. D	12. C	37. E	12. C		12. B	37. A
13. C	38. E	13. C		13. C	38. B	13. C	38. B	13. C		13. C	38. E
14. A	39. E	14. D		14. E	39. D	14. D	39. C	14. D		14. E	39. A
15. C	40. A	15. B		15. C	40. C	15. B	40. E	15. D		15. D	40. D
16. B	41. D	16. C		16. B	41. B	16. E		16. E		16. E	
17. E	42. C	17. D		17. B	42. C	17. D		17. E		17. E	
18. B	43. B	18. D		18. A	43. E	18. A		18. B		18. A	
19. A	44. B	19. A		19. B	44. A	19. E		19. E		19. A	
20. A	45. A	20. A		20. C	45. B	20. A		20. C		20. E	
21. D		21. B		21. B	46. E	21. B		21. E		21. B	
22. C		22. C		22. E	47. A	22. A		22. B		22. C	
23. E		23. C		23. A	48. E	23. C		23. C		23. C	
24. D		24. C		24. C	49. A	24. C		24. D		24. C	
25. D		25. D		25. D	50. A	25. A		25. A		25. A	

HOW TO SCORE YOUR DIAGNOSTIC TEST

After you have checked your answers to the diagnostic test against the key, you can calculate your score. For the two verbal sections (Sections 1 and 6; section 4 was experimental, so ignore it completely, because it doesn't count), tally up the number of blanks and the number of incorrect answers. To calculate your verbal "raw score," use the following formula:

$$\text{Verbal "Raw Score"} = 85 - \text{blanks} - \frac{5}{4}\text{ (incorrect)}$$

As you can see, blanks lower your "raw score." For example, let's say you left 16 questions blank and had 15 incorrect. Your verbal "raw score" would be 85 minus 16 minus $18\frac{3}{4}$, which equals $50\frac{1}{4}$. The closest integer is 50. Using the chart on page 283, you can see that a verbal "raw score" of 50 equals an SAT of 510.

Figuring your math score is a little trickier, because some of the questions have five answer choices and some have just four. In sections 2 and 5, count the number of blanks, the number of incorrect *regular* math questions, and the number of incorrect quantitative comparisons. To calculate your math "raw score," use the following formula:

$$\text{Math "Raw Score"} = 60 - \text{blanks} - \frac{5}{4}\text{ (regular incorrects)} - \frac{4}{3}\text{ (comparison incorrects)}$$

Again, blanks on the math section lower your "raw score." Let's say you left 14 questions blank, had 10 regular incorrects, and 7 comparison incorrects. Your math "raw score" would be 60 minus 14 minus $12\frac{1}{2}$ minus $9\frac{1}{3}$, or $24\frac{1}{6}$. The closest integer is 24. Using the chart on page 319, you can see that a math "raw score" of 24 equals a SAT score of 440.

SCORE KEY TO DIAGNOSTIC TEST

	Reported Score				Reported Score				Reported Score		
Raw Score	SAT-Verbal	SAT-Math	TSWE	Raw Score	SAT-Verbal	SAT-Math	TSWE	Raw Score	SAT-Verbal	SAT-Math	TSWE
85	800			50	510	680	60+	15	280	360	32
84	780			59	500	670	60+	14	280	350	30
83	770			48	500	660	60+	13	270	340	29
82	760			47	490	650	60+	12	260	340	28
81	750			46	490	640	60+	11	260	330	27
80	740			45	480	640	60+	10	250	320	26
79	730			44	470	630	60+	9	240	310	25
78	720			43	470	620	60+	8	230	310	24
77	710			42	460	610	60+	7	230	300	23
76	700			41	450	600	60	6	220	290	22
75	690			40	450	590	59	5	210	280	21
74	680			39	440	580	58	4	210	280	20
73	680			38	440	570	57	3	200	270	20
72	670			37	430	560	56	2	200	260	20
71	660			36	420	550	55	1	200	250	20
70	650			35	420	540	54	0	200	250	20
69	650			34	410	530	52	–1	200	240	20
68	640			33	410	530	51	–2	200	230	20
67	630			32	400	520	50	–3	200	230	20
66	620			31	390	510	49	–4	200	220	20
65	610			30	390	500	48	–5	200	210	20
64	610			29	380	490	47	–6	200	200	20
63	600			28	370	480	46	or			
62	590			27	370	470	45	below			
61	580			26	360	460	44				
60	580	800		25	350	450	43				
59	570	780		24	350	440	41				
58	560	760		23	340	430	40				
57	560	750		22	330	420	39				
56	550	740		21	330	410	38				
55	540	730		20	320	410	37				
54	540	720		19	310	400	36				
53	530	710		18	310	390	35				
52	520	700		17	300	380	34				
51	520	690		16	290	370	33				

AFTERWORD

About The Princeton Review Course

The Princeton Review course is a six-week course to prepare students for the SAT.

Students are assigned to small classes (eight to twelve students) grouped by ability. Everyone in your math class is scoring at your math level; everyone in your verbal class is scoring at your verbal level. This enables the teacher to focus each lesson on your problems, because everybody is in the same boat.

Each week you cover that one math area and one verbal area. If you don't understand a particular topic thoroughly, some other courses expect you to listen to audiocassettes.

Not so with The Princeton Review. If you want more work on a topic, you can come to an extra-help session later in the week. Classes in extra-help are optional, so usually they are even smaller than regular classes, allowing still more personal attention. If after coming to an extra-help class you still don't understand a concept, or you simply want more practice, you can request free private tutoring with your instructor.

Four times during the course you will take a diagnostic test that is computer evaluated. Each diagnostic is constructed according to the statistical design of actual SATs. Indeed, some of our questions are actual questions licensed directly from ETS.

The computer evaluation of your diagnostic tests is used to assign you to your class, as well as to measure your progress. The computer evaluation tells you what specific areas you need to concentrate on. We don't ask you to spend time on topics you already know well.

Princeton Review instructors undergo a strict selection process and a rigorous training period. All of them have done exceedingly well on the SAT, and most of them have gone to highly competitive colleges. All Princeton Review instructors are chosen because we believe they can make the course an enjoyable experience as well as a learning one.

Finally, Princeton Review materials are updated each year. Each student is assigned a manual and workbooks that are designed specifically for his or her level. If you're strong at math but weaker in verbal, you'll receive the upper level math materials. Of course, if you advance beyond these we'll give you more advanced materials. Each person receives materials that are challenging, but not overwhelming.

Is This Book Just Like Your Course?

Since the book came out, many students and teachers have asked us, "Is this book just like your course?" The answer is no.

We like to think that this book is fun, informative, and well written, but no book can capture the magic of our instructors and course structure. Each Princeton Review instructor has attended a top college and has, himself, excelled on the SAT. Moreover, each of our instructors undergoes several weeks of rigorous training.

It isn't easy to raise SAT scores. Our course is more than fifty hours long and requires class participation, quizzes, homework, four diagnostic examinations, and possibly additional tutoring.

Also, for a number of reasons this book cannot contain all of the techniques we teach in our course. Some of our techniques are too difficult to explain in a book, without a trained and experienced Princeton Review teacher to explain and demonstrate them. Moreover, this book is written for the average student. Classes in our course are grouped by ability so that we can gear our techniques to each student's level. What a 900-level Princeton Review student learns is different from what a 1400- or 1600-level students learns.

We're Flattered, but . . .

Some tutors and schools use this book to run their own "Princeton Review course." While we are flattered, we are also concerned.

It has taken us seven years of teaching tens of thousands of students across the country to develop our SAT program, and we're still learning. Many teachers think that our course is simply a collection of techniques that can be taught by anyone. It isn't that easy.

We train each Princeton Review instructor two hours for every hour he will teach class. Each of the instructors is monitored, evaluated, and supervised throughout the course.

Another concern is that many of our techniques conflict with traditional math and English techniques as taught in high school. For example, in the math section we tell our students to avoid setting up equations. Can you imagine your math teacher telling you that? And in the verbal section, we tell our students not to read the passage too carefully. Can you imagine your English teacher telling you that?

While we also teach traditional math and English in our course, some teachers may not completely agree with some of our approaches.

Beware of Princeton Review Clones

We have nothing against people who use our techniques, but we do object to tutors or high schools who claim to "teach the Princeton Review method."

If you want to find out whether your teacher has been trained by The Princeton Review, or whether you're taking an official Princeton Review course, call us toll free at 1-800-955-5585.

If You'd Like More Information

Princeton Review sites are in dozens of cities around the country. For the office nearest you, call 1-800-955-5585.

ABOUT THE AUTHORS

Adam Robinson was born in 1955. He graduated from Wharton before earning a law degree at Oxford University in England. Robinson, a rated chess master, devised and perfected the "Joe Bloggs" approach to beating standardized tests in 1980, as well as numerous other core Princeton Review techniques. A free-lance author of many books, Robinson has collaborated with The Princeton Review to develop a number of its courses.

John Katzman was born in 1959. He graduated from Princeton University in 1980. After working briefly on Wall Street, he founded The Princeton Review in 1981. Beginning with nineteen high school students in his parents' apartment, Katzman now oversees courses that prepare tens of thousands of high school and college students annually for tests including the SAT, GRE, GMAT, and LSAT.

Both authors live in New York City.

The Princeton Review
Diagnostic Test Form ○ Side 1

Completely darken bubbles with a No. 2 pencil. If you make a mistake, be sure to erase mark completely. Erase all stray marks.

1.
YOUR NAME: (Print) Last First M.I.

SIGNATURE: DATE: / /

HOME ADDRESS: (Print) Number and Street

City State Zip Code

PHONE NO.: (Print)

IMPORTANT: Please fill in these boxes exactly as shown on the back cover of your test book.

2. TEST FORM

3. TEST CODE

0	A J	0	0	0
1	B K	1	1	1
2	C L	2	2	2
3	D M	3	3	3
4	E N	4	4	4
5	F O	5	5	5
6	G P	6	6	6
7	H Q	7	7	7
8	I R	8	8	8
9		9	9	9

4. REGISTRATION NUMBER

0	0	0	0	0	0
1	1	1	1	1	1
2	2	2	2	2	2
3	3	3	3	3	3
4	4	4	4	4	4
5	5	5	5	5	5
6	6	6	6	6	6
7	7	7	7	7	7
8	8	8	8	8	8
9	9	9	9	9	9

5. YOUR NAME

First 4 letters of last name				FIRST INIT	MID INIT
A	A	A	A	A	A
B	B	B	B	B	B
C	C	C	C	C	C
D	D	D	D	D	D
E	E	E	E	E	E
F	F	F	F	F	F
G	G	G	G	G	G
H	H	H	H	H	H
I	I	I	I	I	I
J	J	J	J	J	J
K	K	K	K	K	K
L	L	L	L	L	L
M	M	M	M	M	M
N	N	N	N	N	N
O	O	O	O	O	O
P	P	P	P	P	P
Q	Q	Q	Q	Q	Q
R	R	R	R	R	R
S	S	S	S	S	S
T	T	T	T	T	T
U	U	U	U	U	U
V	V	V	V	V	V
W	W	W	W	W	W
X	X	X	X	X	X
Y	Y	Y	Y	Y	Y
Z	Z	Z	Z	Z	Z

6. DATE OF BIRTH

MONTH	DAY		YEAR	
○ JAN				
○ FEB				
○ MAR	0	0	0	0
○ APR	1	1	1	1
○ MAY	2	2	2	2
○ JUN	3	3	3	3
○ JUL		4	4	4
○ AUG		5	5	5
○ SEP		6	6	6
○ OCT		7	7	7
○ NOV		8	8	8
○ DEC		9	9	9

7. SEX

○ MALE

○ FEMALE

SCANTRON® FORM NO. F-591-KIN

Begin with number 1 for each new section of the test. Leave blank any extra answer spaces.

SECTION 1

1	A	B	C	D	E	26	A	B	C	D	E
2	A	B	C	D	E	27	A	B	C	D	E
3	A	B	C	D	E	28	A	B	C	D	E
4	A	B	C	D	E	29	A	B	C	D	E
5	A	B	C	D	E	30	A	B	C	D	E
6	A	B	C	D	E	31	A	B	C	D	E
7	A	B	C	D	E	32	A	B	C	D	E
8	A	B	C	D	E	33	A	B	C	D	E
9	A	B	C	D	E	34	A	B	C	D	E
10	A	B	C	D	E	35	A	B	C	D	E
11	A	B	C	D	E	36	A	B	C	D	E
12	A	B	C	D	E	37	A	B	C	D	E
13	A	B	C	D	E	38	A	B	C	D	E
14	A	B	C	D	E	39	A	B	C	D	E
15	A	B	C	D	E	40	A	B	C	D	E
16	A	B	C	D	E	41	A	B	C	D	E
17	A	B	C	D	E	42	A	B	C	D	E
18	A	B	C	D	E	43	A	B	C	D	E
19	A	B	C	D	E	44	A	B	C	D	E
20	A	B	C	D	E	45	A	B	C	D	E
21	A	B	C	D	E	46	A	B	C	D	E
22	A	B	C	D	E	47	A	B	C	D	E
23	A	B	C	D	E	48	A	B	C	D	E
24	A	B	C	D	E	49	A	B	C	D	E
25	A	B	C	D	E	50	A	B	C	D	E

SECTION 2

1	A	B	C	D	E	26	A	B	C	D	E
2	A	B	C	D	E	27	A	B	C	D	E
3	A	B	C	D	E	28	A	B	C	D	E
4	A	B	C	D	E	29	A	B	C	D	E
5	A	B	C	D	E	30	A	B	C	D	E
6	A	B	C	D	E	31	A	B	C	D	E
7	A	B	C	D	E	32	A	B	C	D	E
8	A	B	C	D	E	33	A	B	C	D	E
9	A	B	C	D	E	34	A	B	C	D	E
10	A	B	C	D	E	35	A	B	C	D	E
11	A	B	C	D	E	36	A	B	C	D	E
12	A	B	C	D	E	37	A	B	C	D	E
13	A	B	C	D	E	38	A	B	C	D	E
14	A	B	C	D	E	39	A	B	C	D	E
15	A	B	C	D	E	40	A	B	C	D	E
16	A	B	C	D	E	41	A	B	C	D	E
17	A	B	C	D	E	42	A	B	C	D	E
18	A	B	C	D	E	43	A	B	C	D	E
19	A	B	C	D	E	44	A	B	C	D	E
20	A	B	C	D	E	45	A	B	C	D	E
21	A	B	C	D	E	46	A	B	C	D	E
22	A	B	C	D	E	47	A	B	C	D	E
23	A	B	C	D	E	48	A	B	C	D	E
24	A	B	C	D	E	49	A	B	C	D	E
25	A	B	C	D	E	50	A	B	C	D	E

The Princeton Review
Diagnostic Test Form ○ Side 2

Completely darken bubbles with a No. 2 pencil. If you make a mistake, be sure to erase mark completely. Erase all stray marks.

Begin with number 1 for each new section of the test. Leave blank any extra answer spaces.

SECTION 3		SECTION 4		SECTION 5		SECTION 6	
1	A B C D E	1	A B C D E	1	A B C D E	1	A B C D E
2	A B C D E	2	A B C D E	2	A B C D E	2	A B C D E
3	A B C D E	3	A B C D E	3	A B C D E	3	A B C D E
4	A B C D E	4	A B C D E	4	A B C D E	4	A B C D E
5	A B C D E	5	A B C D E	5	A B C D E	5	A B C D E
6	A B C D E	6	A B C D E	6	A B C D E	6	A B C D E
7	A B C D E	7	A B C D E	7	A B C D E	7	A B C D E
8	A B C D E	8	A B C D E	8	A B C D E	8	A B C D E
9	A B C D E	9	A B C D E	9	A B C D E	9	A B C D E
10	A B C D E	10	A B C D E	10	A B C D E	10	A B C D E
11	A B C D E	11	A B C D E	11	A B C D E	11	A B C D E
12	A B C D E	12	A B C D E	12	A B C D E	12	A B C D E
13	A B C D E	13	A B C D E	13	A B C D E	13	A B C D E
14	A B C D E	14	A B C D E	14	A B C D E	14	A B C D E
15	A B C D E	15	A B C D E	15	A B C D E	15	A B C D E
16	A B C D E	16	A B C D E	16	A B C D E	16	A B C D E
17	A B C D E	17	A B C D E	17	A B C D E	17	A B C D E
18	A B C D E	18	A B C D E	18	A B C D E	18	A B C D E
19	A B C D E	19	A B C D E	19	A B C D E	19	A B C D E
20	A B C D E	20	A B C D E	20	A B C D E	20	A B C D E
21	A B C D E	21	A B C D E	21	A B C D E	21	A B C D E
22	A B C D E	22	A B C D E	22	A B C D E	22	A B C D E
23	A B C D E	23	A B C D E	23	A B C D E	23	A B C D E
24	A B C D E	24	A B C D E	24	A B C D E	24	A B C D E
25	A B C D E	25	A B C D E	25	A B C D E	25	A B C D E
26	A B C D E	26	A B C D E	26	A B C D E	26	A B C D E
27	A B C D E	27	A B C D E	27	A B C D E	27	A B C D E
28	A B C D E	28	A B C D E	28	A B C D E	28	A B C D E
29	A B C D E	29	A B C D E	29	A B C D E	29	A B C D E
30	A B C D E	30	A B C D E	30	A B C D E	30	A B C D E
31	A B C D E	31	A B C D E	31	A B C D E	31	A B C D E
32	A B C D E	32	A B C D E	32	A B C D E	32	A B C D E
33	A B C D E	33	A B C D E	33	A B C D E	33	A B C D E
34	A B C D E	34	A B C D E	34	A B C D E	34	A B C D E
35	A B C D E	35	A B C D E	35	A B C D E	35	A B C D E
36	A B C D E	36	A B C D E	36	A B C D E	36	A B C D E
37	A B C D E	37	A B C D E	37	A B C D E	37	A B C D E
38	A B C D E	38	A B C D E	38	A B C D E	38	A B C D E
39	A B C D E	39	A B C D E	39	A B C D E	39	A B C D E
40	A B C D E	40	A B C D E	40	A B C D E	40	A B C D E
41	A B C D E	41	A B C D E	41	A B C D E	41	A B C D E
42	A B C D E	42	A B C D E	42	A B C D E	42	A B C D E
43	A B C D E	43	A B C D E	43	A B C D E	43	A B C D E
44	A B C D E	44	A B C D E	44	A B C D E	44	A B C D E
45	A B C D E	45	A B C D E	45	A B C D E	45	A B C D E
46	A B C D E	46	A B C D E	46	A B C D E	46	A B C D E
47	A B C D E	47	A B C D E	47	A B C D E	47	A B C D E
48	A B C D E	48	A B C D E	48	A B C D E	48	A B C D E
49	A B C D E	49	A B C D E	49	A B C D E	49	A B C D E
50	A B C D E	50	A B C D E	50	A B C D E	50	A B C D E

FOR TPR USE ONLY	V1	V2	V3	V4	M1	M2	M3	M4	M5	M6	M7	M8

Ms

Tues / Thursday

March 27th 29th

Paula

DATE			